ALSO BY STUART SCHNEIDERMAN

Jacques Lacan
Rat Man
An Angel Passes

SAVING
FACE

SAVING

America and the Politics of Shame

FACE

STUART SCHNEIDERMAN

Alfred A. Knopf New York *1995*

Grateful acknowledgment is made to Helen Epstein for permission to
reprint excerpts from Children of the Holocaust by Helen Epstein,
copyright © by Helen Epstein.

Library of Congress Cataloging-in-Publication Data
Schneiderman, Stuart.
Saving face : America and the politics of shame /
by Stuart Schneiderman.—1st ed.
p. cm.
Includes bibliographical references and index.
ISBN 0-679-40969-6
1. National characteristics, American.
2. National characteristics, Japanese.
3. East and West.
4. United States—Civilization—1970- —Psychological aspects.
I. Title.
E169.12.S35   1996
973.92—dc20   95-22998   CIP

For my mother and my father

Washington . . . deplored the adversary theory which sees government as a tug-of-war between the holders of opposite views, one side eventually vanquishing the other. Washington saw the national capital as a place where men came together not to tussle but to reconcile disagreements.

—JAMES THOMAS FLEXNER

Manners are of more importance than laws. Upon them, in a great measure, the laws depend. The law touches us but here and there, and now and then. Manners are what vex or soothe, corrupt or purify, exalt or debase, barbarize or refine us, by a constant, steady, uniform, insensible operation, like that of the air we breathe in. They give their whole form and color to our lives. According to their quality, they aid morals, they supply them, or they totally destroy them.

—EDMUND BURKE

The English, more than any other people, not only act but feel according to rule. . . . The greater part of life is carried on, not by following inclination under the control of a rule, but by having no inclination but that of following a rule.

—JOHN STUART MILL

In the past and up to the very present, it has been a characteristic precisely of the specifically American democracy that it did *not* constitute a formless sand heap of individuals, but rather a buzzing complex of strictly exclusive, yet voluntary associations.   —MAX WEBER

Contents

SAVING
FACE

Introduction

Fresh from her victory in the Cold War, America awoke to find herself confronted with a new and, in many ways, more difficult challenge. This other struggle—for money and markets—had been going on for years: the nation had been engaged in economic competition against Japan and the rest of the nations of the Far East.

Moreover, we seemed to be losing. At the close of the American century we could no longer assume that everyone would have to play by our rules.[1] Alarmists were even predicting that the next century would belong to the Pacific Rim.

For a time Japan seemed to be like an octopus. A large head located on a small island sent out tentacles that stretched around the globe in a "diaspora by design."[2] As the 1990s dawned, the Japanese "bubble" economy had burst, however, and the bloom was off the chrysanthemum.

Even so, from 1965 to 1990 Japan and the leading nations of the Far East enjoyed economic growth rates that far outdistanced those of any other part of the globe. According to the World Bank,

Japan, Hong Kong, Indonesia, Malaysia, Singapore, South Korea, Taiwan, and Thailand had an average annual growth rate that was more than double those of both the developed and the developing world. And these nations, hardly the most democratic, also maintained the most equitable distribution of income.[3]

Throughout the Far East Japan had already supplanted America as the nation to emulate. As Deng Xiaoping's China modeled itself on the Japanese postwar success and became the world's fastest growing economy, the newly democratized Russia entered into an economic free fall. While some were proclaiming the final victory of Western liberal democracy, others feared that the United States was about to become a Third World nation. Both were no doubt exaggerated.

To defend democratic values we began to denigrate the Far East—reveling in each story of Japanese corruption and Chinese despotism. We consoled ourselves by thinking that in some final triumph of justice we would win and they would be punished. Perhaps that was why we continued to produce far more lawyers than engineers, while Asian nations were turning out far more engineers than lawyers.

In the ultimate indignity, Japan became a nation for the United States to emulate. American business leaders streamed to Japan to see how they had done it; American politicians sought to copy Japanese industrial policy. And *Fortune* magazine recommended, "The most important thing that Westerners can learn from Asians is how to motivate workers. The region's success is often explained in terms of cultural forces, including close family ties, a strong belief in the value of education, a penchant to save for the future. Those Confucian values are much the same as what Americans once called the Puritan Ethic. There's nothing exotic about the strength of Asians: They just work hard at everything. So can Westerners."[4]

But we believed ourselves to have largely surpassed the Puritan work ethic. How could anyone expect the Woodstock generation, whose consciousness had been formed in the crucible of Vietnam, to embrace such reactionary uptightness?

Fortune, among many others, was telling us that we were at risk of losing out to Asia because we had lost touch with something fundamental in our own tradition. Believing we were saving our souls, we had sacrificed economic development for hedonistic pleasures, family solidarity for self-fulfillment, rigorous educational standards for creative self-realization, social order for one of the most crime-ridden nations on earth.

As the children of the generation that won World War II and the Cold War, those of us who make up the Woodstock generation (the baby boomers) certainly do not want to be remembered as hippies and Yippies, yuppies and buppies. We do not want to think that our own best contribution to the American century was sex, drugs, and rock 'n' roll.

Too often people cast the new competition between West and East as a conflict between democratic and authoritarian values. Our virtuous idealism arrayed against their corrupt pragmatism. Our individualism facing off against their lockstep conformity. Our creativity versus their anthill mentality.

Cultural anthropologists have promoted the divisions by analyzing East and West in terms of whether shame or guilt provides the basis for social organization.[5] Supposedly, as Ruth Benedict argued in *The Chrysanthemum and the Sword*, America is the ultimate guilt culture, Japan the ultimate shame culture.

Theoretically, the difference is this: a shame culture provides a uniform code of conduct to promote civility, propriety, dignity, integrity, and honor. Group cohesion is more important than individual expression, and good behavior is encouraged by knowledge that the consequence of deviation is expulsion from the group. The behavior of each individual reflects well or badly on the group reputation.

A guilt culture attempts to control behavior by passing laws and punishing transgression. The guilty party is treated as an individual: he alone is punished; his group has no responsibility for his misdeeds. On the other hand, anyone who does not break a law has the right to act with the greatest freedom, to do what he wants, when he wants to, unmolested by considerations of how he looks to others. The effect of personal behavior on group cohesion is trivialized. Each individual is free to pursue a course of action that will ensure his soul's salvation.

Applying these terms to Japan and America produces the following caricature. The Japanese are all business; Americans are seeking self-fulfillment. The Japanese are conformists; Americans are individualists. The Japanese manufacture electronic widgets; Americans produce software, art, and culture.

But are we really so different from the Japanese? Most Americans would be profoundly offended to hear that they would sacrifice their honor on the altar of self-fulfillment. In enterprises where self-respect is a primary social value—in the military, in commerce, in corporate cultures—America is still the most powerful nation on earth.

A brief examination of history further serves to refute the caricature of America as a guilt culture. Pre-revolutionary America would certainly count as a shame culture. Public interest prevailed over private concerns; homogeneous communities maintained standards of proper behavior by shaming deviants; people were held responsible for the behavior of their fellow citizens.[6] Moreover, society was hierarchized and stratified; each person was expected to act according to his proper station and role.[7]

Common customs, ceremony, and ritual served to create and maintain the ties that bound people together in communities.

The American Revolution changed things but in the sense of expanding the shame culture, not of replacing it with something else. The American Revolution created a nation as a federation of self-governing and cooperating local communities. National government would unite them by providing a uniform national identity: it would defend against foreign invasion, conduct relations with foreign governments, regulate commerce between the states, ensure the integrity of a single currency, and perform those worthwhile functions that were beyond the will or the means of the states.

The American Revolution extended the practice of respect throughout the body politic rather than reserve it for an élite class of gentlemen.[8] And it reformed the decadent aristocratic love of idleness that had characterized European gentility. Gordon Wood wrote: "The Revolution brought respectability and even dominance to ordinary people long held in contempt and gave dignity to their menial labor in a manner unprecedented in history and to a degree not equaled elsewhere in the world."[9] Eventually, these reforms would provide the ground for flourishing corporate cultures.

The American nation served to connect communities that still retained the independence associated with Protestant congregations; it lacked the central power found in the Roman Catholic religion and in those nations whose political cultures received a decisive influence from it.[10]

America was more like a tribe, less like a centralized state. The political model of guilt culture sees society as an aggregate of disparate individuals seeking personal gain at the expense of others. Each individual's innate propensity to sin must be controlled by a coercive central power. More concerned with soul than outward appearances, it will forgive almost all forms of deviant behavior, while harshly punishing differences of opinion.

Since guilt culture is based on the inner voice of the individual conscience, it emphasizes belief in dogma. Such a state aspires to universality and homogeneity of belief. A shame culture, however, relies on ceremonial norms: good manners, public decency, propriety, and dignity. With less need for uniform belief Anglo-American nations could legitimate opposition. In allowing discussion and debate they solidified consensus by respecting differing opinions; thus, these nations were among the first to permit a change of government by peaceful means.[11]

In his controversial book *Tribes*, Joel Kotkin argued that world trade and commerce has been directed by five great transnational tribal cultures. Members of these tribes have achieved disproportionate success and influence because they value group cohesion, hard work, education, dignity, decorum, and integrity.

An extended family spread out through the world provided a ready-made network of trustworthy business associates, all of whom were dedicated to the same goal: maintaining the group's reputation. And, living as aliens in cultures not their own, they were especially concerned with maintaining an appearance of propriety; they all had very strict rules governing everyday life.

The most powerful Asian tribes are the Japanese and overseas Chinese, with the overseas Indians fast assuming international prowess. The economic miracles in Taiwan, Hong Kong, Singapore, Indonesia, Malaysia, and southeastern China have been directed by overseas Chinese. In the West there are two great tribes: the first is the Jewish; the second, Kotkin asserts, is the Anglo-American. Of all the global tribes, the one with the most influence and importance is the Anglo-American.

Beginning from a small island, this tribe branched out through the world and created the United States, Canada, Australia, and so on. International business, commerce, trade, and diplomacy take place in the English language according to rules established by the Anglo-American tribe. From parliamentary democracy to the Industrial Revolution to the abolition of slavery to the emancipation of women, this tribe has set global standards. Those who, like the Chinese in the eighteenth century, refused to follow the lead of the British were left behind in the global race to industrialize.[12]

However much it began with a WASP élite, the Anglo-American tribe is unique for being an open, not a closed, tribe. As Arthur Schlesinger wrote, "The smelting pot thus had, unmistakably and inescapably, an Anglocentric flavor. For better or worse, the white Anglo-Saxon tradition was for two centuries—and in crucial respects still is—the dominant influence on American culture and society. This tradition provided the standard to which other immigrant nationalities were expected to conform, the matrix into which they would be assimilated.''[13]

These tribal groups have learned to succeed in world markets; they do not tolerate failure; they do not expose loss; they see no dignity in poverty.[14] If something is wrong within a family, all members hold it as a secret.[15] They choose to exhibit in public only the most exemplary behavior. Protecting the group's reputation is an individual's primary social responsibility.

The successful tribes value education as a way to move up the social hierarchy. They believe in merit, not aristocratic entitlement. They value achievement that can be measured objectively: in science, mathematics, business, banking, engineering. They are pragmatic, not idealistic, the best examples of advanced shame cultures.

When one group enjoys disproportionate success in worldly pursuits, others often believe it to be a criminal conspiracy. Instead of emulating its success, they come to resent it. Those who suffer higher rates of failure become convinced that the game has been fixed, and that they are the victims of the success of others.

The less successful groups may tax the more successful with guilt for having succeeded: the victor's gains are ill-gotten; profits must be confiscated, capital redistributed. Above all, those who win must be punished; they should not be allowed to enjoy the fruits of their success.

All the dominant global tribes have at one time or another been designated as criminal conspiracies. In the West the Jewish people have most often been persecuted for being too successful and too influential.

Are the Anglo-Americans, the Japanese, the overseas Chinese, the Jews, and the overseas Indians hardworking, highly disciplined people who have achieved success because of their moral character or are they basically cheats and rogues? Are they honorable people who have made occasional mistakes, or are they dishonorable people who have tried to dissimulate their fundamental venality behind a mask of propriety?

In different terms, should a more successful group be emulated for its positive qualities or punished for its mistakes? Should a less successful group seek to improve itself by working harder or should it seek legal redress?

We do not need to decide the issue with absolute certainty. Groups that achieve a consistent record of success in different places at different times under different laws in different markets deserve to be granted a presumption of honesty.

Punishing those who have garnered honest success has never worked. If a society decides to demean a successful group, it will be glorifying values that are associated with failure. Making your suffering into an indictment of someone else does not improve your condition.

The great global tribes have all known how to avoid shame; their behavior in the marketplace has not been determined by the requirement to control sinful impulses. They seek pride and honor, not innocence and soulfulness. As Benjamin Franklin resolved, "In order to secure my Credit & Character as a Tradesman, I took care not only to be in *Reality* Industrious & Frugal, but to avoid all *Appearances* to the Contrary." What better definition of the importance of saving face?

Saving face is quite distinct from saving your soul. Face is a public presentation of self; as Franklin stated, it concerns creditworthiness, character, industry, and frugality. These qualities are real when one earns a reputation for being an honorable participant in a market through consistently ethical behavior. Reputation is never a mere matter of appearance. And yet, appearance also matters; it is another aspect of face.

Saving face is avoiding shame, not only for yourself, but for everyone else in your group. Groups for whom cohesion is critically important are meticulous in their practice of respect; most especially these are military organizations, corporations, and families.

Saving your soul is entirely another matter. Your soul is the most private, personal, unique part of you. Requiring people to conform to group norms is often taken to be inimical to the soul's growth, development, and ultimate salvation.

In a shame culture your membership in the group and your role within it are the most important aspects of your identity; you are obliged to defend both. You will defend yourself against any attacks on your status—disrespectful gestures that would deprive you of prestige—by refusing to be treated in that way. You may withdraw from the dialogue, reassert your own position, show anger, or express your hurt and allow the other person to apologize. In some extreme cases you may be obliged to defend your membership in the group, or the group's values, by employing violent means.

This is the most extreme case, and extremes do not make the rule. "Saving face" de-emphasizes dramatic confrontations in favor of civility. Its paradigm is conflict-avoidance and conflict-resolution, not conflict-promotion. Drama occurs only when the everyday modes of civility break down, or when one is dealing with someone who does not respect them.

Perhaps, as Roger Fisher and William Ury suggest in *Getting to Yes*, the expression has a "derogatory flavor" in English. But they add, "This is a grave misunderstanding of the role and importance of face-saving. Face-saving reflects a person's need to reconcile the stand he takes in a negotiation or an agreement with his principles and with his past words and deeds."[16]

One can never save face at the expense of someone else. In the simplest bartering, the buyer pays more than he proposed and the seller receives less than he asked. Both, however, walk away thinking that they have gotten a good deal. Beyond the requirement to save your own face, you must always ensure that your competitor can save his.

Competition does not produce equal outcomes, for that would destroy any incentive to improve oneself. Some receive more or less than others; but all receive something. Competitive markets work to preclude divisions where the few have everything and the many have nothing. These latter gross disparities often provoke the most dramatic social confrontations.

All human societies have notions of honor. Their practices often differ sharply. Groups that promote violent punitive actions to defend their honor and pride are not shame cultures. Taking the least offense against honor to be a criminal action, not a failure of propriety, they seek to punish the offender, not to restore decorum. In the end they produce blood feuds, not civility.

Shaming is about ostracism. The ultimate penalty is ignominy, not torture and beatings. Montesquieu disputed Chinese boasting about their sense of honor by saying that nothing in that country got done without someone being beaten.[17] The same applies to those southern European cultures that supposedly have a strict code of honor but in which this involves constant fighting and an almost codified disrespect for women under the notion of machismo. Nor will I count as honor-bound the antebellum culture of the Southern plantation owner whose sense of "honor" required him to engage in brawls and feuds but did not allow him to dispense with the exploitation of slave labor.

In contemporary Japan almost no one considers violence to be a legitimate response to an insult.[18]

No one has failed to notice that America has had eminent representatives of both shame and guilt cultures.

In the early days of the Republic the difference was represented by the political opposition between Alexander Hamilton and Thomas Jefferson. The intensely proud Anglophile Hamilton believed that the most secure foundation for the nation would be to render it creditworthy; thus he nationalized the Revolutionary debt held by the states and created a national bank.

Hamilton favored industry, manufacturing, capital markets,

and trade. He, like Abraham Lincoln, placed the interest of the union over the rights of factions and states.[19] If our nation is closer to industrial England than to agrarian France, we owe it to Hamilton and his fellow Federalists.

A corporatist, market-oriented theory federalism at its best promoted national unity in order to avoid conflict among the groups that constituted the nation. Establishing a valid currency in which to conduct interstate and international commerce was one of its fundamental achievements. Also, it offered people a national identity modeled on the identity granted by membership in local communities.

Jeffersonian liberalism saw the interests of individuals and individual groups as primary. Where the Federalists were horrified by conflict and rebellion, Jefferson hailed the French Revolution, even to the point of initially accepting the Reign of Terror.

Idealistically, the Jeffersonians sought to free individuals from the constraints of groups and to free local groups from the power of the national government. Personal identity would derive from actualizing one's humanity more than from being a citizen of the American nation. No personality had more facets than Jefferson's.

The Francophile Jefferson favored a concept of individual liberty and democracy based on the rural agrarian lifestyle. The rural farm was self-contained and self-subsistent, autonomous and independent; it grew its own food and could therefore avoid the corrupting influence of commerce, trade, and markets. Jefferson's closest colleague, James Madison, wrote, "The class of citizens who provide at once their own food and their own raiment, may be viewed as the most truly independent and happy. They are more: they are the best basis of public liberty and the strongest bulwark of public safety."[20]

The Virginian slaveholders believed that living off the land (and someone else's labor) was the best way to remain virtuous.[21] Thus the Puritan work ethic was institutionalized by Hamilton, not Jefferson. Hamilton's defender, historian Forrest McDonald wrote, "Certainly devotion to work was not to be found among slaveowners, nor among their slaves, nor among the Scotch-Irish herdsmen who dominated the interior uplands, nor among the majority of yeoman farmers.''[22]

Of course, the two conflicting claims managed to find a modus operandi. Hamiltonian federalism made the machine run; Jeffersonian liberalism provided the brakes. ''The Jeffersonian tradition has had as its principal function acting as a censor of the demonic side of capitalism, speculative excess.''[23]

Saying that the interests of the marketplace can be well served by a judicial system that limits its excesses places us on the side of harmony and consensus. A guilt culture, however, sees capitalists preying on innocent people through rigged markets; only legislation and regulation can protect the people from predatory capitalists. Those who believe in sin and guilt hold that markets are intrinsically corrupt, ultimately that they should not exist.

American shame culture did not end with the inauguration of Thomas Jefferson. Beyond the reach of the national government local communities continued to practice traditional values.

During the presidency of Andrew Jackson, hardly a period of domestic tranquillity, Alexis de Tocqueville described how Americans used shaming to promote the values of hard work and family cohesion: ''All those quiet virtues that tend to give a regular movement to the community and to encourage business will therefore be held in peculiar honor by that people, and to neglect those virtues will be to incur public contempt.''[24]

On marriage and family, Tocqueville considered America to be exceptional in relation to the rest of the world: ''In America all those vices that tend to impair the purity of morals and to destroy the conjugal tie are treated with a degree of severity unknown in the rest of the world.''[25] Even in a time of considerable social ferment America retained her grounding in shame culture.

Asking whether America is a shame or guilt culture is like asking whether Americans are pragmatists or idealists. Do Americans seek to find solutions to practical problems, or do they hold to ideals that all citizens take as absolute truths?

The pragmatist tests his assumptions against reality; if they do not work in practice, they are discarded. The idealist disregards the judgment of reality; when his policies fail he blames others and works to punish them. He seeks a consensus of belief about who is at fault. Idealists excel at rationalizing failure.

The pragmatist represents the values of shame culture, the idealist the values of guilt culture. The one values what works, the other what people believe. The one derives from the military, the other from religion. The one is relentlessly this-worldly; the other believes in an ultimate otherworldly vindication.

Samuel Huntington has argued the case that America has assimilated people with different backgrounds and customs by proposing an ideology to which they could all adhere. As he described them, American ideals are liberal, individualistic, democratic, and egalitarian.[26]

Huntington held that in the absence of common rituals and ceremonies, of common national identity and national character, America offered membership in its community through common belief. This has a religious flavor, as though people were being welcomed into a congregation formed around a set of sacred texts.

Do Americans really all believe the same thing? Abraham Lincoln noted that North and South did not hold to the same concept of liberty: "With some the word liberty may mean for each man to do as he pleases with himself, and the product of his labor; while with others the same word may mean for some men to do as they please with other men, and the product of other men's labor."[27] Some people wish to be free to play the game, others to be free to break the rules.[28]

The cohesiveness of America does not lie in uniformity of opinion or in the documents that founded her institutions. The durability of America's institutions lies in the character of the people who have led them and the victories they have garnered

in economic and military competition. If America had been subjected to repeated military humiliations; if she had not been able
to provide a comfortable lifestyle for her citizens; if the leaders
of the dominant social institutions had been inadequate, corrupt,
or ridiculous, the population would long since have lost faith in
sacred documents.

Institutions do not function in a vacuum. Bright ideas do not
dictate social realities. People respect government because those
who represent the national interest command respect in their persons. Leaders provide the face of institutions, and if face is not
maintained society will break apart in a battle over the correct
interpretation of texts.

It took more than the Constitution to bring the nation together.
The nation needed a living symbol to provide its face. And his-
torians declare that the incontestable prestige of George Washington fulfilled that need.[29]

Noting that George Washington was, among the founding fathers, the one most aware of civility and etiquette,[30] Gordon Wood
emphasized the importance of an extraordinary act of humility at
the foundation of the American nation: "The greatest act of
[Washington's] life, the one that gave him his greatest fame, was
his resignation as commander in chief of the American forces.
Following the signing of the peace treaty and British recognition
of American independence, Washington stunned the world when
he surrendered his sword to the Congress on December 23, 1783,
and retired to his farm at Mount Vernon. . . . This self-conscious
and unconditional withdrawal from power and politics was a great
moral action, full of significance for an enlightened and republi-
canized world, and the results were monumental."[31]

Wood noted the critical importance of Washington at the Constitutional Convention. "His presence and leadership undoubtedly
gave the convention and the proposed Constitution a prestige that
they otherwise could not have had."[32]

Once in power, Washington was especially aware that he had
to appoint the most qualified and meritorious men to office. Nep-

otism, cronyism, and the use of ideological litmus tests were clearly not the way to build a nation.

America functions according to prescribed rituals and ceremonies that are practiced in common: whether pledging allegiance to the flag or voting or participating in a town meeting or serving on a jury or doing military service. The strength of the nation lies in the ability to offer a national identity to people who come from diverse backgrounds . . . regardless of their beliefs.

Thus the basis for American success. But, as we know from studying the psychology of individuals, being successful has a great deal to do with knowing how to deal with failure. If Vietnam is any indication, we have not done very well at this of late.

For a nation to maintain face it must take its failures as aberrations caused by poor leadership. When leaders do not take responsibility for failure, then the political and social order will be threatened. If a failure is not someone's mistake, it reveals a basic flaw about the nation.

In concrete terms: Was Vietnam an expression of some basic truth about America, or was it, and the attendant social chaos it caused, simply an error? Or, to load the questions somewhat differently: Did America during the Vietnam period and its aftermath finally learn to confront its ghosts and demons, or would the nation's problems have been confronted in a less divisive, more constructive fashion if Vietnam had never happened?

Was Vietnam something that had to happen given the nature of the American beast, or was it the product of a series of errors made by an immature and inexperienced president, his excessively idealistic staff, and his arrogant successor who could not admit to error?

One way of putting it might be: Should we feel shame or guilt over Vietnam? Given the disruption caused by Vietnam, the nation has been faced with two options: one requires that we restore pride, reassert dignity, and reaffirm integrity by reviving an indigenous but somewhat dormant shame culture. The other counsels accepting a degree of social disorder because we deserve it, and because it frees us to be autonomous individuals pursuing spiritual growth by repudiating corrupt institutions.

Do we need now to restore our sense of shame through civil behavior and respect for the feelings of others or to build a new world based on the endless drama of guilt and punishment? Should we respect the achievements of those leaders who built the nation or discredit them wherever possible for their flaws?

If the right to criticize the government were anything like the panacea the legal profession takes it to be, Vietnam would have been America's finest hour. Whatever went wrong in Vietnam it did not derive from the failure to protest. Nor has the nation corrected itself by placing its faith in regulators, litigators, and advocates.

Legalistic remedies have broken the nation into warring factions: extremes are glorified and the middle ground of consensus, cooperation, and productive enterprise has nearly been lost in the din.

Many have recently begun to experience some shame over the currect state of America. This will count as progress so long as we do not wallow in the feeling, but move quickly to restore and maintain our pride, our honor, and our dignity. So long, in other words, as we act to save face.

I

A Conflict of Cultures?

On December 3, 1984, poisonous methyl isocyanate started leaking from a storage tank at a Union Carbide insecticide plant in Bhopal, India, causing one of the worst industrial accidents in history. Eventually, more than three thousand people were killed; another three hundred thousand were exposed to the poison. Two thousand animals perished and another seven thousand were severely injured.

Four days later Union Carbide chairman Warren Anderson flew to Bhopal to assess the damage. He was immediately placed under house arrest and charged with negligence and corporate liability. The U.S. State Department had to intervene to free him.

Indian authorities, however, advised Anderson to leave the country quickly because his safety could not be guaranteed. To the local citizens, his visit was "perceived not as an expression of genuine sympathy, but as an attempt to pre-empt lawsuits."[1]

They knew whereof they spoke. On December 8 San Francisco lawyer Melvin Belli filed a $15 billion class action suit against Union Carbide. Two days later frenzied American lawyers started arriving by the planeload in Bhopal, tramping through the streets to sign up clients for the thousands of lawsuits that were to follow.

Defending victims of the "system" has long been a part of the social mandate held by American attorneys. Yet the spectacle of liability lawyers flocking to Bhopal in search of fees dishonored that principle, dishonored the legal profession, and, ultimately, dishonored the nation.

Union Carbide's attorneys were equally shameless. They sought to defend the company "by denying liability and . . . [continuing] the battle in the courts as long as possible." They wanted to shift blame from the parent company to its Indian affiliate and attempted to lower the cost of a settlement by asserting that the value of life in developing countries was lower than in advanced industrial nations.[2]

The overriding need to protect the company against litigation, coupled with an emphasis on technical mastery, made it impossible for company executives to respond to the psychological issues involved. Strategic response was undermined by the presumption of corporate guilt. No one imagined that the company, motivated solely by its sense of responsibility and its concern for its reputation, would apologize voluntarily and make a fair offer to the victims of the accident.

Much has recently been written about competition between American and Japanese cultures in the matter of industrial efficiency and productivity. Let us examine the different ways they deal with the psychological effects of corporate failure.

In August 1985 a Japan Air Lines plane crashed, killing 520 passengers and crew. The event became "a national crisis for the Japanese, who often view themselves as members of a great extended family."[3] In response, the company acted quickly to transport relatives of the victims to a command post it had set up.

In a scene that remains vivid in memory, the president of Japan Air Lines stood at the foot of the stairs of the arriving airplane and bowed deeply to each relative. At a news conference earlier he had said, "I can't find appropriate words to express my apology."⁴ Two days later he announced that he would accept responsibility by resigning his office. Together, Japan Air Lines and the plane's manufacturer, Boeing, negotiated a settlement of damages for the victims of the crash.

In Japan a chief executive is obliged to offer a shamefaced apology when his company has done something wrong. This ceremonial acceptance of responsibility applies whether or not the executive himself acted to cause the failure. Yet the Japanese distinguish between those managers who actually make mistakes and those who take responsibility for their subordinates. Both resign, but the latter are more easily reintegrated at some other post than the former.⁵

The basic principle dates from the time of Confucius. W. T. de Bary described its early articulation: "The ruler and his dynasty alone are made to bear responsibility for the sufferings of the people; there is no scolding of the people themselves for breaches of faith or derelictions of duty, nor are the people's sufferings seen as retribution visited upon them for their sins."⁶

Good leadership requires the capacity to accept responsibility for failure. Leaders always maintain an appearance of dignity and propriety; they are willing to tell small lies to cover up small failures that can be corrected internally. But when a major public failure occurs, there ought to be no thought of cover-up. Under such circumstances the good leader faces shame and offers a sincere apology.

This requires the group to accept that certain failures are incontestably real. Part of the formation of social consensus involves agreeing on what constitutes failure. So long as everyone agrees on which real events can compromise a leader there will be no problem in allocating responsibility.

Sometimes the term "saving face" is employed to describe

leaders who refuse to face shame. An arrogant leader does not admit to either error or failure. He might deny that the trauma has taken place or else, more commonly, blame someone else—his predecessors, his subordinates, the press, the cultural élite. Such leaders are not "saving face"; they are masking their shame.

Leaders who avoid shame in circumstances where they have failed will become tyrannical or ineffectual. They might even take control of the organs of public communication to present only those stories that save them from shame. Such leaders have no face to save. Either they rule by force or they do not rule at all.

Shame and guilt provide different approaches to leadership. The contrast stands out most clearly when a group has to face failure.

To understand how this works we need to understand the difference between these two sanctions. I will distinguish them sharply. Shame occurs when you do not do something you are supposed to do; guilt occurs when you do something you are not supposed to do. Shame involves failing to perform socially prescribed tasks. Guilt occurs when you commit an act that is prohibited by society.

Shame feels like being bereft and isolated for having failed one's group; guilt feels like the anxious anticipation of an impending and inevitable punishment for having broken a law.

Shame and guilt are not disconnected as autonomous spheres. Groups employ mechanisms of guilt and punishment when a deviant member lacks a sense of shame. If people have a sufficient sense of honor and decency to perform their social obligations and to recognize when they fail, the mechanisms of guilt and punishment may remain dormant.

Our own courts often take into account the accused's prior record and standing in the community. These, accompanied by a sincere expression of shame through an apology, often convince judges that the person is unlikely to commit further crimes. A perpetrator who shows himself to be shameless—that is, smug, arrogant, distracted, unable to acknowledge the harm he has done—is more likely to receive a harsher punishment.

The experience of shame involves a heightened sense of self-awareness. Not so much about how one feels about oneself, but of how one looks to others. When an individual realizes that his behavior places him at risk of being ostracized, he will rally all his resources to repudiate his shameful behavior and repair the damage to his reputation.

An individual whose status is threatened by public insult will repair his reputation by rejecting the implications of the insult. He feels anger and is obliged to save face by, for example, expressing the anger and allowing the offending party to apologize. He is not shamed by an insult; he would be shamed if he let it go unanswered or if he overreacted.

We observe a strange twist when there is too much shaming. A group that systematically shames an individual and refuses to allow him any face-saving response is treating him as someone whose behavior can only be controlled through enticements of reward and threats of punishment. Erik Erikson explained, "Too much shaming does not lead to genuine propriety, but to a secret determination to try to get away with things, unseen—if, indeed, it does not result in defiant shamelessness."[7]

When citizens feel they have been coerced by threat of physical punishment into behaving a certain way in public, they will be more likely to misbehave in private,[8] in order, strangely enough, to retain some sense of an identity. When people are repressed, rebellion is face-saving.

Shame cultures educate by persuasion, by showing the right way to do things; leaders provide an example for others to follow. Guilt cultures educate by fear of the consequences of doing the wrong thing; they evoke universal laws that disregard the vagaries of individual character and achievement.[9] This becomes more necessary when leaders are setting bad examples.

A wide range of mistakes may cause shame. From an airline's failing to ensure the safety of passengers whose lives are in its care, to using the wrong fork at a dinner party, to discovering that one's fly is open in public, to going back on one's word. Shame means that one has failed to observe any one of a large number of socially correct behaviors, whether of etiquette, politeness, obedience, or courtesy—up to and including the successful performance of a professional duty, as in a general's responsibility for his troops.

Shame is about rules and roles: following the rule and fulfilling the role. Every social role brings with it a considerable number of obligatory behaviors; failure to perform them correctly means that one is inadequate to the role. This makes it more difficult to continue to command respect. And without credible authority, one can only rule by force.

When shame is the dominant sanction, people accept that failure was an isolated unintentional occurrence that does not reflect one's moral character. And yet, having become associated in the public eye with uncharacteristic behavior, one must apologize publicly in order to accept the fault and vow that it will not be repeated. Anyone who does not experience shame at failure is asserting that the behavior was intentional and is likely to be repeated. Society will then tax him with guilt and impose coercive constraints.

Guilt assumes that one has violated a prohibition. A criminal act requires society to extract payment, usually in the form of punishment but also in the form of civil liability. Only the guilty party as an individual is punished; he alone suffers incarceration. At the same time, the shame for his actions is felt by his family and community.

While breaches of propriety should only cause feelings of shame or embarrassment, criminal acts may cause both shame and guilt. The corporate executive who is caught embezzling has committed a crime for which he alone is punished. But he should also feel shame for failing to uphold the duties of his office, which include responsible management of corporate funds. His family will share his shame, but not his guilt.

Shame and guilt represent two different ways of obtaining proper social behavior. Shame teaches a child that soup must be eaten with a spoon; guilt teaches him that soup may not be eaten with a fork. Shame need not prohibit or forbid; it shows what the correct social actions are and requires people to perform them. It assumes that the child's fondest wish is to be socialized into the world of adults. Guilt assumes that the child really wants to reject the unnatural practice of table manners.

Guilt tells what not to do. In its purest form it will not tell the child how to eat soup; it will simply list the wrong ways to eat soup. A clever child, of course, will hear these prohibitions and immediately find a loophole. Tell him that he should not eat his soup with a fork and he may respond by eating it with a knife, a cup, or his hands. Obeying the letter of the law, he will oblige you to invent more and more prohibitions.

A persistent parent might finally resort to rewards. If he believes that humans are motivated by less than honorable means, he will offer a new toy as a reward for avoiding bad table manners.

In more dramatic form, when human society attempts to civilize sexual behavior only through prohibitions, it will not limit itself to the incest taboo. If the primary constraint to your sexual expression is a law that makes your family members unacceptable sexual partners, your choice of partners and behaviors is so immense as to become unwieldy. If society proposes to favor traditional conjugal ties only by using prohibitions, then it will have to produce an extraordinary list of sexual taboos—pedophilia, premarital sex, adultery, homosexuality, perversions, masturbation, and so on. If it does not need to regulate behavior by taboo it will be less agitated about sexual deviations in private.

When sexuality becomes regulated by guilt, all tabooed acts have to be named and imagined to be avoided. And each time they are imagined the individual will experience guilt for thinking of sinful acts. But he will also experience desire, since the impulse to translate the fantasy into action has been blocked. Paradoxically, the more sex is associated with guilt the more people take their illicit desires to be their true desires.

The alternative approach, also part of our cultural heritage, declares conjugal relations to be a social obligation. Failing to live up to this obligation causes shame. Marriage is the only relationship implicating sexual activity that does not incite people to imagine what is going on between the sheets. It does not identify the participants by their sexual acts. As long as married couples add new members to society, the group has no need to know what they do in their private moments.

When criminals are punished for their crimes, society produces justice. And yet when guilt is the dominant sanction, justice becomes an ideal. The battle cry of guilt culture declares that everything would be wonderful if only there were more justice. And yet, there is never enough justice. . . .

Shame concerns local custom and convention; table manners are therefore a good example of how society inculcates proper behavior in this context. Guilt traffics in universal taboos. Based on religious ideals, which hold that mistakes violate God's law, guilt does not worry about things like table manners; its arena is larger, more cosmic, and far more dramatic. For this reason it promotes itself as more powerful than shame. God may decide to punish our iniquities by burying the earth in a meteor storm; thus why bother to be civil and courteous?

Beyond courts and prisons, guilt requires an inner policing mechanism called conscience. You feel guilty any time you know that you have done wrong; thus you have an internal policeman standing watch next to all of the STOP signs that he has strewn across the roads you travel. To protect you from your self-destructive tendencies, guilt culture will place a STOP sign at every driveway you pass.

The more these signs constrain your movement, the more you will be tempted to run them; unnatural, unreasonable, and excessive constraints produce a desire to transgress, and define your psyche as a constant struggle between these forces. If you are always aware of the penalty for running STOP signs, your conscience will force you to control your impulses to do so. To regulate them guilt culture will force you to confess your wishes and do proper penance.

An act of penitence may wipe away the stain of a specific sinful act; it does not erase the tendency to sin or the risk of temptation. When you make a mistake, there are advantages to seeing it in terms of guilt. Cleansing one's soul with self-flagellation is easier than restoring a damaged reputation by engaging consistently in socially acceptable behavior.

Self-punishment provides a way to numb the bad feelings that accompany occasional transgressions. But society will seduce people into accepting an irrational excess of regulation by offering extravagant gifts for good behavior. Confession of guilt accompanied by avoidance of sin produces eternal life.

The more miserable a sinner you are the more you will be open to receive a gift of divine love. You never feel all bad about guilt, because guilt places your soul on the path to redemption. Get in touch with your guilt, expiate it thoroughly, and you will receive an eternal reward.

For those who prefer earthly rewards, guilt cultures tend toward hedonism and decadence. One need but compare the British stiff upper lip with French *joie de vivre*. British shame culture is heavily honor- and duty-bound; French guilt culture has mastered the art of culinary decadence. Or compare, as a friend once suggested, the elegant sophistication of Chinese cuisine with the raw simplicity of Japanese food. Guilt culture always offers a reward for the torments of conscience.

Shame is another story: as an emotion it is properly intolerable, and has no redeeming features. When you feel that there is no saving grace to your failure, that there is nothing you can do immediately to make the pain go away, no lesson to glean, no virtue to develop, then you are feeling shame. When you cannot avoid the reality of failure, make up for the loss, or escape responsibility, you are feeling shame. No one embraces shame willingly.

Shame motivates most major psychological changes. Someone who truly experiences shame will do anything to ensure that he will never have to go through it again. Strictly speaking, however, he will only have truly progressed when he learns to do what he is supposed to do because he likes doing it, and not because he is trying to avoid shame.

The distinction between shame and guilt cultures dates at least to Confucius. He defined them as differing principles of governance: "If you lead them by regulation and try to keep them in order by punishment, the people will manage to avoid punishment but will have no sense of shame. If you lead them by virtue and keep them in line by rites, the people will have a sense of shame and regulate themselves."

The renowned cultural anthropologist Ruth Benedict wrote one of the best applications of the distinction between shame and guilt cultures. Preparing *The Chrysanthemum and the Sword* as a field manual for an American army occupying a defeated Japan in 1946, she chose to distinguish Japan as a shame culture from the United States as a guilt culture.

Benedict's definitions focus on the moral dimension of social behavior: "A society that inculcates absolute standards of morality and relies on men's developing a conscience is a guilt culture. . . ."[10]

Absolute standards for moral behavior transcend community norms. They allow an individual to defy his community and feel confident within himself that his virtue will reap its final reward. If he does not honor community standards, he will still feel that he is obeying higher laws that are more relevant to his task of finding salvation.

On the other side of the cultural divide, "true shame cultures rely on external sanctions for good behavior, not, as true guilt cultures do, on an internalized conviction of sin. Shame is a reaction to other people's criticism."[11] If we are concerned about how we look to others and believe that our self-worth will be given or taken away by those others, then we are functioning according to shame.

Guilt and shame cultures have fundamentally different views of self-respect, or face. According to Benedict, self-respect in Japan involves maintaining one's role and position, acting within the situation that presents itself, avoiding conflict and drama, doing nothing to provoke criticism, and doing what is necessary to achieve success.[12] Thus people are seen primarily as social beings striving to perform social obligations properly.

In a guilt culture, self-respect is defined otherwise: "even if thoughts are dangerous a man's self-respect requires that he think according to his own lights and his conscience."[13] Being in conflict with social institutions counts as a sign of moral virtue. Making up one's own mind, defying public opinion, refusing to conform—these aspects of radical individualism form the basis of what guilt culture counts as self-respect.

Nowadays many people believe that self-esteem increases as an individual learns to disregard what others think, how they react, or even the consequences of his actions. The dominant moral principle, often taken as a commandment, is to express yourself and get it all off your chest. Mental health professionals sometimes assert that people fall ill from pent-up emotion, and that if they ventilate it publicly they will feel better. Evidently, the obligation to say everything, to tell the whole truth, and to bear witness embodies the values of guilt culture.

When an executive in a shame culture offers a shamefaced apology, he is not ventilating emotion in the interest of cleansing his system. He is performing a social ritual for the good of the group; his well-being as an individual is identical to his performance of acts that serve the group. Effectively, he is cleansing the group of himself.

A guilt culture must promote a constant awareness of the criminal impulses that are assumed to inhabit everyone's psyche. Only by being aware of these impulses can the individual be sufficiently vigilant to control them.

A shame culture prefers people to deal with failures in private because the more we expose them the more we are putting thoughts in people's minds.

Moreover, any behavior that is constantly displayed in public will come to feel normal. If many people use drugs in public or talk about using drugs in public, then drug use becomes normal and anyone who does not conform becomes abnormal. Destigmatizing by overexposure does not just tolerate deviancy, it encourages it.

Shame and guilt cultures hold different views of human motivation. The one assumes that people are motivated by the duty to preserve their honor and reputation; society will then be organized to encourage this tendency. The other assumes that people seek to gratify themselves and to avoid pain; society will then be organized to reward obedience and to punish transgression. The first system characterizes the successful global tribal cultures; the second characterizes primitive cultures and cultures in decline, whether through despotism, disorganization, or decadence.

A soldier who fights because he fears retaliation is not as effective as one who fights for national honor. The first will be doing only what he has to do to avoid punishment; the second will do all that he can to achieve something positive. Similarly, a soldier who fights to plunder a defeated enemy will not be as effective as one who fights to fulfill his duty.

Shame culture begins with the Confucian notion that Ronald Dore called "original virtue."[14] The Chinese sage posited that people are normally motivated by a will to be virtuous members of harmonious groups. Dore summarized the point: "If you start from the assumption of original virtue, then something else follows. You assume that bonds of friendship and fellow-feeling are also important, and a sense of loyalty and belonging—to one's community, one's firm, one's nation—and the sense of responsibility that goes with it. And you would be likely to assume that economic institutions which bring out the best in people, rather than the worst, make for a more pleasant and peaceful, and probably in the end more generally prosperous society.''[15]

Institutions attempt to bring out the best in people by taking them at their best. Mistakes are almost always forgiven if the person apologizes with sufficient sincerity.

Taking people at their best involves teaching them proper social behavior. People function best when they are working to achieve what society requires of them. They become dysfunctional when they are wasting energy avoiding actions prohibited by law.

If culture inculcates the habits of good behavior, it will eventually bring out the normal tendencies of all people to do what is right. If the tendency is normal, neither carrot nor stick will be needed to obtain the proper response. In the Confucian world showing the right way constitutes the essential act of teaching.

In shame cultures the pain of failure is taken so seriously that every effort is made to ensure success. It is not sufficient to gear society toward avoiding failure, because that could most easily be achieved by avoiding all competition. Cowardice, then, is labeled the ultimate failure—failure to engage in society.

These cultures attempt to ensure success by obliging everyone to engage in rigorous training. People practice rote learning, exercise drills, repetitions of the same set of actions over and over again until doing things right and well becomes almost second nature.

Failure cannot be avoided all the time. Thus a shame culture teaches people how to fail with dignity, never to blame others, whether colleagues or opponents. Accepting defeat graciously does not mean being proud of losing.

Generally, shame cultures take failure to be an isolated event,

something that the individual would never willingly repeat. Therefore, they make every effort to restore his membership in the community. When groups shame people, they should do so only very
rarely and should also provide a ritual means of reintegration.[16]

The first step to reintegration requires the individual to accept
full responsibility for his error. Since this saves the community
the trouble of a trial, it counts as a gesture of conciliation. When
Japanese corporate executives resign their offices in disgrace, they
usually withdraw temporarily from society, eventually to be reintegrated into the life of the group. They become consultants,
advisors, or even vice-presidents, but they do not return to the
role of presenting the public face of the company.

More radically, in traditional Japan leaders who failed were
obliged to commit ritual suicide, seppuku. As Chu Chin-ning
stated, ''Suicide restores respect to those who have been dishonored by failure.''[17]

In politics, original virtue, as opposed to original sin, has
found its best embodiment in a government where people elect
representatives to conduct the business of the state. Republican
government requires trust in the judgment of citizens; it also requires citizens to trust the judgment of their representatives. As
James Madison wrote in *The Federalist* No. 55, ''As there is a
certain degree of depravity in mankind which requires a certain
degree of circumspection and distrust: So there are other qualities
in human nature, which justify a certain portion of esteem and
confidence. Republican government presupposes the existence of
these qualities in a higher degree than any other form. Were the
pictures which have been drawn by the political jealousy of some
among us, faithful likenesses of the human character, the inference
would be that there is not sufficient virtue among men for self-
government; and that nothing less than the chains of despotism
can restrain them from destroying and devouring one another.''

In the West guilt cultures derive from biblical and philosophical
sources. Emphasizing spiritual growth, they disregard the petty

obligations of community life in favor of an ideal world that would provide personal fulfillment. For guilt cultures, sin is the natural state of people living in less-than-ideal societies.

People who maintain guilt as their frame of reference are not concerned with whether the system functions or how well it functions. They would not care if the system ground completely to a halt in the pursuit of truth and justice. Effectively, this is what the Chinese did during their Cultural Revolution, when revolutionary justice destroyed all social institutions and when just about nothing functioned.

Guilt culture does not encourage a basic human impulse to do the right thing, because it assumes that left to their own devices, human beings will do the wrong thing. Society must impose laws to constrain the propensity to sin and must grant rewards to encourage correct behavior. Laws are the most perfect representation of ideas. They are beyond custom, beyond ceremony, beyond propriety, and beyond the persons who implement them; they are imposed on, not adapted to, reality.

The constraints of law are compensated by a general license in favor of anything that has not been forbidden, that is, anything you can get away with. Too often this license is applied to what are called ''rights.'' Guilt culture promotes itself as the champion of the individual, of his rights and freedom.

The will to sin and the counterforce of law exist in a state of social tension. Thus guilt culture always contains conflict and drama, because even if competing interests are controlled by laws and contracts, the human wish to exploit and abuse can never be eliminated. At the limit, guilt culture predicts that people will repose in a harmonious society when they cease to be human.

Oriental shame cultures tend to see the individual as a social reject, bereft of family and friends. His condition is held up as an example of the penalty inflicted on those who fail to conform. These shame cultures believe that guilt cultural values—like free expression, independence, autonomy—can only threaten social order.

The genius of Anglo-American politics lies in its ability to respect the rebellious individual, the nonconformist. As a pragmatic system it trusts but does not worship tradition: the fact that things have always been done one way does not mean that they need always be done that way. Tradition is accepted as a guideline subject to modification. Respect for tradition does not require anyone to be its slave.

Evidently, this differs significantly from societies that force the populace to be tyrannized by the past and from societies that make revolutionary behavior into a way of life.

Rather than see the individual threatening the interests of the dominant shame culture, our tradition invented a way for him to contribute to social stability and the improvement of policy. At the same time it has incurred the risk that the rights of the individual become so disruptive that they rend the social fabric in its entirety, as happened during our Civil War.

The heroic individual is a fixture in American civilization; at best, his role is to correct a malfunctioning culture, not to become the standard against which we need all judge ourselves. Society calls on the hero episodically, and it is not the destiny of each and every one of us to be such a hero. Obviously, not everyone has accepted this limited role for the individual.

Ralph Waldo Emerson wished to supplant American shame culture in favor of individual creativity. In his essay "Self-Reliance," he sought to make individual fulfillment a way of life: "Society everywhere is in conspiracy against the manhood of every one of its members. Society is a joint-stock company, in which the members agree, for the better securing of his bread to each shareholder, to surrender the liberty and culture of the eater. The virtue in most request is conformity. Self-reliance is its aversion. It loves not realities and creators, but names and customs."[18]

Emerson opposed custom, convention, conformity, and consistency. He saw the isolated individual as innocent, but corrupted by society. Social propriety could only throttle the full expression of individual creativity.

He thereby elevated a useful way of correcting society's mistakes into a way of life. If society conspires to hinder the individual's search for self-fulfillment, only the force of law can protect him from the group. In our day those who want to see government protecting the individual against the workings of the marketplace present their arguments under the banner of "rights." Guilt culture takes "rights" to be the enemy of respect, and holds the good of the individual to be in conflict with the good of the nation as a whole.

At the origins of the Republic, Alexander Hamilton disputed the idea that society, in the form of government, was the enemy of liberty. In *The Federalist* No. 1 he wrote: "On the other hand it will be equally forgotten, that the vigor of government is essential to the security of liberty; that, in the contemplation of a sound and well informed judgment, their interest can never be separated; and that a dangerous ambition more often lurks behind the specious zeal for the rights of the people, than under the forbidding appearance of zeal for the firmness of government. History will teach us, that the former has been found a much more certain road to the introduction of despotism, than the latter, and that of those men who have overturned the liberties of republics the greatest number have begun their career, by paying an obsequious court to the people, commencing Demagogues and ending Tyrants."

In *The Federalist* No. 9, Hamilton sought to guard against a phenomenon that sounds like the worst excesses of our own special interest groups, whereby we would, in his words, be "splitting ourselves into an infinity of little jealous, clashing, tumultuous commonwealths, the wretched nurseries of unceasing discord and miserable object of universal pity and contempt."

Excessive individualism causes societies to fragment into groups at war with each other. When people come to believe that groups, like individuals, are motivated by original sin and that the success of one can only take place at the expense of the other, these groups become factions. When a nation fragments into warring factions, each led by its own demagogue, this usually gives rise to calls for a larger tyrant to force these groups together into one nation.

Throughout our history the concept of the individual has allowed open debate and even rebelliousness. Currently, however, individuality has become an ideal: many now believe that you should judge each person as a unique and autonomous being, disregarding any qualities associated with others who belong to his family or social group.

I call this an ideal because it cannot happen in reality. If there were someone you could deal with only as an individual, he would have nothing in common with anyone you had ever had any dealings with or had ever known anything about. Under this condition you would be facing a monster. I will disregard the metaphysical question of whether such a being could exist.

Every human being has characteristics that allow you to identify him as human; therefore you treat him in a way that is appropriate to a human being but not to a chaise longue. Other characteristics lead you to associate him with groups: he belongs to a family, a community, an ethnic group, and perhaps a religious congregation. He probably works for a certain company or practices a profession. Each of these groups has a reputation constructed over many years by a record of success or failure. We commonly think that a person comes from a good neighborhood, or went to a good school, or works for a good company. We judge people by whom they call their friends, whom they marry, and by whom they dissociate themselves from. It is impossible to see the person as disconnected from all groups.

A reputation is always subject to modification, depending on the behavior of other members of the groups one belongs to. A group's leaders will embody the group's reputation in the example they set, the successes they achieve, the apologies they offer, and the judgments they make about what constitutes acceptable behavior within the group.

A culture does best when it respects an individual's innovative contributions without thinking that each and every person in the society needs to become a self-contained individual.

When we talk of "culture" today we are not referring to the same thing as Ruth Benedict and her colleagues. Usually, we think of "culture" as comprising the arts and the media, the forms of public expression that are separate from governance, business, and the professions.

By culture, Benedict meant "the patterns and standards traditionally handed down"[19] to an individual from his community. Culture sets down a certain number of policies, values, and principles that will direct the course of one's life. It will define the right things to do and the right ways to do them by using the examples set by people who are leading real lives within socially determined rules and roles.

These aspects of culture are transmitted through ceremony and ritual. Pledging allegiance to the flag is a concrete gesture that is performed in the same way by all citizens. The uniformity of the practice joins people as members of a single group. And it also connects them to others who engaged in the same ritual in the past.

A military culture is constituted by ritual salutes, showing the colors, sharing common songs and common meals, wearing the same uniform, undergoing the same training, and participating in behaviors that are prescribed by the group. In a shame culture, group cohesion is produced by public behaviors, not by private beliefs.

Think of a culture as a game. The game has been going on for some time, it has its rules and players, and past matches have shown that some strategies are better than others. All of this is given to you; you are free to enter the game and to play it to the best of your ability. Within this framework you may be clever and creative, but you do not have the right to play by your own rules. And if you choose to persist with a losing strategy, the game does not have any obligation to make you feel like a winner.

In places like China and Japan the influence of culture manifests itself as ancestor worship. This represents a literal application of the fact that "face" has a concrete, as well as a metaphoric, meaning. Shame cultures put faces on the system of inherited behavioral prescriptions and social policies; they thereby humanize the relationship to culture. Ancestors receive honor for having maintained, and even enhanced, community standards.

Ancestors exist as practical examples of something that is achievable because it has already been achieved. They do not represent ideal or divine beings who are worshipped for doing things we will never accomplish ourselves.

Shame cultures value those who live lives of quiet dignity fulfilling their social and personal obligations; these individuals serve as the best examples for others, especially the young. A child will honor his or her ancestors by becoming a vice-president, a firefighter, a professor, a lawyer, a parent, and by fulfilling the same social obligations that governed the ancestors' lives.

The role models proposed by guilt culture are unique and inimitable, and they always come in pairs: the saint and the sinner, the famous and the infamous, the tyrant and the rebel. The important point is that their example cannot be emulated. No matter what happens, your child will not grow up to become Oprah, Larry Bird, Hamlet, Oedipus, Ted Bundy, Mao Zedong, or Martin Luther King.

Whether they exist in a courtroom, in a theater, or on television, the personalities that serve as role models in guilt culture live lives of constant drama. They are each uniquely themselves, they are one of a kind, they cannot be reproduced. Of course, you cannot have a society made up of celebrities and fictional characters. Nevertheless, they are the truest individuals.

In times of social crisis—as in our own Cultural Revolution —people model their behavior on what they see in the famous or the fictitious. Some even perform the most repulsive actions in order to create their own little island of fame. Preferring the order of drama to no order at all, they believe that being a character in a public drama is the antidote to social anomie.

So people idolize Elvis and denounce their parents; they imitate Beavis and Butt-head and mock those who earn a living, bring up children, and otherwise function as "pillars of the community." At a time that we find serial killers endlessly fascinating, the idea of being a "pillar of the community" sounds like a stale joke.

If we are more prone to imitate what we see in art, this suggests that we have blurred the boundary between real and make-believe. Television presents real events as though they were fictional and fictions as though they were real.

But are the artists at fault, or are they reflecting something about our leaders? After all, at the summit of this confusion the American people elected a Hollywood actor president for two terms.

The confusion began with the first truly telegenic president, John Kennedy. Kennedy's qualifications were flimsy at best, but he seduced the nation with his charm and wit. His was the only presidency that asked to be judged in reference not to actual achievement but to a mythical kingdom. Behind the hype about Camelot, the Kennedy presidency was short on accomplishments and ought to be held accountable for getting the nation involved in the worst foreign policy mistake of our times, Vietnam.

The blurring of boundaries must originate at the top. When leaders play to the camera as though they were acting a part, people become confused about what should be emulated and what is fiction. Eventually, everyday people will come to emulate fictional characters: they will value charm over substance and seek any means to express individual quirks. The more a leader shares what is private about his personality, the more he will be loved by the people and the poorer will be the example he sets for decorous social behavior.

The better a leader communicates the greater the chance that he can trick his listeners into ignoring the evidence of their own experience. He may convince them that things are wonderful when they are not, or that things are awful when they are perfectly fine. At the limit, demagogues can convince people that reality does not exist, and that nothing can possibly happen to disprove their vision.

Like the perfect lover, the ideal political leader never makes mistakes. Not only is the emperor not wearing the new clothes he imagines, but his subjects, upon being informed of the subterfuge, see it as a call to love him better. Can they, through their eyes, dress him in imperial finery, denying their knowledge of what does and does not constitute ceremonial dress?

When the insignia and trappings of office become costume, the world becomes a theater, and nothing is real . . . not calamity, not misery, not defeat, not even success. Thus no action need be taken. Like spectators in a theater, who know they have no influence on events, the citizenry will seek to cultivate their aesthetic sensitivities, that is, to get in touch with their feelings.

It is never enough to know how things go wrong. To set them right we need to understand the principles that regulate normal social relationships. We do not want human contacts to be a permanent drama, a permanent passion play, a permanent trial. But what is required for things to be otherwise? The basic requirement falls upon those who assume positions of responsibility in society. They have the greatest influence on social behavior. Leaders must always maintain the dignity of their office, act with decorum and integrity, and set an example fit for others to follow. They show benevolence in assuming their role; they give to the people but do not take from them. And this mix of good character traits must always contain humility: the ability to see one's own failings and correct them so that the group does not have to undergo the trauma of removing a leader by force.

Leaders who indulge in emotional outbursts, express their confusion and indecision, or who expose their private matters in public will often produce more of the same in the rest of the populace. The leader's sex life should not be a matter of public discussion. No one can command respect when his fly is open or when he has shirked a public duty.

Social harmony is not imposed by a leader. It is produced by practices that others emulate. These must be enacted by all members of society in the commerce of everyday life. They are characterized by good manners, propriety, civility, decency, and courtesy.

Among the other principles that regulate everyday social interaction to produce harmony in a shame culture Benedict isolated a principle of reciprocal exchange. She was impressed by how many interactions between individuals in Japan were controlled by requirements to keep emotional ''accounts'' in balance.

Every time anyone did a favor or offered a gift to someone else, a debt was contracted; the recipient was bound on his honor to repay it . . . sooner rather than later. Benedict saw clearly that this system functioned according to an economic calculation about the exchange of feelings. ''Love, kindness, generosity, which we value just in proportion as they are given without strings attached, must have their strings in Japan. And every such act makes one a debtor.''[20]

Extremes are always excluded. Too generous a gift is impolite, even insulting, because it imposes too great an obligation on the receiver. No gift at all is also impolite: first, it takes the other person's feelings for granted, and second, it represents a wish to take without giving.

However fervently we pay lip service to the ideal condition where affection is offered with no strings attached, in our culture people often make very strict calculations about what they have done for whom, and about who owes them what. The rules may be looser than in Japan, but people have a very clear sense of social reciprocity, even if they prefer to believe that their motivations are more noble. But, then again, why is it less noble to take other people's feelings strictly into account?

A shame culture requires civility and propriety of each of its members, on a permanent basis. Each person gains confidence by knowing unambiguously what he needs to do in order to maintain his status in the group.

Sometimes we feel that ritual bowing and scraping, gestures of respect and humility, formal exchanges of business cards, are insincere expressions of artificial hierarchies.

Everyone seems to hate hierarchical forms of address. And yet the opposite, rudeness and familiarity, does not have very much to recommend it. And it has its own price. Not only does familiarity breed contempt, as the saying goes, but familiarity also produces anger and hatred. These become a breeding ground for tyrants.

A social hierarchy with many steps allows for the most equitable distribution of goods in society. As well, it shows a practical means to social advancement: one small step at a time, not a giant leap across a social chasm. The alternative to hierarchy is not equality, but a society like we see in many Latin American nations: the few own everything, and the many own nothing.

Of late, Japan has stood out as the most flagrant example of shame culture. Japan may seem strange and foreign, but in recent years it has become increasingly real to us. As our own social interactions become more impolite and indecent and as our society becomes increasingly crime-ridden, we look with some awe at a relatively crime-free Japan.

Observers are often astonished by the number of minor rituals the average Japanese person has to go through on a daily, even an hourly, basis. Japanese people know what they have to do, how they must do it, toward whom, when, and where. Social contact is orchestrated through a series of gestures that everyone knows and that everyone follows. Knowing that with this person you must bow at fifteen degrees and with that one at thirty degrees, and that you must use this pronoun and this verb form with this person and that pronoun and verb form with that one, seems to us to be almost like living in a straitjacket.

Such a system provides a powerful sense of group cohesion; individuals have an unshakable sense of belonging to the group, and they know exactly what they have to do to continue to maintain their membership. Few people experience psychic distress for not knowing whether or not they belong anywhere.

An obvious example of the orchestration required in a shame culture exists in the workplace. Here we see another level of reciprocal exchange. Relationships are based on a primary social contract: the company promises to provide lifetime employment for the employee; in return the employee dedicates his efforts and pledges his loyalty to the good of the company. While the Japanese practice of this contract has frayed recently, the American practice has collapsed under mass layoffs and an increasing reliance on outside suppliers and temporary workers.

A certain number of virtues are required of an efficient and diligent employee. He needs to know his job and his place within the company; he needs to be loyal to the company and respectful of his superiors. But the subordinate cannot simply follow orders out of fear of reprisal; he can function optimally only if he respects his manager's judgment and if he knows that his manager respects him.

Hierarchy is clearly the rule. Beyond pep talks and indoctrination sessions a Japanese corporation trains new employees to perform a number of respectful acts; every interaction between executive and subordinate will reflect the different positions each occupies within the hierarchy. The subordinate will bow somewhat deeper than his boss, will walk slightly behind his boss in the hall, will enter the elevator after his boss, and will offer honest opinions when asked.

When he begins his employment the subordinate will spend days being drilled in all the proper gestures of respect. He may not have specific reasons to respect his executive supervisor, but he will be taught to act as though he does. Confucianism teaches that performing the proper social rituals and ceremonies, even if you do not know why, produces the right feelings toward others.

Corporate life also includes spiritual and disciplinary training. Employees are inducted into the group by going on retreats, visiting temples, and enduring special hardships together. Companies have uniforms, badges, songs, and mottoes. Everyone is taught the daily ceremonies for opening the store, commencing work, or starting physical exercise. Employees are also encouraged to spend their off-duty hours together, whether drinking or going to baseball games or family outings. And no individual criticizes a co-worker to his face. Such tactics would subject the other person to embarrassment.[21]

This does not mean that no one ever utters any disparaging remark. Criticism has its appropriate time and place. Outside work, under cover of alcohol, a low-level manager may criticize his supervisor in the most violent terms. Even though the behavior does not threaten his face, the supervisor, evidently, will do well to take heed. If the supervisor were criticized to his face, he would have a greater obligation to save face than to change his way of treating his employees. Thus direct confrontation would be counterproductive.

The rule of avoiding confrontation extends to everyday polite conversation. To the shock of many Westerners the Japanese tend to tell others exactly what these others want to hear. No value is placed on self-expression or self-assertion; the goal is harmony, not conflict and dispute. People are trying to get along, not to impress others with the superiority of their wit or their intellectual acumen.

Shame cultures minimize verbal in favor of gestural communication. To avoid offending people you must be able to read facial gestures. If you see that someone is about to take offense at something you are saying, you can stop before you give offense. Avoiding conflict takes precedence over resolving conflict. Nothing is to be gained by talking things out, revealing all wounds, sharing all pain, and telling others exactly what you think of them. Western openness often produces unacknowledged psychological damage. Insults launched in the heat of passion are held to be truths, undermining trust and confidence. At times, to overcome the feeling of vulnerability they have gained from having confessed too much and made themselves look irretrievably bad, people feel obliged to sever social ties.

Sharing secrets is a very serious gesture; you would abuse it if you poured out your soul to the person standing next to you on the subway. Revealing too many intimate details too often to too many people places undue burdens on them. The rule of reciprocity makes them feel obliged to offer up their own family secrets, and many of your acquaintances do not know you well enough to do so freely.

Shame cultures prefer friendship to the mixture of aggressiveness and possessiveness that often characterizes romantic love. As we shall see, guilt cultures promote passionate attachment as a primary social value. Disparaging ceremony and ritual, they have few other ways to connect people.

Where friendship is dominant you wish the best for your friends and feel happiness for their success; it reflects well on you to have successful friends. When romance is dominant, you will resent others their success, feeling that the fruits of success are a limited resource and that "they" have taken something away from you. Romance both requires and produces conflict.

Friendship is a nonbinding, noncontractual social link that ought to dominate the divisive effects of romantic love. Friendship values consistency, loyalty, and steadfastness; romance finds its resource in surprise, conflict, frustration, and excitement. In our civilization, Aristotle offered the best articulation of the central importance of friendship in his *Nicomachean Ethics*, whereas Freud thought that society was held together by libidinous strivings that always need to be held in check.

Meanwhile, back in America, a telling symptom of what happens when the values associated with guilt become dominant lies in what is called the self-esteem movement. Self-esteem is the guilt-cultural version of "face": it emphasizes how you feel about yourself, no matter how others see you. It transcends the conventional to vault you into the absolute. Let us examine how it works in practice.

In Plainfield, Indiana, a few years ago, a middle school decided that everyone who wanted to be a cheerleader would be accepted on the squad. To promote the psychological health of its students the school abolished tryouts; no one would be permitted to fail in a competition. Having discovered that students who did not win a place on the cheerleading team lost self-esteem, the school felt that it had little choice but to admit everyone. The same policy was extended to all other extracurricular activities.

Somewhere else in America, a has-been Hollywood producer named Julia Phillips wrote her memoirs. Having co-produced some of the best movies of the 1970s—*Taxi Driver*, *The Sting*, *Close Encounters of the Third Kind*—Phillips used her book *You'll Never Eat Lunch in This Town Again* to expel an anguished cry of rage against the system that she blamed for making her waste her considerable fortune on cocaine and dissolute living. Her behavior ruined her reputation; therefore she blamed not only the system but also her mother.

She made a fool of herself before associates, friends, and family; what was left but to expose her failings to public scrutiny? Phillips was proud of her shame; she exhibited her failures like so many badges of honor; she exulted in her newly enhanced self-esteem.

These two relatively minor events highlight the serious flaws in current thinking about self-esteem. The cheerleaders have clearly not gained any self-esteem. If everyone is accepted, then being a cheerleader loses its value; wearing the uniform cannot signify any positive achievement.

Because of this policy, the squad became too large and disjointed to cheer effectively. When the story was carried on CNN and in *The New York Times*, the spectacle of a seventy-two-member cheerleading squad subjected the school to ridicule. When the same policy was applied to the school band the disharmony was even more jarring.

We can only regret that children were held up to ridicule because some parents and educators had a skewed sense of self-esteem and wished to spare their children the pain of competition and the joy of achievement.

Here we see on a small scale a group in disarray. Children are not held to standards; they are acceptable no matter what they do or how they behave. The honor of belonging to the squad is degraded for everyone because it cannot be earned by anyone. No one learns what it means to have a place in society, to function as part of a harmonious group, to perform at a certain level of competence. All that is required is a wish to be a cheerleader, and presto, the school makes the wish come true.

The Hollywood producer presents a different facet of the problem. Her good feelings about herself are so powerful that she does not care what anybody thinks about her. Effectively, they function like a drug.

She may revel in overcoming her shame, but I suspect it was a deficient sense of shame that got her into trouble in the first place. If she had cared about how she looked to others, she would perhaps have comported herself with greater dignity. If she had been more willing to take responsibility for her own behavior, she would have been less prone to indulge herself.

Now, in order to assure the world that her deplorable behavior was not just an aberration, she perpetuates it by telling as many dirty secrets as she knows about anyone who had the misfortune to cross her path. Perhaps the men who control Hollywood, like men in other industries, were somewhat reticent and diffident about granting executive authority to a young woman. Still and all, they did do it. Has Phillips helped or hurt her cause by showing that she cannot be trusted with the kinds of secrets that people who work together closely know about each other, and that her loyalty can be sacrificed in the interest of having a best-seller?

Her goal is to indict the system. Instead of maintaining her dignity, she has made her life into a symptom of the intrinsic corruption of the system. It is as though she, and many others who have written such books, were saying that the only honorable thing to do when caught in such a degenerate world is to make one's life a testimony to its evils. Indecorous self-exposure and betrayal of confidence are presented as good signs, worthy of emulation by those who seek high self-esteem.

People make mistakes; sometimes achieving too much success too soon causes them to go off the track. Once this happens, however, an individual with a sense of shame will seek to erase the memory of his bad times from the minds of his friends and associates. He will allow such episodes to pass under a discreet silence. He will want to show that if you deal with him in the future you will not be dealing with a deviant.

Advertising your failures does not accomplish this goal. Attempting to humiliate and ridicule your former friends and family is not a sign of moral character either. Even if the public display of stigmata elicits some sympathy, it will not win you any respect.

In both of these cases self-esteem is taken to be a property of an individual, something that he feels at the expense of the group. If we saw each cheerleader's self-respect as depending on the level of accomplishment of the squad, then it would be defined as it usually is, according to each person's contribution to the group's performance.

Those who are excluded from the squad should understand that they would better serve both themselves and the school by engaging in activities where they can develop other talents and interests.

Phillips assumes that the best way to feel good about herself is to make others feel bad about themselves. High self-esteem belongs to the heroic individual who has the courage to stand out from the crowd to denounce the group that has refused to accept him. Too often, however, he himself has rejected the group's values and principles, and has little claim to its respect.

The current American interest in self-esteem has promoted cultural policies whose purpose is to abolish shame. Recognizing that shame results from failure and that failure inheres in the nature of competition, many educators and psychologists have sought to abolish competition. No one should be judged as better or worse, as having more or less.

This policy derives from a too literal application of the idea that all people are equal. As Christopher Lasch wrote, "We do children a terrible disservice, however, by showering them with undeserved approval. The kind of reassurance they need comes only with a growing ability to meet impersonal standards of competence. Children need to risk failure and disappointment, to overcome obstacles, to face down the terrors that surround them. Self-respect cannot be conferred, it has to be earned."[22]

Self-esteem has become another term for false pride. When we read that the math scores of American eighth-graders are lower than those of their fellows in the other major industrialized nations, but that they have the highest opinion of their own ability, we know that something is radically wrong. These students are not only the least capable, but they are also the most deluded about their ability. If they base their self-esteem on their beliefs instead of their scores, they will take severe offense at anyone who would recognize them for what they can actually do instead of what they think they can do.

The Hollywood producer typifies the second part of the strategy. By taking pride in shameful behavior she is participating in a more or less organized campaign to desensitize people to shame. The more people expose their private lives in public the more such behavior will become normal and customary. Instead of fearing being caught with their pants down, people take their pants off voluntarily and demand to be respected for their candor. In trying to subvert conformity they create a situation where self-exposure becomes a new badge of honor.

Together these two policies elevate the individual at the expense of the group's interests. Having identified and smoked out the demon shame, having laid all emotional suffering at its doorstep, they seek to conquer it by giving people the power to be themselves: free, creative, and equal, unencumbered by society's strictures and structures.

Since shame concerns how you look to other people, you may overcome it by ignoring other people, denouncing them as unworthy of judging you, or by seducing them into seeing you the way you want to be seen. The desensitization program seeks to undermine social obligations and to promote frank and open relating.

These methods of education propose that guilt in itself can socialize people. Their defenders worship the morally superior individual and seek to save him from community standards and practices. You will have more freedom to do whatever you please if the only constraint on your behavior is your knowledge of which acts are explicitly prohibited by law.

It is generally admitted that there are no pure shame or guilt cultures.[23] I disagree with those who identify shame culture with primitive methods of socialization and guilt culture with "literate and urban cultures."[24] In fact, I consider the opposite to be closer to the truth. Those groups that have assumed leadership roles in advanced industrial societies have promoted civility as a primary social virtue and have shown respect for the greater number of people.

Guilt cultures tend toward superstition: their rituals expiate guilt more than affirm group membership. Since all gains are illgotten, some part must be sacrificed to the god from whom they were stolen, the better to forestall punishment. Those who deprive themselves of goods show that they know how to expiate guilt. Those who do not will inevitably be punished by losing it all. Cultures operating according to these rules use ritual to avoid danger, not to promote civility.

Shame culture derives from the marketplace, not the bullring. It promotes civility with sophisticated codes of social conduct. Instead of raising the fist of confrontation, it extends the hand of respect. The true measure of such a culture is the extent to which the leadership élites "give face" to the rest of society.

A culture that systematically brutalizes women falls short of our standards for showing respect to people. No culture can pretend to value reciprocal respect while practicing foot binding, wife beating, or genital mutilation. Such attempts to produce good behavior by threat and punishment characterize guilt cultures.

In comparison to imperial Chinese or southern Europeans, the Puritans who settled the Massachusetts Bay Colony "sternly enforced" the rule that a husband could neither beat nor verbally abuse his wife.[25] One man was charged as a criminal for saying that his spouse was not his wife but a servant.[26] In this as in other situations, David H. Fischer writes, "The object of these proceedings was not punishment or retribution, but the restoration of good relations within the family."[27]

Such are the ways and means of a shame culture.

Shame cultures tend to be moral; they do not pretend to be perfect. The existence of flaws does not in itself disqualify a culture; the failure to remedy them over a long period of time does. The standards against which cultures are judged are those of the most successful groups; no culture should be excluded or included on the basis of its resemblance to some ideal state, even if we take that state to be our own.

Even if the United States is a shame culture, it is still clear that many Americans find something not quite right, even grating, at times frankly repellent, in Oriental cultures. However wonderful things appear to be in Singapore these days, we have great difficulty believing that Lee Kuan Yew's authoritarian capitalism is really as benevolent as it appears, or that it has not been purchased at the price of severe restrictions on personal freedom. How would you like to be fined $250 for spitting on the sidewalk, even more for failing to flush a public toilet?

Such anecdotes, commonly known, beg the question: Is it true that people behave with more civility in Singapore and Japan because they are more fearful of punishment? No one gets caned in Japan; and yet, civility is the rule rather than the exception.

Ultimately, people who do not spit on sidewalks and do flush public toilets are simply considerate of the feelings of others. They are as considerate as they would be toward members of their own family. Many cultures value cleanliness as a sign of respect toward others. Where fines prohibit indecorous public behavior, do people show propriety because they are being forced to do so or because it feels natural despite the threat?

A lot of people believe that the Japanese are simply putting a good face on things. Behind the surface appearance, behind the pro forma public apologies, behind the extraordinarily ritualized and ceremonial modes of interrelating must lie a seething mass of powerful emotion struggling to get free.

Through the eyes of Western intellectuals, Japan appears to embody a repressive social order that sacrifices pleasure to convenience, truth to appearance, creativity to conformity. Of course, there is some truth to the charges. But we are also missing something. Japanese people need not experience any of this as repressive; they often rejoice over the fact that they live in comfort and security. And given the choice, many of them may well prefer their way of doing things. They may be paying a price—as we are—but they may believe that giving primacy to civil behavior is worth the repression of their impulses to be obnoxious.

According to many of our mandarins, Oriental shame cultures ought not to work. Our best thinkers hold to the belief that truth will out over appearance, that no one can be truly happy unless he can exercise his creativity to the fullest, and that social order must be based on liberty, democracy, and equality. If these are truths, then Japan and the four Asian Tigers must be frauds.

The more important reason, many intellectuals intone, is that human relationships are based on power, not on pride, prestige, and self-respect. The word "power" has become a shibboleth in certain circles these days, and it exemplifies the belief that coercion is the ultimate truth of human society.

Guilt-ridden thinking holds that people are not searching for a harmonious mean, but that they are either indulging or repressing their impulses toward exploitation. It also believes that people want to force others to obey and will abuse any advantage that comes their way. Satisfying a guilty pleasure in a dark corner will always prevail over a concern for how things look to others.

Freud offered one of the strongest secular versions of human-kind's thrust toward sin: "Lusts which we think of as remote from human nature show themselves strong enough to provoke dreams. Hatred, too, rages without restraint. Wishes for revenge and death directed against those who are nearest and dearest in waking life . . . are nothing unusual."[28] Freud even pretended that people were not sufficiently cognizant of evil: "We lay a stronger emphasis on what is evil in men only because other people disavow it and thereby make the human mind, not better, but incomprehensible."[29]

Will truth overcome the hypocrisy of surface appearances? If you believe that justice is always done, you will also believe that the suppressed force of truth will erupt in democratic revolution. Wouldn't we be better off disregarding the veneer of face?

The human face is an apt representative of surface and superficiality; our religious tradition has denounced it in favor of the soul. We have been taught that the inscrutable Oriental face is a locus of lies and deceit; the more inscrutable the face the more repressed the person. Guilt culture holds that the face ought to be a window to the soul.

Both face and soul concern the moral dimension of human life; the first values living in harmony with one's fellows; the second, living in harmony with the angels. Shame and guilt cultures maintain a fundamentally different approach to the question of building moral character.

In a shame culture appearances are kept up and rituals are followed scrupulously in order to build character from the outside in. If you want to build character, it is better to pretend that you have it than to prove that you don't.

Pretending to have character requires you to follow social conventions, customs, and ceremonies—whether you believe in them, understand them, or feel what they are supposed to be expressing. The more you do this the easier it will become; you will come to understand why you are doing what you are doing as you enjoy the benefits it confers.

To answer this, guilt culture will always retort, But would it be worth losing your soul to save your face? You should never suppress your soul's feelings in order to save something that is superficial and meaningless. When your soul is submitted to its last judgment, will God care whether you ate your soup with a fork or a spoon?

Face is not an image you don like a mask to go out in public. Think of it as psychological capital, something you inherit from those who have come before you and will seek to preserve for those who will come after. Your reputation, credibility, and dignity are qualities that you invest in your personal relationships. You choose your friends and colleagues carefully because once you are connected with them, your reputation will rise or fall in tandem with theirs.

No one ever deals with you as a unique individual. Everyone you meet makes judgments about your character based on his experience of the behaviors of other members of your family or community.

Face belongs to groups. You have it because you belong to certain groups—family, company, community, nation. Belonging is conferred through participation in the group's ceremonies and rituals and through the ability to act in public as a dignified representative of the group.

Psychological capital belongs to the group; each individual has a share in it and a responsibility to maintain it. It is distributed equitably but not equally. The leader has the most; his actions are most pertinent to the group's reputation and credibility. When something goes wrong, his shame is the greatest.

Face is not about whether you have a nice personality, or whether people like you for your personal qualities. Based in the marketplace, it tells whether people trust you enough to do business with you. Since the marketplace is made up of competing groups, doing business also means trusting your colleagues, resting assured that you are not out there on your own without support.

When people form friendships or relationships they create new groups. If you invest your psychological capital—to say nothing of time and energy—in a new friend you expect to benefit from that friendship. If a new friend proves to have values inferior to yours, to have a reputation that makes people think less of you for associating with him, then you are likely to withdraw from the friendship . . . to cut your losses.

Social standing is not equivalent to economic prosperity, but it cannot exist if the two are wildly out of balance. A man who cannot support his family will have lost face, no matter what other qualities he maintains. But a man who supports his family through honorable enterprise will have more ''face'' than one who has accumulated wealth through dishonorable means.

Investments of psychological capital are regulated by one's sense of shame. Well-tuned shame tells you whether you are gaining or losing face, whether you are succeeding or failing in your social relations, whether to get closer to someone or to distance yourself. It tells you when you have to work harder to be a worthy member of the group and when your values are askew.

With individuals it often happens that this regulatory function gives imprecise readings. As the cliché says, people lose touch with reality. Some are thick skinned, others thin skinned. Some are too sensitive to criticism, making the least slight into a matter of momentous consequence that can only be remedied through the most extreme means. Others are insensitive to the insults that are wearing away at their social standing, until one day they wake up to discover that they have been acting slavishly and have not known it.

If there are extremes in the sensitivity to shame, then there must also be a reasonable mean, one that avoids suggesting that we need never feel shame or that we need always feel it.

The only way to know whether one's shame barometer is properly calibrated is to test it against a rigorous analysis of the specific situations that have or have not produced shame. This requires objective analysis of one's standing in a community, the reputation of the groups to which one belongs, the correctness of a specific action or inaction, and, most especially, the objective, measurable consequences.

Effectively, the primary motivating factor in human psychology is the requirement to maintain one's self-respect, to save face. Psychological theorists have made a significant error by developing a concept of self-esteem that only fits within guilt culture.

Nevertheless, the dominant issue in post-Freudian psychotherapy is shame. Psychologists now tend to emphasize the importance of identity, selfhood, self-respect, and dignity. They are almost hyperaware of the disastrous effects of psychological trauma, and have become very sensitive to the shame involved. The problem may be ill-defined, but the direction is correct. If capital markets are normally subject to speculative excesses, why shouldn't the marketplace of ideas be granted the same tolerance?

And we ascertain noble motives even in those who believe that psychotherapy should lead people to defeat shame. This may be wrong, but it does represent one aspect of clinical experience: when the full power of shame attacks an individual, a conscientious therapist will immediately try to stop the overwhelming mental anguish it causes.

Thus, it is not surprising that therapists tell their patients that the opinions of others do not matter, and that each person is a unique and autonomous individual, accountable only to his own standards.

Psychotherapists see on their patients' faces what it really means to lose face. Freud notwithstanding, it is not so much that therapists have difficulty being looked at, but that they are pained by what they see. Watching another person's face disintegrate, lose its features, crack before your eyes to the point where it is unrecognizable, chastens you. Therapists usually respond with compassion, as would any normal person.

This tells us why Freud invented psychoanalysis as a theory of guilt, and why it has been such a seductive theory. The internal torment, brooding self-doubt, constant self-questioning, futile actions, interminable delays, and crippling inhibitions that characterize someone who feels guilty for all the sinful impulses that fill his soul—none of this will cause the person's face to disintegrate.

The guilt-ridden neurotic appears before a therapist wearing a mask. Some call it ego, others narcissism, yet others personality.

Fortunately it is always the same mask, so at least we know whom we are dealing with. Or so we imagine.

People can live with neurotic guilt in a way that they cannot live with shame. Those who feel such guilt are often not threatening to themselves or to others; they are crippled by conscience, disconnected from normal social relations, lacking in ambition, unwilling to take risks, able to love a little if they are allowed to keep their mask on, and to work a lot if the work is ineffective. Such people have always been good candidates for long-term psychotherapy.

Psychotherapists have erred in basing their theories on what happens in the nursery rather than in the marketplace. Thus they have been remiss in not testing their theories in the crucible of historical and political realities. The psychology of the individual cannot be disconnected from the groups and times he inhabits.

Here psychological theories can contribute to our understanding of political events. No nation can function effectively unless its leaders maintain honor, dignity, and integrity. It is nearly impossible to read about great historical events or even to follow an analysis of presidential leadership without taking account of issues of credibility, integrity, humiliation, and national disgrace.

To take an example almost at random, historian Simon Schama identified the cause of the French Revolution as follows: "The Revolution, after all, had begun as a response to a patriotism wounded by the humiliations of the Seven Years' War." He adds that the conflict between king and revolutionaries was over who could better "regenerate the patrie," in other words, save national face.[30] Of course, the revolutionaries did not succeed; rather, they fell into guilt culture by unleashing an orgy of revenge and retribution in an effort to establish justice. Finally they produced enough anarchy to open the door to a military dictator in Napoleon.

How much do we now allow ourselves to become agitated in the pursuit of national honor? How far are we willing to go to avoid national disgrace? A classic American statement on these matters was made by Alexander Hamilton. Writing in *The Federalist* No. 15, Hamilton identified the ultimate political horror. By direct implication he was arguing that passage of the Constitution would be face-saving: "We may indeed with propriety be said to have reached almost the last stage of national humiliation. There is scarcely any thing that can wound the pride, or degrade the character of an independent nation, which we do not experience. Are there engagements to the performance of which we are held by every tie respectable among men? These are the subjects of constant and unblushing violation. Do we owe debts to foreigners and to our own citizens contracted in a time of imminent peril, for the preservation of our political existence? These remain without any proper or satisfactory provision for their discharge. Have we valuable territories and important posts in the possession of a foreign power, which by express stipulations ought long since to have been surrendered? . . . Are we in a condition to resent, or to repel the aggression? We have neither troops nor treasury nor government. Are we even in a condition to remonstrate with dignity?"

If these words ring more hollow today than they did during the constitutional debate, the simple reason, in a word, is Vietnam. The debate about Vietnam was saturated with appeals to national pride and dignity. Effectively, the failure of our Vietnam policy discredited the notion of basing foreign policy on considerations of saving face. And if it discredited this one application of face saving, it also discredited others.

The issue then is whether saving face is a bad idea, one that ought to yield to considerations about guilt and innocence, punishment and redemption, or whether it was badly applied in Vietnam. Did we pursue a bad policy because we wanted to save face or because guilt would not allow us to accept either success or failure? If we spent that much time and blood because our leaders were trying to cover up their failures, then the issue was not about face at all, but about masking shame and asserting ego.

2

Facing Trauma: America in Vietnam

No one can seriously doubt that America was humiliated in the jungles of Vietnam. The nation staked its prestige on its ability to save South Vietnam from a communist takeover. We may not have lost the war, but we did lose face. America's confidence in her mission, her values, and her worth was undermined by the experience of Vietnam.

If we had dealt with the trauma through the mechanisms of shame culture, the leaders would have stepped forth, taken responsibility, and held themselves accountable. For the most part this did not happen.

What did happen was that a policy failure was compounded with a failure to admit error. As a consequence, the nation divided itself into warring camps contesting the true story of what happened, why it happened, who made it happen, and what it meant.

Guilt cultures produce stories to account for traumas. First, they construct histories to convince the public, sitting as a jury, of who should be blamed and punished. Such histories are presumably factual; they are produced by the media. Second, these cultures produce fictions about the event to show what it means about the nation as a people, a culture, a tradition. In the case of Vietnam the most important fictions were movies. From *Apocalypse Now* to *Born on the Fourth of July* to *Platoon* America's filmmakers sought to highlight those incidents, whether real or imagined, that could dramatize what the event was saying about us.

No one was ever put on trial because of the nation's Vietnam policy. When Lieutenant William Calley was tried for the massacre of civilians at My Lai, there was no consensus about whether or not this was really relevant to the overall conduct of the war. Some believed it emblematic; other saw it as an aberration. Lieutenant Calley was more scapegoat than leader.

Perhaps because Congress had great input into the formation of policy—from voting the Tonkin Gulf Resolution to funding the war to precipitating the fall of South Vietnam by cutting off funds—there were no congressional investigations after the conflict ended.

Lyndon Johnson chose not to run for the presidency in 1968, but he did not admit that Vietnam had been a failure. He thereby ducked an election where his leadership could have been adjudged by the voters.

Eventually, Richard Nixon was held accountable, but that was for Watergate. Presumably, it was peripheral to Vietnam.

If a leader accepts responsibility for a failure, expresses shame, and resigns in disgrace, he is saying that he has misled an honorable nation. If he insists that he made the right decisions, or that his errors were caused by others, then the failure must be placed on someone else's account.

The nation will then mobilize to find and punish the culprits. This produces social conflict and divisive politics. The obsession with inculpating some while exculpating others will overwhelm the practice of respect at all levels of the society.

Political pragmatism requires leaders who can acknowledge

their own mistakes. A great leader can change course when reality judges his policy a failure. Leaders who do not trust reality often turn minor failures into major calamities. The more they believe in their own vision the more they will need a ready supply of scapegoats. Trusting only the strength of their own convictions, such leaders are faithful to ideology and faithless to their subjects.

In psychology, when a trauma produces lingering aftereffects and a distinct change in behavior we say that the person suffers a neurosis or a syndrome. Since the term "Vietnam syndrome" has already become part of the political vocabulary, referring to the nation's inability to use military power effectively abroad, I will use the term "neurosis" to describe the cultural fallout of the Vietnam debacle. Effectively, Vietnam produced a national depression that we attempted to expunge by making it into a neurosis.

A trauma is like a broken ankle; if it is not treated properly you might develop a limp. The limp is like a depression. The limp will slow you down and make you less effective. If you believe the limp is punishment, you may accept it as just, revolt against its injustice, deny its reality, or mask your features so that no one will recognize who is limping. Thus you will have made it into a neurosis.

What are the characteristics of a national neurosis, when the nation's policymaking and legislative functions are infested with considerations of guilt and punishment?

When a divided nation cannot muster the consensus or the will to undertake consequential acts, we would expect to see passion dominate over action. What matters is how deeply you feel, not what you actually do or achieve. Beliefs will become more important than conduct because people are convinced that nothing can be done to change anything. If the leadership has been unwilling to accept responsibility, then the corruption that produced the failure must be systemic; it must be tucked into every corner of the nation's institutions. Revealing corruption and producing justice will take precedence over helping the society function to produce economic growth and to restore national honor.

A nation will ultimately become incapable of using military force judiciously, at the right time, in the right place, under the right circumstances. Having lost the reasonable middle ground, it will veer between two extremes, either gun-shy or trigger happy. Political life will become a succession of traumatic missteps.

When a trauma occurs the nation will seek what any courtroom seeks: to discover the truth of what happened. Whatever the value of this process, knowing what happened in the past will not cure the neurosis. Knowing how you broke your ankle or how it was mistreated will not cure your limp. If someone concocts a fiction that shows your limp to be a metaphor for your moral character, such an exercise will not restore your ability to run or to dance.

Only a real action can refute the pervasive malaise that declares one to be incapable of acting effectively. Only an act can show that the trauma no longer exerts a decisive influence on behavior and character. This tells us why the Persian Gulf War was proclaimed the end of the Vietnam syndrome and the Vietnam neurosis. In the gulf, America was no longer the nation that had stumbled and bumbled its way through the Vietnamese jungle and the Iranian desert. And yet, it takes more than a single victorious action to cure a neurosis. Only when that action comes to set the standard for future conduct can we say that the neurosis has been overcome.

How did Vietnam come about? Who engaged the nation in this war? At the time of the initial engagement most people accepted that the legitimate interests of the United States were at stake in Vietnam. From "the best and the brightest" of the Kennedy and Johnson administrations to the gray eminences of the American foreign policy establishment, there was initially a consensus about the need to intervene in Vietnam.

Vietnam was a tale of three presidents. John Kennedy led the nation into Vietnam; he risked American prestige on a situation he did not understand and did not think out sufficiently. When Robert Kennedy was pursuing the presidency in 1968, he declared that history would hold his brother's administration responsible for the initial mistake.

Lyndon Johnson was elevated to the presidency on November 22, 1963, but he did not escalate the conflict until after he had won the office in his own right, in 1964. Johnson believed in power, and he dealt with politics in terms of power; ultimately he never understood why he could not overpower the Viet Cong. Today, public opinion holds Lyndon Johnson responsible for Vietnam.

Richard Nixon was elected president in 1968 with a secret plan to get us out of Vietnam. "Peace with honor" was his slogan. His policy can be called honorable disengagement. Nixon inherited an impossible situation, commenced a de-escalation of the conflict, and finally, after four years and some twenty thousand additional American deaths, got us out of Vietnam. He may have believed that he made the best of an awful situation, but he did prosecute the war for four more years. When the last American helicopter lifted off the roof of the embassy in Saigon in 1975, the pathetic picture of American defeat made "peace with honor" little more than an empty slogan. We were a long way from Iwo Jima.

All three presidents were decent men, motivated by the best intentions, receiving the best advice and counsel. And yet, they all bear responsibility for one of the greatest foreign policy failures in American history.

The easiest way to rationalize failure is to say that one has done the best that could have been done under the circumstances. But if another president, facing similar problems, acted differently, then the claim of being so much flotsam thrown around on the tides of history becomes invalid.

Throughout the Vietnam War the figure who cast the longest

shadow was Dwight Eisenhower. When some argued that we could not simply withdraw from Vietnam, others could recall that Eisenhower had done just that in a war he inherited: Korea. When some argued that we had to go to war in Vietnam, others could recall that Eisenhower had been implored by the French to enter the fray against North Vietnam in 1954 and that he had demurred. And when some argued that great leaders could not take responsibility promptly for a foreign policy failure, others could recall that Eisenhower had done just that when a U-2 spy plane was shot down in the Soviet Union.

The parallels are inexact, granted. But the public opinion of Vietnam was influenced by the idea that if Eisenhower had been in charge, things would surely have happened otherwise.

What distinguished Eisenhower from his successors in the area of military policy was simply that his prestige was unassailable; he did not have to prove anything to anyone in order to be respected. Eisenhower brought prestige to the office; the others took prestige from the office. And as a military leader Eisenhower knew best how to function within a world of "face."

Eisenhower was a reluctant warrior. The reluctant warrior knows what leadership means, knows what his responsibilities are; he has a sense of humility. The gung-ho novice sees war as an occasion to prove himself, to demonstrate his manhood; he is lower on the hierarchy; fewer people depend on him; he makes war a point of personal pride, not a point of moral obligation.

Whether for reasons of youth, arrogance, or an excessive concern for being one's own man, three successive presidents failed to follow the example Eisenhower set in handling the pressure to intervene militarily in Vietnam in 1954.[1]

Having fought against Ho Chi Minh's forces with America's financial backing, the French called upon their ally in 1954 when their troops were being pinned down at Dien Bien Phu. Eisenhower believed that the French were militarily inept, unreliable, and decadent; he did not want to risk American prestige on such an ally.

When the French made their formal request for American air strikes in April 1954, Eisenhower told his secretary of state, John Foster Dulles, that such an action would be "completely unconstitutional and indefensible."[2] At a meeting of the National Security Council on April 29 Eisenhower stated, "To go in unilaterally in Indochina or other areas of the world which were endangered, amounted to an attempt to police the entire world. If we attempted such a course of action, using our armed forces and going into areas whether we were wanted or not, we would lose all our significant support in the free world."[3]

For someone who understood "face" the political capital of the American presidency needed to be husbanded and deployed judiciously.

Soon after he entered office, John Kennedy watched a popularly elected government in South Vietnam being severely threatened by a local insurgency. Without having grasped the situation, he dispatched 16,500 troops to advise and train the South Vietnamese army. As undersecretary of state George Ball said: "I don't think Kennedy had any real appreciation of the way in which the U.S. would be progressively drawn into a deeper and deeper involvement."[4]

When the administration's ally President Ngo Dinh Diem started persecuting Buddhist monks by shooting up their pagodas, the monks responded by setting themselves on fire in the streets of Saigon. Faced with an embarrassing ally, Kennedy approved a plot by Vietnamese generals to overthrow Diem and his brother Ngo Dinh Nhu. Later, Kennedy had doubts, but the coup occurred anyway. When it led to the murders of Diem and Nhu, the United States found itself responsible for political assassination.

Now American prestige was directly involved in the outcome of the civil war in Vietnam. This was the decisive act of engagement.

John Kennedy did not know how to deal in prestige; he had precious little to deal with. His currency was charisma: charm, wit, and spirit . . . that young, well-polished look. But charisma loses its luster when it crosses borders; foreign leaders take it to be a sign of weakness. Therefore a charismatic leader will either make a show of force or retire from the game.

Kennedy felt that he had to prove himself; after the fiasco of the Bay of Pigs he could not afford another failure. His Russian counterpart, Nikita Khrushchev, was certainly not taking him seriously. George Ball described one of Kennedy's problems: "Although he [Kennedy] maintained an outward appearance of aplomb and invulnerability, he never forgot that the American people were comparing him with Eisenhower, a looming father figure whose established reputation not only for overwhelming military but for political victories had given him political self-assurance."[5]

After losing prestige in the Bay of Pigs and with the erection of the Berlin Wall, Kennedy decided to recover some of it with a show of force in Vietnam. Having failed to convince Khrushchev of American determination in their Vienna summit, he confided in James Reston. As Reston reported: "It was now essential to demonstrate our firmness, and the place to do it, he remarked to my astonishment, was Vietnam!"[6]

Calculations concerning prestige are fundamental to understanding what happened and what might have happened. These calculations allow us to measure the influence of the person of one or another leader. Situations change depending on who the players are.

Regarding the oft asked question of whether John Kennedy would have withdrawn from Vietnam in 1965, Theodore Draper wrote: ". . . Kennedy did not have the prestige in foreign affairs to take a step which would have marked him as the president who had lost a war even before the United States had made every effort to avoid such a historic loss."[7]

After John Kennedy was assassinated in Dallas, Lyndon Johnson picked up the mantle of the fallen leader. Johnson was sorely lacking in charisma, but he made up for it, especially in domestic policy, with his incomparable understanding of the workings of power.

Whatever Kennedy would or would not have done, Lyndon Johnson believed that he was following the course laid out by his predecessor. Not only was he served by the same advisors—Dean Rusk, Robert McNamara, Walt Rostow, McGeorge Bundy, George Ball—but the circumstances of his accession to the office made it impossible for him to feel other than committed to continuing Kennedy's policies.

Whatever John Kennedy would have done had he been president in 1965, the nation was traumatized by his assassination, and this may well have contributed to the conduct of Vietnam policy.

To speculate about the collective national psyche is perhaps frivolous; one can neither prove nor disprove assertions. Nevertheless, I would speculate that one reason for striking out against Vietnam might have been to avenge an unresolved crime. Were we punishing communists in Vietnam because there was no one else to punish? Certainly, we were not trying to win the war.

It was a grave miscalculation. An unacknowledged psychological motive corrupted foreign policy. Worse, if we were punishing someone other than the guilty party, we would become guilty of our own injustice. In any event, something sent policymakers off the track; the war was directed by people whose behavior bespeaks guilt. Did Lyndon Johnson ever feel that the presidency was legitimately his? Did he feel guilt for having ascended to the office through a criminal act?

The Johnson administration did not have a plan for winning the war; neither did it have a plan for securing the peace. It refused to attack and it refused to withdraw.

Henry Kissinger described the moral tone of the leadership. Speaking of Robert McNamara's "deep feeling of guilt for having acquiesced in the decisions that made it both inevitable and inconclusive," he added, "This same ambivalence had come to affect the Administration's conduct of the war, compelling its tentative character, its oscillation between periods of violence and escapism."[8]

The Johnson administration's failure became increasingly obvious as people saw that we were losing face. Two decisive instances were the Tet offensive and the bombing of North Vietnam.

The Tet offensive was a series of military attacks launched by the North Vietnamese and Viet Cong during the Vietnamese New Year's celebration in February 1968. This well-coordinated assault on various cities and towns in Vietnam caused considerable military damage but was eventually beaten back by American and South Vietnamese forces. Military leaders have stated that after Tet the enemy was sorely depleted militarily, thus that the battle represented a significant allied victory.

And yet, having occurred at a time when the American administration was touting its successful prosecution of the war, the Tet offensive destroyed its credibility. The humiliating fact was that after three years of warfare a ragtag bunch of guerrillas and a Third World army could still launch an effective offensive against us.

The loss of face at Tet undermined American public support for the president's Vietnam policy. As Kissinger wrote, "Henceforth, no matter how effective our actions, the prevalent strategy could no longer achieve its objectives within a period or with force levels politically acceptable to the American people."[9]

Throughout the public debate on Vietnam the wisdom of using the full force of American air power was subject to considerable dispute. Why did bombing become of such central importance? Michael Charlton and Anthony Moncrieff isolated a central issue. The image of a superpower punishing a small country was too much for many fair-minded people to bear: "the disproportion of means began to lead to a discrediting of the ends."[10]

While Rusk, McNamara, Rostow, Bundy, and Johnson may have felt obliged to prosecute the war because they loved John

Kennedy, Richard Nixon would not have been motivated by the same considerations.

And yet, while pursuing an honorable disengagement, Nixon did make the war his own. Even if we accept that Nixon had no other viable alternatives, he must still bear responsibility for his conduct of the war.

Having built his political career on his zeal as an anti-communist crusader, Richard Nixon was ill-equipped to walk away from a fight with communists. Where Kennedy had led with charisma and Johnson exercised power, Nixon believed, as he always had, in the virtue of strength. He failed to realize that if one does not take prestige firmly into account, demonstrations of strength will represent simple posturing.

Nixon's policy of honorable disengagement may be defensible, but in reality it became a way to avoid facing failure. Nixon saw two options, neither of which was politically tenable: to withdraw with an unsatisfactory peace agreement or to obliterate North Vietnam with bombs. Therefore he attempted to find a middle ground. But rather than extract what was best in the differing opinions, he chose what was worst: more war, less public support. In addition, Nixon asserted that he had to continue the war to maintain American credibility.

Would American credibility have been more damaged by a withdrawal than it was by a quagmire? Nixon may have believed that we had remained good to our commitments, but the national mood after Vietnam was running strongly against further commitments to foreign wars. No potential adversary could have missed the message.

Richard Nixon brought the war to an indecisive and unsatisfactory conclusion. He took someone else's failure and made it his own. After prosecuting the war for four years, at the cost of some twenty thousand American lives, he achieved a peace treaty that no one really believed. Following the example of his predecessors, Nixon not only refused to accept responsibility for the

American humiliation in Vietnam; he declared himself to have succeeded.

Not only did America fail, but American presidents made every effort to "spin" their failure into a success. The most telling image of presidential leadership was a cartoon drawn by David Levine in *The New York Review of Books*. There, as happened in reality, Lyndon Johnson was showing off an abdominal scar he had recently acquired from a surgical procedure. In the cartoon, however, the scar was drawn in the shape of Vietnam.

The simple fact is that no one has yet apologized for Vietnam. Beyond that, no one was held accountable for the debacle. Thus, responsibility was shifted from the commanders to the troops and, finally, to the American people.

Instead of hearing a shamefaced apology for the conduct of the Vietnam War, we have often heard self-righteously defiant claims for the correctness of the policy. And strangely, those who prosecuted the war declared that they did what they did in order to maintain American prestige. But if they all had such a well-developed sense of shame, why did they not accept the fact that the nation had lost face in the jungles of Southeast Asia?

President Lyndon Johnson was anything but apologetic in his memoirs, written before the final peace treaty: "I was going to do what had to be done to protect our interests and keep our promises. And that is what I did."[11] And again: "We had kept our word to Southeast Asia. We had opposed and defeated aggression, as we promised we would. We had given 17 million South Vietnamese a chance to build their own country and their own institutions. And we had seen them move well down this road."[12]

And yet, the greatest military force on earth had been fought to a standstill by a group Johnson thought of as guerrillas in pajamas; we, not they, had sued for peace and insisted on negotiation. Our president, not theirs, had to renounce running for re-election to show his sincere wish for peace. Johnson's view of the war disconnected us from reality. He could hardly be expected to apologize for what he considered a rousing success.

Things are slightly better when we listen to Clark Clifford, who was secretary of defense in 1968. At least he admits to having done something wrong: "We made an honest mistake. I feel no sense of shame. Nor should the country feel any sense of shame."[13] Clifford is wrong, however, to say that shame cannot be associated with an honest mistake.[14]

Leaders are responsible for what happens to their subjects, even, in the most extreme case, if they had nothing to do with the event. The president of Japan Air Lines did not say that a plane crashed because of an honest mistake made by some mechanic and that therefore he need feel no shame.

Henry Kissinger understood this point: "Leaders are responsible not for running public opinion polls but for the consequences of their actions. They will be held to account for disasters even if the decision that produced the calamity enjoyed widespread public support when it was taken."[15]

His point was well taken. But since Kissinger made it while defending his own conduct of the war, it contains a bitter irony. Instead of accepting that leaders "be held to account for disasters," Kissinger attacked the antiwar movement for being unkind to those who conducted the war: "There was no civility or grace from the antiwar leaders; they mercilessly persecuted those they regarded as culpable."[16] Beyond its transparently self-serving purpose, this statement fails to note that if our leaders, as Kissinger admitted later, had sought congressional approval for their policy, they would have largely silenced their critics.

The antiwar movement may well have been excessive, and it may even have been disloyal in defending an enemy that our own soldiers were fighting against; it ought not, however, to be taxed with guilt by someone who was directly involved in prosecuting an undeclared war for four years with insufficient public support.

The initial putative justification for the war was the Tonkin

Gulf Resolution, but that Resolution was repealed by Congress in May 1970. So from May 1970 to January 1973 there was not even the appearance of the war being approved by Congress.

The most acute controversy about the issue of apologizing for Vietnam was generated by Robert McNamara's *In Retrospect.* There McNamara echoed Clark Clifford: he was wrong; he made a mistake. He did not add that he need feel no shame, but manifestly McNamara did not feel the need to apologize. Instead he confessed.

Apology serves the group; confession serves the individual. Apology indicates shame: the person who apologizes sincerely does not offer an explanation and does not couch his apology in the assertion of a newfound identity as a sage. This would make it appear that he had profited from failure. "It is an odd, modern sort of confession," Mickey Kaus wrote of McNamara in *The New Republic*, "that becomes the occasion for such well-publicized self-congratulation."[17]

No shame from McNamara, but much guilt. By his account Vietnam was conceived and prosecuted by wonderful people. They received the best advice from the most esteemed experts. They followed this advice, all the time knowing in their souls that they were wrong. No one else, McNamara appears to believe, could have done otherwise.

While pretending to take responsibility for Vietnam, McNamara casts the net of blame. He criticizes right-wing congressional hawks, cold warriors, military leaders, Eisenhower, the wise men, and so on. All of these people presumably failed to give better advice. McNamara taxes himself, Kennedy, and Johnson with not standing up to the Republican right. His purpose is transparently to exculpate the Democratic left.

Beyond blaming others for making him prosecute the war despite himself, McNamara leaves the impression that his decisions were based on fear. Fear tied our hands. We feared the Russians, so we could not do this; we feared the Chinese, so we could not do that. The general anxiety did not yield to reality checks. When the defeat of communism in Indonesia refuted the domino theory, no one drew a conclusion that would mitigate the fear.

No one imagined that "the best and the brightest" who prosecuted Vietnam were not nice people. They were, however, neither sufficiently experienced nor competent in these matters to formulate or conduct the policy. Thus they had to rely on the advice of others, and had to invoke analogies with other historical events, like Munich and Korea. They did not have enough experience to evaluate Vietnam on its own terms.

We did not need to hear from Robert McNamara that the Vietnam War was pursued by tortured souls who were deeply divided about what they were doing. Kissinger's analysis of Johnson administration conduct of the war said as much twenty years before.

The war itself provided ample evidence: on the one hand, we were dropping a massive amount of explosives on a primitive country, to little military avail; on the other, we were begging for peace negotiations. No adversary could have doubted that our peace-seeking warriors were begging to be saved from the darker side of their nature.

McNamara shows that Vietnam policy was crippled by the guilt of its proponents. For those who believe that getting in touch with one's guilt feelings represents the best way to conduct government policy his book provides a sobering rebuttal.

If anyone should have known how to face the shame of failure, it should have been the military leadership. Who better to understand honor? Soldiers do not march to the beat of public opinion polls; they are not motivated by the reward/punishment dyad; they represent the spirit of self-sacrifice, of doing a job honestly and well because it is their duty.

If we were to ask the question "What price honor?" of a soldier, it would count as a grievous insult.

How can you even think to put a price tag on your dignity, your integrity, or your reputation? To do so suggests that, if the price is right, your honor might be for sale. Obviously, no amount of money could compensate the opprobrium that would fall upon you if you exchanged your honor for lucre.

Honor involves a sacred duty. Maintaining one's honor is the most important responsibility a human bears. It represents his duty to himself, his family, his community.

And yet, in a bizarre episode that could only have happened in America, General William Westmoreland, the commanding general of American forces in Vietnam, once pegged his honor at $120 million. Imagine what the price would have been if he had won the war.

Westmoreland affixed this price in a libel suit he filed against CBS in response to a 1982 documentary titled "The Uncounted Enemy: A Vietnam Deception." The program asserted that Westmoreland had purposefully underreported enemy troop strength to his civilian superiors, thus leading them to make the wrongheaded decisions that embroiled us in Vietnam.

If CBS News intended to exculpate the civilian leadership, its own motives were hardly of the most noble sort. Responsibility is not mitigated for receiving false information.

The suit went to trial in 1985, but after eighteen weeks of testimony by the general's subordinates, much of it supporting CBS, Westmoreland dropped the suit. CBS did not disavow the program or pay any damages. The general justified his decision by saying, "I figured it was the best I could get."

Westmoreland had previously rejected the opportunity to respond to the program by a public statement; he chose the courts as a place to restore his honor.

Assuredly this was the first time in human history that the commanding general of a defeated army felt that he should sue to protect his reputation. In this single gesture, Westmoreland repudiated the central principle of military psychology; the commander is responsible for what happens to his troops, no matter what: in victory the glory is his, in defeat the ignominy rests on his shoulders. He makes no excuses, blames no one else . . . not the politicians, not the press, not the public, and certainly not his soldiers. Military tradition tells us that the leader of a defeated army must, at best, resign in disgrace.

In terms of social psychology the salient fact about Vietnam is that no supreme leader, not the president, not his senior advisors, not the commanding general, was willing to stand up and apologize. Worse yet, they masked their shame with the name of honor.

Kissinger was acutely aware of the importance of such issues: "As a leader of democratic alliances we had to remember that scores of countries and millions of people relied for their security on our willingness to stand by allies, indeed on our confidence in ourselves. No serious policymaker could allow himself to succumb to the fashionable debunking of 'prestige' or 'honor' or 'credibility.' "[18] But can a nation engage its honor while circumventing the Constitution's provisions for declaring war? Kennedy, Johnson, and Nixon all mistook their own ego for national honor.

Kissinger presented an argument against unconditional withdrawal, not an argument against going to Congress, rallying the nation, forming a consensus behind the war, and prosecuting it. If that were not conceivable, then the war should have been stopped. At the least this would have been a constitutional solution. Nixon should have been held accountable for his decisions, even if there was no truly satisfactory alternative. That is the burden of leadership.

One need not debunk the notion of honor to state that the peace concluded at Paris did not solve the problem of "honor." The United States lost face in Vietnam; nothing about the final peace treaty restored American honor.

Having recently pulverized the Nazi war machine and brought the imperial Japanese military to ruin, the United States could not save face by fighting North Vietnam to a standoff. If a lightweight contender fights the heavyweight champion to a draw, he wins a substantial moral victory. The heavyweight champion may not lose his title, but he does lose face. He may protest that he is still champion, but now every boxer on earth will consider him vulnerable to defeat.

Richard Nixon may have believed that he restored national honor, but he was still forced to resign the presidency eighteen months after the conclusion of the Vietnam War. Those eighteen months were filled with attacks and recriminations, an impeachment vote by a House committee, a president so worried about defending himself that he could not provide leadership. Beleaguered and embattled, Richard Nixon finally had to resign his office.

Nixon was going to be impeached for, among other things, an obstruction of justice that rose out of the Watergate burglary. No one ever suggested that he be impeached and tried because of Vietnam. But is this the way a nation treats a leader who has rescued national honor? It is the way a nation treats someone who has tried to "cover up" defeat with empty talk about honor.

I believe that if Richard Nixon's Vietnam policy had succeeded, the Watergate spectacle would not have happened. There are always scandals in government, and many presidents, American and otherwise, have engaged in unsavory practices. The question becomes, Why at that time and in that place did that scandal become a national obsession? The answer, in my view, is Vietnam.

The amount of abuse heaped on Nixon—merited or not—could not have been entirely dissociated from the fact that he had prosecuted the war for four years, at considerable cost in lives, money, and national unity, for a highly dubious peace treaty that no one imagined the North Vietnamese would respect.

Watergate allowed the nation to forget the trauma of Vietnam. It was highly useful in that regard. It permitted the nation to remove from office one of the principal commanders of that war. Richard Nixon resigned the presidency, but he never apologized for Watergate. For want of that his was not an honorable disengagement.

Affixing signatures to a peace treaty in Paris did not spell the end to the conflict between the United States and North Vietnam. It inaugurated an after-war period where the hot war was transformed into a cold war.

For want of an apology the war did not end entirely in 1973. For want of a formal recognition that we had failed, many people continued to deny the evidence of reality. They waited for something that would make it appear that we had not been humiliated.

Some citizens came to see Vietnam as a skirmish in a larger conflict; maybe we lost a battle, but we could still save face by winning the greater war. They declared that the fall of communism vindicated our sacrifice, because world communism would not have collapsed had we not stood firm in Vietnam. That dubious proposition retained little appeal.

An admission of failure through an apology would have provided a ceremonial closure to Vietnam. For want of such a gesture Vietnam remained an open question—in the words of some, an open wound—dramatized by the issue of those who did not return and whose fate remained unknown: the prisoners of war and the missing in action, POW/MIAs.

This issue provided the last chance to maintain that we were an honorable people. The failed policy of the civilian leadership should not have dishonored those who carried out their orders. And would not have if the civilian leadership had been willing to acknowledge its error in a timely and sincere fashion.

Failure to provide a proper burial for the dead can provoke the most excruciating drama. Witness Sophocles' *Antigone*, the great tragedy of filial piety. In providing a ceremonial burial for her brother Polynices, Antigone defied an edict of her uncle Creon prohibiting such a burial for one who was fighting against the state. Her moral action closed the unhappy history of the family of Oedipus.

Codes of both family and military honor posit a sacred obligation to respect the dead. Soldiers are honor-bound not to leave their fallen comrades—injured or dead—behind on the field of battle. For the families of the POW/MIAs there can be no higher moral duty than to offer a proper rest to their loved ones and no greater anguish than being unable to do so.

For some the plight of these families offered another occasion to gain something that resembled a face-saving exit from Vietnam. And yet, in no other recent American war has the POW/MIA issue taken on such symbolic significance. Many more were left behind in Korea and World War II. The real impossibility of bringing everyone home or accounting for all of the dead usually does not make this a sign of having shirked a sacred duty.

Supporters of the POW/MIAs took the most adversarial stance: they insisted that economic and diplomatic sanctions were the only way to force the Vietnamese to deliver over to us their records and the remains of our servicemen.

By demanding that the Vietnamese grant us access to all of their files and all of their territory we were posturing as conquerors. Surely, we were looking for them to make a gesture that resembled surrender in order to feel that we had not lost face. Perhaps the Vietnamese saw their ability to hold back information as an assertion of the sovereignty they had gained at an enormous cost. They had not ceded to military pressure and had fought us to a standstill. What made us imagine that they would act differently when faced with political or economic pressure?

Others argued that cooperation between the two countries, and diplomatic recognition of the Vietnamese state, would best facilitate opening the doors to the Vietnamese archives. They proposed that we extend a hand of friendship, that we give face to the North Vietnamese.

Since many of those who supported this position had spent the war years trying to befriend North Vietnam, they did not have the credibility to offer something that resembled a capitulation. Besides, North Vietnam had flagrantly violated the terms of the peace agreement, especially those provisions that concerned the POW/MIAs, and had invaded Cambodia in 1978.

Vietnam began cooperating on the POW/MIA issue in 1988

and completed her withdrawal from Cambodia in 1989. By 1991 George Bush began the process that would lead to normal relations.

Perhaps the restoration of diplomatic relations with Vietnam in 1995 will serve to put the entire episode behind us.

The only problem with this gesture was the identity of the person who made it.

The fact that it fell to America's most famous draft evader to offer diplomatic recognition to Vietnam produced some measure of outrage, and not just among the POW/MIA families.

This gesture of conciliation should have been cloaked in humility. No one should have felt vindicated by it and no one should have felt repudiated.

When Richard Nixon went to China he was admitting publicly that isolating and antagonizing China had failed. As the American politician most closely associated with that policy, Nixon was humbling himself by traveling to Mao Zedong's capital; his act produced an immediate national consensus for the new open door to China.

Bill Clinton's recognition of Vietnam was largely accepted as the right thing to do. But Clinton could not do it on his own authority. A score of military officials, veterans, and former POWs surrounded him at the ceremonial announcement as though only *their* presence could grant the right amount of gravity and dignity to the ceremony.

Thereby, Clinton was the wrong man who did the right thing. By structuring the ceremony to disconnect his presidential action from his personal conduct during the war, Clinton did not appear to be vindicating the antiwar movement or repudiating those who had fought in Vietnam.

Rather than negotiate the trauma of Vietnam through the mechanisms of shame, we dealt with it by constructing a guilt narrative.

Shame cultures produce social order out of ceremony and ritual; they tend not to rely on stories to create this order. Shame cultures use narratives to sustain social harmony, not to examine social conflict. They celebrate victory, glorify heroes of the nation, and assert the nation's history of success. Washington crossing the Delaware, Teddy Roosevelt leading the charge up San Juan Hill, Edison inventing the lightbulb, are typical stories invoked to build national pride. They show leaders exemplifying the nation's values. A national hero is an ancestor writ large; he presents the nation's face.

Shame cultures care more for social order than for truth. But, significantly, they are most concerned with people's feelings. How would the parents of a soldier who had died in a war feel if they discover that he was killed by his own troops or that he had been murdering babies?

There are a lot of things shame cultures simply do not want to know about. And often it is not just the autocrats who do not want the people to know; the people themselves have a considerable personal stake in believing in themselves, in their honor and dignity and integrity. Upon this basis they rebuild shattered honor after a defeat.

In a shame culture people want to hear stories about those whose behavior is worthy of emulation. Deeds of heroic ancestors are often brought forth for these purposes. These stories show the hero overcoming adversity by following the rules; they do not show him learning to live with failure. Instead of plumbing the depths of motivation, they portray decisive action that resolves dilemmas.

Nor do they attempt to portray human conflict, interior or exterior. The heroes of shame narratives are not filled with conflicts; they face their fears, overcome their doubts, and act to affirm the order of society. They are constant and do not undergo transformations in the course of the narrative. And they are also leaders—in charge of and responsible for an army, a government, a business. Corruption is not their reason for being.

Guilt narratives are another story. They are built on conflict and mystery. A criminal faces off against a detective or a judge:

the detective seeks to remove the criminal from society, the criminal to get away with his crime. These are mysteries because something has gone seriously wrong in a society and no one has stepped forward to claim authorship.

The detective story represents this genre well, especially in the modern version typified by Sherlock Holmes. If there were no crimes, Holmes would have no reason to exist.

Such narratives concern what went wrong; they do not show automobiles being built or victories being won. They attempt to convince the reader of the detective's version of events as surely as would a brilliant trial lawyer. They seek a unanimous verdict about the identity of the criminal and the true story of the actions, intentions, and motivations that produced his crime.

Expanding its function, a guilt narrative tries to show that a failure is not an isolated event but the inevitable consequence of fundamental flaws in national character. It takes historical events to be emblematic of tendencies that have always been there, but that have never been acknowledged.

Guilt culture takes a single failure to be indicative, not an aberration. Its goal is to show a pattern of error revealing venal intentions and fundamental character flaws. Guilt culture believes that revealing the truth about the nation will purge it and lead us into a brave new world.

Guilt narratives feed on conflict between those who lead and the rest of the population. Their concern with indicting everyone who holds any authority in the system often borders on the demagogic.

The most compelling guilt narratives take place in reality. Ongoing public drama with criminals and victims, prosecutors and defense attorneys, presided over by sage judges, where we the people sit as the jury has a power to capture the national imagination as few other events, short of war, can. The dogged pursuit of truth —that is, the smoking gun—brings people together in an exercise that serves well to distract them from the real business at hand.

In the post-Vietnam period the most important guilt drama was

Watergate. This extended public spectacle told us that if we were no longer very proficient at war than at least we were good at justice. In the vacuum created by the failure of military and industrial leaders a new class of leaders arose: crusading attorneys; fearless investigative reporters; wise old judges; self-righteous intellectuals.

Exposing dirty secrets and dirty tricks became noble acts. Revealing classified military information was positively heroic. Covering up—one's shame, for example—meant that one was obstructing justice. And obstructing justice—not national disgrace— was pronounced to be the worst crime anyone could ever commit.

Watergate helped transform the nation, temporarily, into a guilt culture. The institutions representing American shame culture had been found wanting in Vietnam; now the other side would have its chance to affect a Cultural Revolution, to abolish shame and to make guilt into a way of life.

Both shame and guilt cultures seek to ensure that the failure never happen again: the first by declaring that the nation was misled, and thus that it need but repudiate incompetent leadership; the second by fostering a revolution against authority and responsibility.

Whereas a shame narrative affirms a nation's institutions and leaders, a guilt narrative denounces its leaders and the principles for which they stand. A guilt narrative can produce a guilt culture when members of society overcome their sense of shame to get in touch with their feelings of guilt. Everyone should learn to feel guilt over citizenship, to indulge in self-criticism, to adjudge himself and his neighbors to be incompetent, inept, and criminal. In some cases this produces a cultural revolution. At the least, politics will become ideologically polarized. Promoting social conflict will become good; destroying your opponents by any means will become public sport. People will wait in vain for a synthesis to emerge out of the raging dialectic. It never does.

When everyone comes to believe that a guilt narrative is true there is only one constructive way to overcome the ravages it produces. Some real event must occur that disproves it. Only a real event can counter a fiction that has become a dogmatic belief. For the United States the Persian Gulf War served this function. If the Vietnam guilt narrative had been true, the Persian Gulf War would not have happened as it did. This war reaffirmed the fundamental American shame culture.

A guilt culture would see the Vietnam conflict as the inevitable consequence of a decade of Cold War–mongering, the inherent corruption of the military institutions, residual colonialist and imperialist cravings, and the venality of capitalism; the event had to happen, and nothing could have prevented it. But if this is taken to be the truth, how can the nation ever act differently in the future?

In a shame culture Vietnam was a mistake caused by weak, inadequate leadership. Whatever the background circumstances, whatever the profits that were gained, a good leader could have avoided the quagmire. Nothing required the United States to involve itself as it did in Vietnam. Nothing about its history or national character forced it to fight indecisively; the nation was simply misled. Thus the reasoning that began with the proposition . . . If Eisenhower had been in charge. . . .

To show how American culture at large attempted to understand and explain what went wrong in Vietnam, I will examine the cinematic presentations of that event.

Movie versions do not limit themselves to telling the story as it happened. Unconstrained by fact, they venture further afield and attempt to find more general significance. If a filmmaker takes an event like the massacre of South Vietnamese civilians by American troops, he will not present it as an isolated occurrence perpetrated by a deranged soldier, but will see it as emblematic of the war effort itself, and perhaps of American national character.

The major cinematic representations of the war do not attempt to restore national pride. They want to show what went wrong, what it means, and who we need to punish to make things right. A constant theme has been the corruption of the system, and the way that individuals attempt to oppose it.

Take the example of Colonel Walter Kurtz in Francis Ford Coppola's *Apocalypse Now*. Kurtz is presented as one of the best the army has produced, a man of uncommon valor and intelligence, on the fast track to military greatness.

Kurtz figures out how to fight the war successfully, only his way is not the army's way. When he suspects that certain South Vietnamese officers are collaborating with the enemy, he has them put to death. Future events prove him right, but his actions have violated government policy and caused problems between Americans and their South Vietnamese allies.

Kurtz comes to appreciate the genius of the enemy. After he vaccinates the children of a Vietnamese community, enemy soldiers overtake the village and amputate the arms of the vaccinated children. Kurtz seeks victory and he does not care what he has to do to achieve this goal. When the military refuses to accept his tactics, Kurtz decides that he cannot function effectively and follow orders, so he goes AWOL and organizes his own insurgency.

Kurtz represents the tradition of the victorious American soldier, one who would obey orders given by competent leaders but who cannot follow ineffectual leaders and wrongheaded policy.

So he gathers a bizarre group of tribesman around him in Cambodia and starts broadcasting his own messages through the countryside. They sound to us like the ravings of a deranged hippie, but evidently they speak to the people in a way that the United States government and its allies do not. With the CIA, the military decides that Kurtz must be eliminated.

The movie recounts the journey of one Captain Willard, whose assignment is to terminate Kurtz's command "with extreme prejudice."

The movie claims to tell why we lost the war. Instead of profiting from the intelligence of those who knew how to get the job done, the government harassed and assassinated those heroic individuals who could, had they been given the chance, have set us on the right track.

The movie's vision is not one-sided. The character of Colonel Kurtz raises significant moral questions. Could the United States have maintained its own values while doing things his way? What would the press have said? How would a Kurtz-led war have looked back home? On the other side, if his was the only way of winning the war and if it was unacceptable, then what were we doing there?

Coppola presents the murder of Colonel Kurtz as showing why we lost the war. We were fighting against ourselves; the only force that could have defeated the American military in Vietnam was the American military itself. This dramatizes the issue of "friendly fire" and makes it representative of the war effort. A nation divided cannot prevail.

The same theme was dramatized in the game of Russian roulette in *The Deer Hunter*; this game represents the self-defeating senselessness of the American gamble in Vietnam. It also holds on to a shred of national pride by asserting that we were not beaten by the Viet Cong.

The moral dilemma of *Apocalypse Now* finds one type of resolution in the later film character of Rambo. Rambo is Kurtz without a functioning intelligence and without self-doubt and introspection. In times of trouble only someone who is chronically outside the system can get the job done.

Rambo is a postwar character; he shows a post-mortem analysis of what went wrong: we did not use our best human resources, but we persecuted them and hounded them and made them social outcasts. Rambo's return to Vietnam tells us that if we had to do it over again, we would get it right.

The Vietnam guilt narrative, as it developed through succeeding films, transformed questions of honor and disgrace into ones of guilt and innocence. These films offered redemption to those who were wrongly punished and meted out justice to those who followed the rules. While *Apocalypse Now* sustained a tone of moral complexity—Colonel Kurtz was not entirely unsympathetic and Captain Willard was not entirely sympathetic; both were too human to represent moral absolutes—another movie from the same period, Hal Ashby's *Coming Home*, presented a more stark contrast.

This movie begins in a veterans hospital; the character played by Jon Voight, Sergeant Luke Martin, has been paralyzed in the war. He is cared for by Sally Hyde (Jane Fonda), the wife of a different kind of soldier, Captain Bob Hyde, played by Bruce Dern. Captain Hyde believes in the war, looks forward to combat, and willingly goes off to fight for his country.

Eventually, Luke Martin and Sally Hyde fall in love—we are led to believe that she did not really love her husband—and they engage in something of an affair.

Finally Captain Hyde returns from the war, injured, not from combat, but from having shot himself in the calf: he was carrying his M-16 on his way to take a shower and tripped and fell. There is no such thing as being injured while acting heroically in battle: How can there be heroes in an undeclared war?

In the final plot twist, we discover that Sally Hyde's affair with Luke Martin has been recorded by military intelligence, which had been stalking him because of his antiwar activities. After Captain Hyde is informed, he confronts both his wife and her lover and eventually ends his personal torment by trying to swim across the Pacific. Justice is done.

Ordinarily, soldiers who are wounded in battle become war heroes. This could not happen in an undeclared war for which the nation was never rallied. Battle scars should be taken to be demonstrations of courage and sources of pride; here they function as stigmata. Wounded veterans were stigmatized by the nation for Vietnam, not for anything they had done, but for being a present reminder of failure.

Coming Home elevates the victim's suffering and grants him some measure of justice. It provides him with the love of a good woman, who incidentally is the wife of a failed soldier. Captain Hyde is not a war hero. He was not injured in the line of duty; his injury functions as a stigma, perhaps even more than does the paralysis of Luke Martin. Where the ethic of a soldier like Bob Hyde does not allow for a new role in society, Luke Martin gains redemption as an antiwar protester.

The stigma of paralysis becomes a sign of vulnerability, and vulnerable signifies lovable. Religion redeems the failure of civil authority by placing an event in a different kind of narrative.

Oliver Stone's *Born on the Fourth of July* represents the apotheosis of the genre. Where Captain Willard had to journey into the heart of Cambodian darkness to fulfill his mission, Ron Kovic undergoes an inner spiritual quest as he confronts his nation's attitude to his sacrifice.

This crippled veteran began as a gung-ho warrior who enlisted to go to Vietnam to fight communists. He ends as an antiwar hero who fulfills his spiritual destiny when he sees the light, comes home, and joins the Democratic party.

The note of political partisanship is intriguing. Having been vilified and harassed at the 1972 Republican Convention, Kovic is shown in the movie's last shot exiting the tunnel that will take him to the podium of the 1976 Democratic Convention. He is surrounded by light as he goes out to join the company of saints and angels.

Out of the darkness and into the light . . . this movie mines the rich tradition of religious conversion experiences; it participates fully in one of the most significant religious myths of our civilization, the myth of redemption of sin. While Nixon is shown as having inherited the war and made it his own, the Democratic party, with its nomination of the saintly born-again Christian Jimmy Carter, is shown to have overcome its guilt for having started and escalated it.

Ron Kovic's personal journey corresponds to the saving of the soul of the Democratic party. His psychological torment results from his unresolved sense of guilt for having killed one of his men in the heat of a confused battle. He essays to make this event emblematic of the entire war.

Kovic had tried to express his guilt to his colonel, who had responded with the shame-culture attitude, that these things happen in combat, that they are best forgotten. But Kovic cannot forget. His guilt for having killed Private Wilson, coupled with his guilt for having participated in the murder of innocent women and children, haunts him and seems literally to make him crazy.

He can only redeem his soul by confessing his guilt. Thus Kovic renders himself to Venus, Georgia, home of the family of Private Wilson. There he confronts Wilson's parents, his widow and son, and finally, after much agony, tells them the truth about Wilson's death.

These parents had received a letter from the marines telling them that their son had died while fighting valiantly in battle. Their dignity and family honor, their long tradition of fighting for the nation, are destroyed by an act that is portrayed as soul cleansing for Kovic but that is best seen as wanton mental cruelty. Wilson's widow says that she will never forgive him.

While the marines had put the best face on Private Wilson's death, Kovic shows no concern for the feelings of others; his primary concern is the state of his own conscience. The moral dilemma represented by this scene shows clearly the difference between saving face and saving one's soul. In the absence of social consensus, a group becomes a collection of individuals, each concerned only with saving himself.

Shame became guilt, and guilt was purged through punishment and confession. The innocence recovered by this process is otherworldly; it will always come up short when confronting this-worldly problems.

In *Born on the Fourth of July*, as well as in Oliver Stone's *Platoon*, American soldiers are more than their own worst enemies; they are also wanton killers of innocent civilians. The nation was divided because the enterprise was criminal.

In *Platoon* the cohesion of a military group is torn apart when the men massacre innocent Vietnamese civilians. Under the circumstances, they ought to feel guilt; they have acted like criminals. Eventually the platoon will be destroyed, as much by conscience as by enemy soldiers. Justice wins out as proper punishment is inflicted.

Other films also communicate the message that we deserved to lose because we are criminals whenever we are not fighting fascists. Whether they tell us that the United States is a corrupt nation or that advanced capitalism can only wish to murder peoples of the Third World, they present American standards of honor and dignity as masks for murderous impulses.

Stanley Kubrick's *Full Metal Jacket* offers two sides of the story. Beginning with a group of recruits in basic training, it attempts to show how the marines make boys into men. This training is depicted as a lesson in unexampled brutality. It climaxes when one of the recruits murders the sergeant who had trained them. This act of ''gratitude'' is justified because the recruit, portrayed as mentally ill, was the only one sufficiently sensitive to experience the full horror of the exercise.

In the second half of the movie these same marines are pinned down by sniper fire and lose their esprit de corps. The movie does not tell us whether they fail because they are enacting bad policies or because their training was a sham. In either case, American male pride is humiliated by a woman.

The enemy force that decimates the squad of marines is a lone woman with a machine gun. Even when they manage to overpower her, she shows herself to be more of a man than they are. The truth of her cause gives her superhuman power while our proud marines, fighting for a corrupt idea, can only be picked off one by one.

Many drew the lesson that communists prevailed in Vietnam because their cause was just. Radical intellectuals saw the Vietnam War as a clear sign of the failure of capitalism and the inevitability of socialism.

If leaders do not take responsibility and are not held to account, then the fault must lie with the system, with the soldiers, with the nation. This view was presented by these and other artworks; they sought to construct a coherent narrative of the American experience of Vietnam.

The most comprehensive were *Apocalypse Now* and *Born on the Fourth of July*. In our time filmmakers produce the cultural artifacts most likely to be considered of mass appeal. As myth or fiction makers, they acquitted themselves properly in a time of national crisis.

With *Born on the Fourth of July*, the story became a national epic. The movie attempted to offer a narrative explanation for who we are, what we were doing in Vietnam, and why the country turned against the war and against the soldiers. It also offered a solution: confess your guilt and vote Democratic!

Understanding what went wrong does not in itself make things right. Oliver Stone's film provided a description but not a solution to the national neurosis; its resource was the myth of guilt, punishment, and redemption. Ultimately, it verged on exculpatory propaganda.

No matter how good or bad it makes you feel, a story is just a story. Stories help us to organize experience, even to process reality, but they cannot restore national pride in and of themselves. They might produce a unanimous verdict or convince us to undergo endless self-criticism. None of this can restore pride. The ravages of failure are only overcome when failure is an isolated event in a series of successes.

How does a country exit a national neurosis? One way was shown in the Persian Gulf crisis and war. Clearly, those who proclaimed that victory in the gulf obliterated the Vietnam syndrome in American foreign policy spoke too soon. But that situation can still provide something of a paradigm for resolving an engrained sense of national failure.

In and of itself a war can only serve as an example of what a nation can do. For it to refute a sense of national purposelessness it must be taken as an exemplary event that defines future actions. Otherwise, it will appear to be a fluke, a consequence of good fortune, not a function of good leadership and national resolve.

If a shame culture sees failure as an aberration, guilt culture would normally hold the same view of success. Seen through the perspective of guilt, a successful action leaves much to be desired: there is nothing to feel guilty about.

Cast against a pattern of consistent failure, success can appear to be a fiction. For some it may even be a trauma. That does not obviate the reality of what happened in the Persian Gulf, but beyond the questions about the conduct of the war and its resolution, the more salient issue will continue to be whether it represents a future course for America, or whether it will go down in history as a lucky break.

Another point is this: the longer a nation lives in the throes of a national neurosis the more people have a stake in its continuation. Enough people believe that the turmoil and torment of the Vietnam period were salutary; they see the peace and prosperity of the 1950s as some kind of spiritual torpor. Historical revisionism even comes to blame the mistakes of the Kennedy and Johnson administrations on Eisenhower: if Ike had solved certain problems, Kennedy and Johnson would not have dealt with them ineffectively.

Life went on during the period of the Vietnam neurosis. People fell in love, had families, established careers; they did so, for better or for worse, within the social context that the nation offered. They formed opinions, engaged themselves politically, and established their own sense of pride and self-respect within the parameters that constituted social reality. People adjusted to social discord and came to have a considerable investment of "face" in it.

Saying that Vietnam was a mistake, that it did not need to happen, that there was nothing to gain from it, that it could have happened otherwise if we had had better leadership attacks the basis for personal self-respect in no small portion of the populace.

Most people will balk at the idea that the lessons they have learned from Vietnam were the wrong ones, that it was not a meaningful reflection of who we are or what we represent, but was simply an instance in which people we idealize failed us.

How then does an event break the hold of a national neurosis? If the neurosis is sustained by a national consensus about the validity of a master myth of guilt and redemption, we can only exit it when the myth is shown to be a fiction, when its premises are proved to be false, and when its vision of America is refuted. Only something real can discredit a fiction that has been taken to be the truth of experience.

The debate over the Gulf War was saturated by the fallout of the myth of American guilt. From both the extreme left and the extreme right there were calls to stay out of the gulf; those who had held leadership positions in previous administrations were constantly on television uttering the most dire forecasts. They saw the nation as incapable of mounting an effective campaign against Iraq. It appeared that they could not imagine that others could succeed where they had failed. The success of Operation Desert Storm shamed no small number of foreign policy experts.

The slogan that dominated the debate and influenced the conduct of the war was, "Not another Vietnam." Whatever the flaws in the Gulf War, it was, most assuredly, not another Vietnam. The only way to show that Vietnam was an aberration was to do it over again and get it right.

In and of itself the Gulf War could not remedy Vietnam, but it was a necessary precondition, a point of reference, from which to conduct future policy. If its lesson is disregarded, then the power of the syndrome will continue in force.

The Persian Gulf War was conducted according to the principles Eisenhower enunciated as the basis for American military intervention abroad. All of them had been disregarded in Vietnam. First, the military action in the gulf was undertaken with an international coalition; second, it was sustained by a congressional resolution; third, it was supported by the American public; fourth, it stayed within its mandate; fifth, it used overwhelming force with the intention of winning as quickly as possible and keeping allied casualties to a minimum. If these are the criteria for success, the action was a success. Perhaps not an unalloyed success, but a success nevertheless.

Was it face-saving? By and large it was, for a simple reason: from the beginning the Bush administration ruled out any compromise with Saddam Hussein. It refused, as Bush himself stated, to give Saddam any face.

Thereby George Bush affirmed a basic principle of face saving. If you negotiate with someone who does not have face, you lose face yourself. If face is based on recognition by others, clearly those others must be respectable members of the community.

Refusing to give Saddam Hussein any face revealed the fundamental ignominy of his position. Fighting someone who does not respect the rules of the game defends those who play by the rules.

When you are invited to play a game against someone who has been cheating with impunity, you must refuse in order to maintain the integrity of the game. Moreover, you must act to divest the cheater of his ill-gotten gains.

As a professional assassin, Saddam Hussein craved the only thing that his type of leadership could never gain—respect. Seeking to be recognized as a great world leader, he wished to corrupt the rules by which all others conducted business by placing his will above international law. Beyond his material interests in Kuwait, this was his psychological goal.

The Gulf War was not perfect; nothing is. Mistakes were made; some things could have been done better. The handling of the Gulf crisis set a performance standard for the conduct of international crises; it was not ideal.

What were its shortcomings? Primarily, that Saddam Hussein survived the war and, in the words of Margaret Thatcher, was not sufficiently humiliated. Her point of view merits notice: when dealing with tyrants, she said, one must be especially clear about the completeness of the humiliation.

The Bush administration defended itself on pragmatic grounds: invading Baghdad would have overstepped its mandate and cost it international and perhaps even American support. Any accident resulting in large numbers of American casualties would immediately have redounded to Mr. Bush's demerit. And military officers found the slaughter of defeated soldiers morally unacceptable. Finally, they might also have pointed out the dangers in excessive humiliation. Distinguished thinkers have long held that the extreme punishment inflicted by the Allies on Germany after World War I paved the way for Adolf Hitler.

In the United States after Vietnam the only segment of the nation that understood shame and acted to save face was the military. The nation might have accepted the myth that common soldiers were criminals or failures, but those who remained in the service and made it their career did not. They rose above the nation's guilt.

In a time of national self-flagellation a military organization restores its reputation not by dwelling on its failures but by accentuating its tradition of success. In many ways the military and large parts of middle America remained untouched by the negative, defeatist images that were being purveyed by those who provided narrative sustenance to the rest of us.

When a trauma becomes a national neurosis one segment of the population must keep itself apart from the emotional turmoil. Otherwise no one will be able to provide the leadership required during the next crisis.

The military's performance in the Gulf War came as a surprise and shock to almost everyone involved. No commentator predicted before the war that most of what the military put on the battlefield would work, and that American casualties would barely enter triple digits. Afterward, these thinkers tried to save their own face by belittling the same Iraqi army that they had previously taken to be an awesome military machine.

The fear of another Vietnam was palpable in the mouths of the people who opposed the war; expecting another Vietnam, they predicted that we would have tens of thousands of casualties and would sink into the Iraqi desert as surely as we had sunk into the swamps of Vietnam. If the only thing you knew about the American military after Vietnam was what you had seen on *60 Minutes*, you would have thought that none of the equipment would work and that our soldiers would be slaughtered in trenches filled with burning oil.

Desert Storm represented a real action that, if the guilt-culture narrative of Vietnam was correct, ought not to have happened.

Victory in battle is not sufficient to restore prestige. To solidify its advantage the nation was obliged to employ it for positive ends. Thus the Bush administration decided to invest a considerable portion of its political capital in a process designed to resolve the Arab-Israeli conflict and to bring peace to the Middle East.

Even that was not sufficient. President Bush dealt with the Persian Gulf crisis with uncommon skill and courage. And yet, in the aftermath of the war, he dissipated his domestic political capital with stunning speed.

As many have noticed, George Bush failed to capitalize on his victory in his address to a joint session of Congress on March 6, 1991. Instead of using his immense popularity to propose a domestic Desert Storm and to exercise leadership on basic economic issues, he chose to make the event an exercise in partisanship. Having brought the nation together, he now, in a single speech, sowed the seeds of further divisions.

Instead of appealing to Congress to act responsibly in the domestic arena, Bush seemed to want to rub the faces of congressional Democrats in their opposition to the war. He delivered an ''in-your-face'' challenge, saying that instead of offering a domestic agenda he would offer them two pieces of legislation, a transportation bill and a crime bill, and give them a deadline to pass them. The underlying message was demeaning; he was saying that he recognized their incompetence and would not be too demanding. At the same time congressional Republicans gloated about how they would use the Gulf War as a club to drive Democrats out of office.

Clearly these tactics did not promote cooperation. They were face-threatening and allowed the Democratic leadership to save face by exercising its own not inconsiderable legislative powers. This did not have to happen. That it did must be counted as George Bush's failure.

A better follow-through to the Gulf War victory was found by Mr. Bush's political adversaries. If the cold war was over and if we were now the reigning world military superpower, it was time to engage the nation in serious economic competition against the European and Asian economic blocs. Such a gesture, accompanied by new economic policies, would have turned the Gulf War into a defining moment in the national psyche.

George Bush lost the 1992 presidential election because his feckless approach to national economic distress seemed to give the lie to the determined leadership he showed in the Gulf crisis.

And yet, Bill Clinton, having seduced the nation into believing that he would launch a vigorous frontal assault on the nation's problems passed the first two years of his presidency looking more like the embodiment of the Vietnam syndrome than like the son of Desert Storm.

This allowed Newt Gingrich and House Republicans to seize the political initiative, effectively reaping the rewards for George Bush's success.

The 1994 congressional elections, in which the voters expressed a severe rebuke of the Democratic party and embraced Republican candidates, represented a decisive shift in the national political agenda.

In 1994 the voters repudiated at once the Great Society programs of Lyndon Johnson and a president who fashioned himself as a JFK clone. Few could recall such a decisive shift in national politics; fewer still saw the Republican takeover to be the consequence of the Gulf crisis.

Elections are rarely decided on who has the better ideas. Something real must sustain the voters' belief that the ideas can be made into policies and that the policies will produce constructive results. For Republicans that reality was the handling of the Gulf crisis.

Congressional Republicans produced a political action program, the Contract with America, accompanied by a promise to hold House votes on each of its ten items within 100 days.

They thereby proposed a plan of attack on social, economic, and political problems. They eventually fulfilled their promise with martial discipline and vigor.

The image of a Republican assault on a difficult set of problems may have recalled the Bush administration's handling of the Gulf crisis. People were not voting for a promise; they were voting for an achievement.

For the first 100 days of Republican rule of the House, getting things done replaced sterile debate and posturing. Moreover, the House Republicans managed to overcome one basic flaw that contributed greatly to the voters' rejection of George Bush: they kept their word. Thus, they understood that if anything undermined George Bush's presentation of himself as a strong, decisive leader it was his failure to keep his ''No new taxes!'' pledge.

House Republicans repaired the damage of this pledge in two ways: first, by presenting a positive program for a concerted attack on the nation's problems, something that a negative policy could never do; and second, by keeping their word where George Bush had lost face by breaking his.

For the moment Republicans seem to be leading the national charge to overcome the curse of Vietnam. They will hold that charge only if their reforms produce results and if they wear the mantle of leadership with dignity and humility.

It remains to be seen whether the Gulf War changed history.

What it ought to do—that is, to change our judgment of Vietnam from something that had to happen as it did to something that could have happened otherwise—it can only do in conjunction with other events. Instead of seeing defeat as coming from historical necessity, we should understand it as the product of bad decision making and inept leadership. Any society or culture, even any individual, must come to this judgment about any traumatic event.

Much of what was going on during the post-Vietnam era came to bear unmistakable traces of unreality and, at best, theatricality. Taking Vietnam to be a sign of our inevitable national decline, as though we were somehow on the wrong side of a great historical wave, people seemed either to be preparing for the revolution that would overtake our way of life or to be turning the end of the millennium into one last orgy before the impending doom.

The influence of the Vietnam War and its aftermath on our own history provides a place to demonstrate the effects of social trauma. It will show how a government's loss of face produces ill effects throughout society.

When guilt culture dominated America in the post-Vietnam period, it produced social dislocation and a cult of personal freedom and expression. Beliefs became more important than institutions; the good of the individual prevailed over the good of the group. The nation tried to heal the scars of Vietnam by a great reign of justice, a purge of the system.

Professor Samuel Huntington called this a "creedal passion period." I will call it the Great American Cultural Revolution.

3

The Great American Cultural Revolution

Meantime on the home front the Vietnam War was producing social turmoil. As government lost respect the body politic broke into factions, each looking out for its own self-interest. When a group loses face, its values and traditions become discredited; at that point each individual feels that he must save himself in the midst of pending calamity.

The leaders refused to see anything wrong in their own conduct. Instead of facing their shame and changing their policies, they masked it by proclaiming their innocence and accusing journalists and protesters of undermining the national spirit. For its part the antiwar movement asserted its own virtue and sought to stigmatize all those associated with the war. Throughout society masking shame became the order of the day.[1]

It manifested itself in the culture of narcissism identified by Christopher Lasch, in the self-indulgence represented by the unholy trinity of sex, drugs, and rock 'n' roll, in revolutionary yearnings for a new social order, in reactionary attacks on the excesses of the young, and finally in the dislocations caused by a transformation of the American work force from well-ordered hierarchies into self-serving disorder. Effectively, the war came home.

The effects linger. Writing in *Time* magazine in 1993, Lance Morrow compared the condition of the American workplace with the way the Pentagon fought the war in Vietnam. Referring to the growth of temporary employment, the shrinkage of large corporations, and the loss of permanent jobs, Morrow declared that American corporations were betraying the American work ethic: "There may be an analogue to this betrayal in the way that the U.S. fought the war in Vietnam. Robert McNamara's Pentagon became intoxicated by computer efficiencies and pseudo precisions and began sending soldiers out to the war alone instead of in cohesive units—the confused young soldiers going like temps dispatched to a 365-day jungle job and then coming home alone. . . . Thus vanished esprit de corps, team spirit, the intangibles that are indispensable to winning. An economy too much addicted to treating its workers like interchangeable, disposable grunts, such as Kelly girls and cannon fodder, may find itself succeeding about as well as America won its war in Vietnam."[2]

The loss of corporate loyalty mirrored the loss of national loyalty. Large numbers of individuals, set free from their moorings in national identity, renounced all reference to tradition and decided to make revolution a way of life.

Efforts to overthrow the government sounded like adolescent posturing, but other social institutions did not survive as well as government did. The Great American Cultural Revolution proposed, and even dictated, new approaches to love and marriage and family. And to minister to the many individuals who were lost in the new American funhouse, it made psychotherapy into a national pastime.

Members of the Woodstock generation, myself included, found other ways to mask the shame about their own activities during the war. It was easier to stigmatize the powers that be than to accept our own failures.

Besides the shame that the nation shared for its ignominious war, the youth of the sixties had other forms of shame to deal with. First, and perhaps the most difficult to admit, was the shame of having ducked a fight, of appearing to have chickened out. How many of us would have protested if we were not threatened with the draft? How much of our self-righteousness looked to others like cowardice? How much did we see ourselves as a privileged élite, willing to leave the grunt work to others? However unjust the war, however incorrect the policy, we suffered by comparison with our fathers who had fought and won World War II. Beginning with our generation, Americans would have a declining standard of living.

Military service has traditionally been one of the most important ways of leading young men across the threshold of adulthood. Young men have always needed to prove themselves under fire by risking their lives for the group in which they aspire to assume leadership. Many members of my generation never faced this challenge. To mask our shame we took to the streets, we protested, we fought as urban guerrillas against the forces of order, we were jailed and harassed, denounced and punished.

Revolutionary actions could make us feel it was not our cowardice but their failure that had gotten us into this situation. But to justify our actions we felt a need to indict not just one policy, but the nation, its traditions, its history. The rationale for revolt must extend beyond a temporary failure of leadership.

Never having served in the military, many of us never developed the skills that such organizations impart: the feeling of being a part of something larger than oneself; the need to maintain order, discipline, and morale; the importance of ritual and ceremony; the value of hierarchy; the relevance of respect; the uses of uniformity and conformity. As the generation that had not acquired these skills came to assume positions of greater authority in the workplace, corporate structure changed significantly to adapt.

Finally those of us who participated, even marginally, in the antiwar movement refused to see that the movement had failed. No evidence exists that the protests shortened the war by one day;

they may even have lengthened it by emboldening our enemies. Besides, no elected government could allow its policies to be made by rabble.

Rebellion derives its value from the possibility that authority might be abused by those who wield it. Intrinsically neither good nor bad, rebellion works if its only goal is to establish legitimate authority. When it sets out to degrade all authority, it tends to produce anarchic conditions that call forth demagogues and tyrants.

Rebellion must occupy a middle ground between those who wish to rebel all the time and those who see no rebellion as legitimate. People in permanent revolt quickly become revolting; people who accept all authority as legitimate make of servility the supreme virtue.

It is one thing to remove a leader who has compromised the dignity of his office, and quite another to destroy the social order by turning the everyday life of citizens into a court of revolutionary justice. The latter was the goal of cultural revolutions according to the model invented by Mao Zedong.

How does a cultural revolution take place? When a guilt narrative, constructed to make sense of a social trauma, moves beyond seeking a consensus of belief and attempts to produce a new world, you have a cultural revolution. Instead of believing that certain people betrayed an honorable tradition, you denounce the entire tradition and demand a radical transformation. Beginning with all those in positions of authority and extending to the artifacts and symbols that produce cultural coherence, a cultural revolution destroys everything in the hope that a new world will rise from the ashes.

Communism was the most extravagant attempt to do this. Holding that capitalism meant exploitation, it sought to eliminate exploitation by eliminating capital. Communists eradicated the cultural hierarchy based on shame and face and substituted one based on the soul, on guilt and innocence, reward and punishment.

This required new social institutions, a new form of government, even a new human being. The more Communist revolutions failed, the more their despots sought to extend the power of the state to control all aspects of everyday life.

Eliminating capital meant eliminating private property. Everything would belong to the state. This could only happen by destroying competing claims to loyalty. Family loyalty had to be attacked; children would be taught not to respect their parents, but to denounce them to the authorities. Family pride could not be deployed as psychological capital but had to be sacrificed to the good of the state.

"Face" is the psychological form of private property. Deprived of his psychological capital, the individual in a workers' paradise lost incentive, initiative, dignity, pride, prestige, and the will to do a good job. Lacking any pride in personal achievement and not being allowed to reap rewards for superior performance, people became economically dysfunctional.

Communism did not fail because it repressed religion; it failed because it did not allow anyone to have any face.

Samuel Huntington has argued that the Chinese and American Cultural Revolutions had much in common. Political authority was attacked in both countries by systematic muckraking and the exposure of corruption.[3] Hierarchy was overturned as the young were given authority over their elders; respectful behavior was considered to be a sign of complicity with criminal conspirators.

No Red Guards roamed the streets of America; no officials were dragged out of their homes for torture sessions and public trials. And yet violent protests and riots occurred in many of America's cities; youth gangs terrorized many of America's urban ghettos. In an increasingly crime-ridden society, personal property was subject to permanent threat. The post-Vietnam period saw among the more "civilized" elements of society a proliferation of efforts to rationalize the most extreme forms of deviant behavior. No officials suffered the fate of victims of the Red Guards;

and yet, many of Nixon's men had their lives destroyed by public humiliation and prison sentences. Few university professors were set upon to be humiliated by their students; many, however, burdened with guilt over their authority and wisdom, repudiated the trappings of their positions in order to act more like students. Such was the strength of the threat they perceived.

Additionally, as Huntington pointed out, in the post-Vietnam period in America a passion to expose corruption[4] was placed against the backdrop of "increasingly unfavorable perceptions of governmental and other institutions. . . ." It "necessarily made moralism and opposition to authority the dominant theme of politics"[5] and leveled social hierarchy in the name of individualism, democracy, egalitarianism. In the United States the "moral convulsion"[6] sought to produce a consensus of belief as a way to transcend cultural diversity.[7] Finally, in the absence of national pride, factions fought each other for the right to special government favors. Reversing John Kennedy's dictum, each group demanded that the country do for it, rather than ask what it could do for the country.[8]

A cultural revolution systematically transforms shame into guilt. When a leader cannot admit to his failure, he will shift the blame and seek to punish scapegoats. More generally, one can produce a guilt culture by punishing success and glorifying failure. If a game is rigged, the winners are cheats and the losers are victims. The same reversal is brought to bear on the meaning of a stigma: instead of being a sign of exclusion, it becomes a badge of honor worn by a rebel who has had the courage to refuse to play by the rules of an unjust society.

Such revolutions make extensive use of shaming to create a guilt culture. If you make a person feel that his dignity is a sham, his honor a convenience, his successes evidence of corruption, he will soon abandon all efforts to act with honor and dignity.

Shaming people indiscriminately does not heighten anyone's sense of self-respect. It makes people feel so totally stigmatized that they are willing to say and do anything to belong to any group whatever. This describes the thought reform that Stalin and Mao used to establish their own revolutions.[9]

In thought reform you take an individual, remove him from his normal social support network, surround him with people who take him to be criminally responsible for every ill that has befallen "the people," induce him to betray his friends, his family, and the values of his own tradition, and welcome him into a new group on the condition that he confess his criminal misconduct.

Thought reform as practiced by totalitarian regimes represents an insidious form of a common strategy for dealing with experiences of shame when face-saving strategies are not available. We should grasp the general concept.

The near universal symbol of shame is nakedness. In shame cultures nakedness represents the destitution of the individual, his state of being rejected by society. Having a sense of shame means knowing that one is naked and trying to hide it.

The leader who has failed will renounce his titles, his insignia, his uniform, his position. Divested of all the trappings of social existence, he sets out on his new path alone, isolated, ostracized. His last bit of dignity obliges him to spare others the pain of witnessing his destitution. He may have no clothes, but he does cover his shame.

Western idealism—religious and philosophical—offers an alternative course. Shame is made an occasion of redemption. You have not really failed, because your failure serves to critique society. If a fine person like you has not succeeded, then clearly there is something wrong with the world. Your destitution may be Christlike, a sign of participation in our civilization's greatest passion. Stigmatized and rejected, you can now set out to serve the god of Christian love by joining a community of the like-minded and redistributing wealth to the poor.

Or you may learn that in your abject nakedness, freed from the duties of your office and the responsibilities of your everyday life, you are now, finally, liberated to serve Eros, the philosopher's god of love. You may discover the meaning of life; you can live to love and love to live.

Guilt culture repugns the titles and symbols of social status; instead it promotes the virtues of romance and desire. Thus it finds a redeeming virtue in nakedness. Naked, all people are equal, just as they were when they were born and before they knew shame. Instead of being a sign of destitution, nakedness becomes a symbol of the egalitarian ideal. Those who hold such an ideal may form a community; if they coerce others to join, they have formed a cult.

Sex is the preferred mode of transmitting original sin, but it is also the great equalizer: knowing no distinctions of rank and honor, it brings people together to produce pleasure out of conflict.

Our Cultural Revolution was also a sexual revolution; many intelligent people believed that sex would demolish capitalism. Obviously, we overestimated the power of sex. Not only do we not identify people socially by the appearance of their genitalia, but we rarely judge them by how much sexual pleasure they experience. Shame cultures specify the face because each person is uniquely identified by its appearance; someone who has no face is unrecognizable. All the world's pleasures would not compensate his loss.

Ordinarily, we see revolutions erupting from below. Therefore, when things go wrong we blame unruly students, the urban underclass, blue collar workers, and other relatively disenfranchised groups. We err in doing so. Responsibility for social disorder ought rightly to be placed with those who hold authority in society. Their example sets the tone for the dissolute behavior that becomes more dramatic when it takes to the streets. Nevertheless, it is difficult to understand how the leadership failure in Vietnam worked its way down the social ladder to impact the lives of everyday citizens. How do you get, for example, from Lyndon Johnson's scar to domestic violence?

Moving down from the top, I begin with the most conspicuous

corporate failure of the Vietnam and post-Vietnam era, the American automobile industry.

For many people Detroit's failure signaled clearly that something was wrong in America. As the United States and Japan competed head to head in the automobile marketplace, Japan was obviously winning. This continued until after the Gulf War, when American automakers began to recapture market share and re-establish corporate reputation.

David Halberstam's *The Reckoning* provides us with a valuable guide to the decline of this industry. Interestingly, Halberstam saw it as beginning in earnest in 1973, the year of the Paris peace accords. The nation that won the most from Vietnam was Japan. If the United States could not hold its own against the least Asian power, how could it compete against the greatest economic machine in the region?

In Detroit as in Washington no one faced shame: ''There was widespread agreement that something terrible had happened to the old-fashioned American work ethic, although everyone seemed to blame everyone else. Everyone had his own scapegoat—the Japanese, the government, the Arabs, Wall Street. No one seemed to accept any responsibility for any actions that might have sapped the country's industrial strength.''[10]

If no one was responsible for what was happening to Detroit, then how could anyone set it right. If the malevolent forces arrayed against you are too powerful, you can become so demoralized that all effort will appear futile. Arrogance eventually gave way to despair: ''In 1966 the American auto industry was at the absolute height of its power, so rich and mighty that its arrogance, its certainty that it *was* America, was almost unconscious. Its leaders were so carefully shielded from the world around them that when they sinned in the construction of cars, they did not seek to correct the sin but sought to find the flaw in their accuser.''[11] Instead of accepting failure, they transferred blame.

The decline of the automobile industry produced personal traumas throughout the region around Detroit: ''There was pain in daily existence as the lives of thousands of citizens collapsed. There were more broken homes, households where the men could no longer face the fact that they had failed as providers and simply left. Social welfare offices reported a dramatic climb in cases of wife and child beating. There was a major increase in suicides. The school system printed up small guide books for students whose parents were unemployed, telling them how to handle certain situations, warning them their fathers were likely to be shorter of temper.''[12]

If a working man loses his job and can no longer support his family, he loses face. The most painful side of this is his having to face a family he can no longer support. When he does not experience his layoff as a temporary setback that will soon be rectified, he will see it as a judgment of his character, declaring him incapable of supporting his family. His wife and children's presence and their reliance on him feel like a perpetual reproach, a mockery of his manhood, a sign of his own moral destitution. He strikes out at them blindly and in rage.

The fact that others are in similar straits does not console him. Instead it causes him to believe that there is no way out of his dilemma. He sees everyone being punished together. The forces that have produced this situation are so powerful that no one can do anything to change them. The sense of despair feeds on itself. All forget what it felt like to be a valued member of a successful group.

The loss of group identity—which had existed in the post–World War II era—was only one element in the growth of American guilt culture. The eighties' buyout mania was based on the idea of taking a corporation, chopping it up, and selling its parts. As a competitive strategy it produced some clear benefits for shareholders. So long, that is, as you ignored the body counts—figured in layoffs.

Corporate officers who took a short-term, bottom line approach to their business clearly showed a diminished concern for the long-term reputation and viability of the enterprise. They did no honor to their predecessors and cared little for how they would be regarded in the eyes of their successors. The short-term goal of profitability prevailed over the long-term goal of gaining market share.

Moreover, profits took precedence over people. When takeover artists like T. Boone Pickens talked about maximizing shareholder value, they violated something that a Japanese executive would have taken for granted: employees are members of one's family, and their well-being must take precedence over increasing the dividend or having a good quarterly report. American business maintained profitability by laying off workers. Instead of thinking about what would happen to the family of the person laid off in a corporate restructuring, leaders thought of how many cents per share would be added to the bottom line. It was as though business success could only occur at the expense of workers. Not surprisingly, productivity suffered.

At a time in our own past when corporations believed that it was essential to respect employees and avoid shaming them by terminating their careers, such things happened much less often. Lance Morrow drew the distinction: ''Twenty years ago, Studs Terkel's *Working* explored the lives of Americans with jobs that seemed like long-term marriages, frustrating, satisfying, boring, rewarding: familiar, anyway, and built on a rock foundation. Careers had a kind of narrative line. It began with something like apprenticeship and then, in the ideal model, proceeded through hard work and merit to raises, promotions, success and eventual retirement with pension. Seniority and experience meant something: work was as close as Americans came to the Confucian. Getting fired was a disgrace: the scarlet letter.''[13]

The takeover and buyout rage demonstrated how unimportant workers were to companies. Lester Thurow declared, ''Company divisions, including the employees, are bought and sold or restructured in a manner reminiscent of kings buying and selling provinces in medieval Europe. As in medieval Europe, the employees are chattel serfs who are not consulted on whether they want to have different masters. Not much corporate loyalty can be expected if one can expect to be treated as a slave and sold to the highest bidder.''[14]

The American worker was often criticized, especially by foreign competitors, for shoddy workmanship and a general lack of interest in doing a good job. Perhaps workers did have a diminished sense of loyalty to their job. But how much loyalty did employers show them?

Whenever possible, workers began looking out for themselves instead of their companies. Like the soldiers in a defeated army they worried about survival and about advancing their own careers. Loyalty to the company counted for little when it was balanced against an opportunity for advancement.

Corporate America will eventually have to concern itself with the psychological costs of downsizing. As *The Economist* observed, ''Job cuts at Eastman Kodak, IBM and Philips have shattered morale and embittered many of those who remain, despite lavish redundancy payments. Massive job-cuts have also led to an exodus of the most talented employees. Confident of finding work at a firm with brighter prospects, the best people are often the first to take the payments that go with voluntary retirement.''[15]

In *Liberation Management* Tom Peters rationalized these policies by imagining that the new corporations are like movie production units: this means that a group of independent contractors come together for a limited period of time, then each goes his separate way. Workers suffer a largely insecure lifestyle in which no one knows where the next job is coming from. How do we expect our citizens to plan for the future or to invest in the future, when they do not know whether they have a future?

Using the arts and entertainment industry as a model provides some sense of liberation from the constraints of hierarchy. But if you look at professions like actor and artist, you will find enormous income disparities between the very few who make it and the many who fail. In contrast, the nations of Asia, with their hierarchical businesses, have the smallest wage disparity between the richest and poorest segments of the population. Certainly, this contributes to social stability and domestic tranquillity.

The larger psychological issue is this: Do people function better in organized groups where they know what is expected of them, what their rewards will be, and what their future will be, or do they become more economically efficient when each individual is freed to create his own job as he sees fit in order to fulfill his own individual talents? Is it more normal to conform or to rebel?

A guilt culture will see the group as inhibiting individual creativity. A shame culture will see people attaining their best levels of performance when they are secure in their group identity. Finally, competition in the marketplace will decide. Historical precedent is, however, on the side of shame culture. No army has ever succeeded without good organization and morale. Nor has any army ever succeeded by allowing each individual to develop his creativity.

Let us return now to the Vietnam era to examine some other consequences of our loss of face. How did the Great American Cultural Revolution start, what were its roots, and how did it grow and develop?

Culturally, one of the first important manifestations of the loss of a sense of shame was the production of what was called a counterculture as part of the antiwar protest movement.

The counterculture promoted a life of fun with sex and drugs; if the nation had lost its sense of shame, why not enjoy it? Hedonistic to a fault, the counterculture represented a new American decadence. In opposition to more venerable European traditions —represented by writers like Sade, Huysmans, Wilde, Beardsley, Baudelaire—the American version did not revel in evil; it proclaimed itself to be both innocent and constructive. Ultimately, Americans are too earnest to excel at decadence.

Followers of the counterculture withdrew from reality to indulge personal pleasures that were proclaimed to be therapeutic.

Finding yourself and fulfilling your spiritual potential would be personally rewarding. The drugs at issue, marijuana and a variety of hallucinogens, were touted as ways to enhance the enjoyment of art, sex, and nature. These would provide new insights, new forms of self-awareness—all of which would make you a better person.

The nation's youth accepted an invitation to undergo therapy through self-exploration and other forms of inner mystical voyages. Everyone was induced to follow his "bliss," and a great deal of bliss was available for all.

If American youth were no longer competitive militarily, this had to mean that they had passed beyond such trivial pursuits and had achieved something of transcendent value: a higher wisdom and greater sexual pleasure.

But what could it possibly mean to have more and better sex, and how could a private experience be judged by objective, publicly verifiable standards? Civilizations in decline and nations that have been humiliated seek such objective standards in increased fertility, more concubines, more sexual conquests, and so on. The man who cannot find a job and who cannot provide for his family decides to demonstrate his manhood by a string of sexual conquests; in place of masculinity we get machismo.

The counterculture encouraged public demonstrations of sexuality, multiple sexual partners, multiple orgasms, and various other performance standards for sexual experience. Similar standards were also established in the world of drug use. Status in that realm was judged by how much, how often, how high, how public, and how dangerous.

Such public demonstrations could only take place if sex and drugs were destigmatized. Private experience would have to become public, and for this to happen, the barriers to public exposure had to come down. No longer could premarital sex be stigmatized for preventing a happy marriage; no longer could out-of-wedlock pregnancy be stigmatized; no longer could the use of drugs to enhance spirituality be subject to social condemnation.

How did people go about destigmatizing these behaviors? Quite simply by publicly announcing, even to the point of bragging, their drug use, sexual exploits, and spiritual experiences. Harvard psychologist Timothy Leary became a guru to many, proposing to lead them on public voyages of spiritual enlightenment with LSD. Author Gay Talese lay claim to the title of champion of the sexual revolution with his book *Thy Neighbor's Wife*, which chronicled his own pursuit of all the new opportunities for pleasure. Sex was so out in the open that a serious author like Talese could recount his experiences with massage parlors, escort services, orgies, and the like as a valid research project. Open communication of fantasy and feeling, personal embarrassment and pain, became so prevalent that people came to require it of friends.

Of course, many people found it all highly offensive. The yahoos who had fought rock 'n' roll in the fifties as a communist plot to weaken the moral fiber of the nation's youth were beside themselves at the counterculture. They formed Richard Nixon's "silent majority" and later Jerry Falwell's Moral Majority. Pious preachers of religious fundamentalism rose up to denounce evil. These masters of blame dispensed guilt through their own national television networks.

Guilt culture always maintains the two sides of innocence and guilt, expression and repression. It sees them as moral absolutes, and it needs them both. You can't have a drama if you don't have an enemy.

The youth culture of the sixties and early seventies gave rise to some not so pleasant aftereffects. When behavior becomes destigmatized, it becomes a normal part of growing up. Once it becomes normal, your failure to participate becomes a sign of abnormality. Despite all the talk of natural tendencies to rebel, most teenagers really want to conform. Mass rebelliousness, as seen in the Chinese Red Guards, derives more from a wish to be a normal member of a group than any innate hatred of authority.

If you did not consume drugs and sex to surfeit and assert the superiority of your jejune opinions, then you were not a good

American teenager. Parents were more concerned that their children were sexually repressed than that they hadn't done their homework.

The sixties counterculture spawned the yuppie phenomenon of the eighties. Then the drug of choice became cocaine, and self-realization was based on less spiritual criteria. It was as though the financial community had drunk some mysterious elixir and had come to realize that youth and inexperience were more valuable than the plodding efforts of those older and wiser. Greed replaced responsible management. Trading in derivates became more important than developing face-to-face relationships.

Instead of gazing at the petals of a petunia while high on hashish, the yuppies consumed lavish meals at upscale restaurants, played with electronic toys and gadgets, bought Italian designer clothing, gold watches, and BMWs. In place of the value granted to insignia in a military organization or to a well-tailored suit, they sought to assert their status by spending and ultimately wasting money. This is one way of retaining a vestige of hierarchy when you have lost face. An extension of the counterculture, the yuppie phenomenon was certainly a form of social decadence.

The yuppies had no shame; they corrupted profit into greed, and sacrificed duty and reputation to the pursuit of excessive wealth. Men who were making more than $1 million a year found their compensation inadequate and engaged in insider trading to accumulate even more. These practices, in turn, provided justification for efforts to police industry, to confiscate profits, and to redistribute wealth . . . in roughly the same way the extremism of the first capitalists gave rise to calls to replace the system with socialism.

The greatest human symbol of the eighties was Ronald Reagan. Even if it was after the fact, no gesture more clearly typified the disregard for ''face'' that characterized the era than Reagan's receiving the world's most extravagant lecture fee from Fjisankei Communications Group in the fall of 1989.

Briefly, Reagan was given $2 million (with an added $5 million for expenses) to deliver two twenty-minute speeches in Japan. He was also persuaded to make a statement supporting the Sony takeover of Columbia Pictures.

As Chu Chin-ning wrote in *The Asian Mind Game*, the Japanese had thereby succeeded in putting a "price tag" on the prestige of the American presidency. They were also signaling to other American politicians that efforts to favor Japanese economic expansion would be well regarded.[16]

Among other consequences of the Cultural Revolution was the devaluing of marriage. The new sexual freedom increasingly won out over more traditional living arrangements. So many people were getting divorced that the state became destigmatized.

Whereas people in the sixties had believed that Nelson Rockefeller's divorce had seriously inhibited his prospects for being president, by the eighties there was no such effect on Ronald Reagan. Divorce became a sign of liberation, largely to the detriment of women and children. Being free of all social responsibilities was touted as the royal road to bliss.

The proponents of the counterculture were the children of privilege. Their actions and pronouncements articulated a new social policy that other, less fortunate members of society tried to emulate.[17] For most segments of the population, making sexual experience a ground for positive self-esteem and destigmatizing out-of-wedlock pregnancy tripled the number of out-of-wedlock births. Among whites this presented a difficult challenge; for black Americans it was a major calamity.

Similarly for drugs. While white Americans moved from psychedelics to cocaine and then, with the demise of the yuppie lifestyle, to something of a restigmatization of drug use, the inner-city ghettos suffered through a far more serious epidemic of the poor man's cocaine: crack. When revolutionary values sifted down to the lower rungs of the social ladder, the results were disastrous.

The pursuit of innocent pleasures during the sixties soon began to show an uglier side. It was not too long before sex began to be associated with child abuse, venereal infections, sexual harassment, and the display of violent pornography. As the sexual revolution revealed a more grotesque visage, reasonable people called for the increasing criminalization of abusive sexual behavior. More laws, more lawyers, more courts, more prisons, were touted as the solution to our problems. As happens in a guilt culture, the excessive public expression of private matters led to social disorder and calls for repression.

If the American Cultural Revolution sought to mask shame by promoting feelings of guilt and innocence, it would naturally have found its institutional defenders in the legal profession. The most important promoters of guilt culture are lawyers.

In the post-Vietnam era the nation's life has been invaded by a litigious band whose adversarial attitudes have undermined confidence in all our social institutions—from government to corporations to families—thereby contributing to an astonishing number of social problems. In its own way this phenomenon derived from the glorification of youth at the expense of age and experience.

Our litigation explosion dates to John Kennedy's New Frontier. Kennedy empowered a new class of mandarins, among whom were many young lawyers and academics. It was not just a new generation that came to power with John Kennedy, but a new class, an academic and intellectual group that did not, for the most part, owe its ascendancy to military or corporate institutions.

Kennedy's people sought to promote integration, to open doors for those who had been closed out, to offer opportunity to those who had been excluded, to grant dignity to those who had been demeaned. People wanted to join the system, to have the same chances for success and failure, to be judged on merit and not with prejudice. The young New Frontiersmen sought to right wrongs through public policy, legislation, regulation, and education.

The assassination of John Kennedy, followed by that of Robert Kennedy, seemed to dash those hopes forever. But Vietnam was the decisive factor. The fact that the new mandarins had been pulling the levers that propelled us into the Vietnam quagmire produced a rush among liberal intellectuals to repudiate the policy by vociferously proclaiming their own innocence. Unwilling to see their heroes as responsible for Vietnam, they blamed the system and sought to make it pay. Their apotheosis was Watergate.

The New Frontiersmen and the other mandarins formed a class I will call the New Advocates. In place of reform from within, they would fight what they saw as systemic corruption. Instead of promoting the value of joining the firm and becoming part of the history of the corporation, the New Advocates attacked corporations as quasi-criminal enterprises whose purpose was to destroy people for the sake of profit. Corporate guilt was a given; only strict legislative and regulatory control could prevent corporations from devouring the innocent public.[18]

Since society's leaders were unwilling to take any responsibility for their failures, our democracy channeled popular resentment by allowing everyone to file lawsuits. Thus could little people take revenge against the rich and powerful: against businesspeople, physicians, clergymen, corporations, and so on. Litigation created an adversarial relationship between rich and poor and held out the promise of limitless recompense.

It may have been more of a myth than a reality. But the pervasiveness of this myth translated a guilt narrative into a framework for social and political relationships.

In fact, however, the little people had better odds with the lottery; the people who got rich at this game were the lawyers. Corporations and other targets of litigation simply bought more insurance and added hefty premiums to the cost of their products. Thereby, the little people ended up paying for it all. One can even argue that the amount of intellectual energy put into courtroom struggles was energy that could have better served to improve product safety and efficiency.

In principle, litigation ought to provoke corporations to fulfill their responsibilities. In some cases this occurs. But it also induces them to make excessive expenditures on legal, as opposed to engineering, talent, and to use this legal talent to see what they can get away with. The new standard becomes whether it is legal, that is, whether the legislature has caught up with whatever is going on, not with whether it is reputable. The litigation game showed why guilt cultural means are ineffective as a way of redressing grievances.

As Walter Olson remarked in his book *The Litigation Explosion*, the wholesale use of litigation to redress social ills is a recent phenomenon, dating to the seventies: "Older lawmakers and judges tended to recognize litigation as a wasteful thing, in its direct expense and in the demands it places on the time and energy of people with better things to do. It was grossly invasive of privacy and destructive of reputation. It was acrimonious, furthering resentments between people who might otherwise have occasion to cooperate."[19]

Through the sixties the American Bar Association promoted ethical canon number 28, which said that "stirring up litigation" was unworthy of the profession. However, "within a few years," Olson writes, "many had come to see stirring up litigation as an inspiring public service, in fact, morally obligatory."[20]

Lawyers, by training, see failure to be the consequence of wrongdoing. They do not trust a corporation to offer compensation on its own and to correct its own errors. They do not trust shame. Malaise and social discontent are ipso facto evidence of unpunished crime. The post-Kennedy generation of lawyers, significantly, was well qualified to attack the functioning of the system, because they had so little experience in making it work. They had not been insiders, but outsiders. They felt that their chance had been prematurely snatched from them by the assassination of John Kennedy, and they fed their idealism on visions of the Camelot that would have been if only. . . .

They set their formidable intellects to the task of finding culprits. Academics and journalists joined in the effort. Investigative reporting arose to offer something of a narrative of what was happening in Vietnam, why it was taking so long, why we were not winning. Journalism placed at the service of judicial inquiry came into its own with Watergate.

The search for victims accelerated in the eighties. Advocates represented the environment, the consumer, women, children, fetuses, the disabled and the handicapped, gays, prisoners, students, any one of the number of racial, religious, and ethnic groups that make up the American system. Business was good, especially for product liability and malpractice attorneys.

The problem was that none of this made anything work better. Advocacy concerns itself with what went wrong in the past, not how to make it better in the future. It emphasizes punishing errors, not producing more efficiently. The threat of lawsuits builds distrust into the system. Contracts do as much. If people trust each other, there is no real need for a hundred-page document detailing every possible way that an agreement can be voided. None of it increases the efficiency of the manufacturing process or adds any value to a product.

Lawyers are mostly superfluous to manufacturing. They drain resources that could be spent on engineering more efficient production. It is one thing to say that lawyers are necessary to a society because they can resolve the most extreme cases of abuse, and quite another to say that they need have their hand in every decision and every piece of paper that an executive signs. It is one thing for lawyers to help mediate and negotiate difficulties; quite another for them to place the threat of lawsuits over every aspect of American economic life.

A society that empowers advocates and makes them essential to the workings of the economy presumes that business is fundamentally corrupt, and that it cannot function fairly unless it is strictly regulated. Only a strong presumption of guilt can grant lawyers power beyond their normal function of correcting excesses. Once this happens, business becomes less inclined to admit error, because there are no longer any innocent mistakes.

By the 1990s a new enemy had emerged on the American political landscape: the faceless bureaucrat.

Government was so concerned about protecting people from evil that it had insidiously come to regulate nearly all aspects of corporate and community life. The faceless bureaucrat came to represent the invisible tyranny of a government that had overstepped its mandate.

The bureaucrat represented the triumph of American legalism; he was the agent through which the strictures of advocates and legislators were applied to the everyday life of far too many citizens. The bureaucrats earned their epithet of "faceless" for applying the same rules indiscriminately, with or without reason. Using regulations to interfere in building, zoning, the environment, product safety, and whatever, bureaucrats became a force that stifled the nation.

Philip Howard's *The Death of Common Sense* chronicled what happened when bureaucrats ceased to exercise their discretion but were reduced to applying rules whether they produced the desired result or not.

What would it be like to live with fewer lawyers? The alternative to onerous contracts is a long-standing relationship. As with friendship, the longer and better you know someone, the more you have had constructive dealings, the more you will have mutual trust and confidence in each other. You will not need to spell everything out, because you know from experience that each partner will do everything within his power to maintain the business relationship.

Contracts can serve a useful purpose when people who do not know each other are obliged to do business. In this circumstance a certain amount of distrust is normal. When people change jobs and neighborhoods often, the sense of basic trust will be less well established. Of course, the more a business holds its employees to be disposable, and the more its own integrity as a corporate entity is subject to takeovers and breakups, the less personal relationships will count.

In America being a lawyer pays better and has more status and glamour than does being an engineer. How can one expect business to run more efficiently when, as Ezra Vogel noted, "charismatic critics of organizations are cheered while hardworking executives who exert themselves to hold organizations together are criticized"?[21]

In the area of affirmative action, the use of legalistic remedies has at times produced an effect opposite the one intended. If hiring a black worker exposes a firm to an increased risk of lawsuits, that worker, all other things being equal, will cost more than a comparable white worker. As Christopher Jencks wrote, "If a firm has to pay black workers more than in the past, and if it also has to be more cautious about disciplining them or passing them over for promotion, it is likely to ask itself whether blacks are worth what they now cost. If its answer is no, it will look for ways of reducing the number of blacks on its payroll. The safest way of doing this is to relocate in an area where few blacks live. . . ."[22] Onerous legal and regulatory constraints require industry to spend its energy discovering creative ways to slip through the law's loopholes.

Psychologically such practices are counterproductive. In an article titled "Green Guilt and Ecological Overload," Theodore Roszak taxed the environmental movement with guilt-mongering to its own detriment: "If we were to compile all the warnings of all the ecology groups, there would be little that we in the industrial world could do that would not be either lethal, wicked, or both. From the dioxin-laced coffee filters we use in the morning to the electric blankets we cover ourselves with at night, we are besieged by deadly hazards. Worse still, many of those hazards make us unwitting accessories to crimes against the biosphere."[23]

As with other advocacy groups, the environmental movement proposes to protect individuals from the system. Worshipping nature to excess, this movement demeans social ties and devalues work within the system.

Rejecting the guilt cultural approach does not mean accepting a filthy environment. It requires people to recognize, as *Business Week* reported, that "publicizing the names of polluters is working better than tough laws.''[24] You can hire lawyers to defend you against lawsuits, but if your company makes the list of the nation's top polluters, the loss of corporate reputation and goodwill is far more difficult to regain.

Responsible corporate behavior is thoroughly consistent with concern for the environment. Special interest groups, however, believe that corporations function like criminal conspiracies, and that advocates must defend the citizen-victims of these corporate predators. In fact, however, shaming a corporation can produce "real declines in emissions [that] are so large that the EPA considers the program a resounding success.''[25]

Whether the cause was abortion or the earth or animal rights, life-or-death matters were far more important than group concerns and the efficient functioning of the "system." How could anyone work within the system if it was intrinsically corrupt and murderous? How many fathers or mothers want to come home to hear their children accuse them of poisoning dolphins, burning down rain forests, producing poverty and malnutrition in the Third World? How many of them, hearing such indictments, will be able to retain the morale and confidence required to do a good job?

Extraordinary intellectual resources are now channeled into the legal system. Too many of the best and the brightest people in our society are spending time suing each other, defending against each other's suits, and micromanaging business to safeguard against future litigation. We thereby waste resources in a conspicuous consumption of intellectual talent that bears some resemblance to those primitive tribal chiefs who demonstrate their power and their guilt by destroying their goods. Only the very rich can afford such indulgence and, even then, not for very long.

Mining the resources of an indigenous tradition, using the force of their own arguments, and exploiting the social dislocations and fragmentation produced by the Vietnam experience, the New Advocates have succeeded in convincing many people that concern for shame and face reveal an unenlightened attitude that is detrimental to the best interests of trial lawyers.

We no longer picture the honest businessman manufacturing a good product, offering it at a fair price, and making a reasonable profit. Instead we imagine him striving to cheat consumers, pollute the environment, and exploit workers. Thus we insist that he be held in check by bureaucratic surveillance, mindless litigation, and the constant criticism of the media élite. The latter guarantees drama and conflict, while the former offers the presumption of decency.

After two decades of intense advocacy, America found herself divided into contentious factions and plagued by rampant criminal behavior. Her businesses were suffering a chronic decline in the growth rate of worker productivity.

The Founders of the American Republic had a special horror of factional politics. When factions believe that their interests supersede the rules of civil conduct in civil society they place us on the road to social chaos.

The issue is simple: Are the interests of any faction more important than the interests of the union? Can the nation sacrifice national pride and honor in order to concede to the demands of special interest groups? Are these groups willing to abandon their claims when they find themselves in conflict with the national interest?

Factions today have found two ways around these questions. Either they identify their interest with the national interest (a cleaner environment is certainly in the national interest; environmentalists make it *the* national interest), or factions discredit the notion of national interest by making it a factional concern. Some people hold that the national interest is really the interest of the ruling capitalist élites. They have denounced the Anglo-American tradition that founded the nation and have encouraged the idea that all customs and traditions have equal value.

On an everyday level this multicultural approach produces social discord and offensive behavior. If two people from two different cultures meet and the proper gesture of greeting for one is a handshake and for the other a bow, one will obviously have to accommodate the other. In our culture the failure to return the offer of a handshake is offensive; in other cultures the failure to return a bow is equally offensive.

The only way to ensure that everyday social interactions do not give offense is for all participants to follow the same code and the same rules. You cannot play a game where one team is playing American football and the other team is playing English football.

The American Cultural Revolution declared that losing face was not such a bad thing, because the experience could enhance the effort to save one's soul. Public exposure of one's faults, public confession of sin, became de rigueur. Ostentatious displays of wealth were good, as were exhibitionistic displays of one's sexual prowess. The Revolution soon became an integral part of everyday life.

Obnoxious and insulting behavior became acceptable. Infatuated with their rights to free speech, people believed it acceptable to walk up to someone who was overweight and berate him for being disgusting and repellent. They felt that they had the right to accost people on the street for wearing furs. Smokers were commonly harassed. Rude language became a sign of freedom, as was other conduct unbecoming gentlemen. At times appointments seemed made to be broken; few felt the obligation to respond to telephone calls promptly or to honor commitments to anything other than self-fulfillment.

Is it a good thing to disregard the requirements of saving face? People would be far less glib about this if they understood what is involved in a loss of face. I will present a picture of what it is like to lose face, or what it means, as the Chinese say, to have "no face." In traditional Chinese culture "no face" is the ultimate human horror.

In American history the closest approximation of having "no face" is being black in America. The most eloquent presentation of this condition can be found in the writings of James Baldwin. The title of one of his books, *Nobody Knows My Name*, renders well the sense of having no face. Roughly speaking, if you have no face you will either be ignored, treated as though you are not there, or else taken to be a threat by your mere presence. Black Americans played a dual role in the American Cultural Revolution. On the one side, their own struggle for civil rights and respect got caught up in the guilt cultural mode that invaded other aspects of public life. But on the other side, black Americans became role models for the privileged youth who were leading the Revolution.

If a shame culture encourages all citizens to emulate those who have achieved the greatest success, a guilt culture seems to turn that formula upside down. After Vietnam many among the privileged came to emulate the underprivileged; failure became a badge of honor, allowing one to escape the shame associated with being part of an élite that had lost a war.

As the Revolution matured, new waves of people claimed to be victims of the ruling power élite. And they identified themselves with those who had the most legitimate claim to being victims. They may have felt that blacks would feel better for having so many sympathizers, but holding up a group as the ultimate victim does nothing to encourage it to build on its successes and to develop its own reputation for honorable behavior. Why would you want to give any group a stake in failure? This may represent a version of white guilt, but many black Americans found it demeaning to be used as examples of the unbridled indulgence of sex, drugs, and rock 'n' roll.

The culture of the black community provided one of the social role models so ardently sought by American cultural revolutionaries. It seemed to be an alternative to a culture based on hierarchy, class, status, achievement, and saving face. It had achieved a dubious success in escaping the nefarious influence of fathers to form an indigenous American matriarchy.

And yet not having face is hardly something that serious people should aspire to. Is it not better to offer the underprivileged access to the American mainstream than to idealize their disadvantage?

Blacks have been treated with disrespect, but it is no consolation to say that they have "soul." Having "soul" and being part of a religious community represents a fallback position, but it is not an adequate substitute. For those who have suffered a loss of face, belonging to a religious community saves them from complete isolation; it does not compensate for reintegration into society.

But before we discuss these issues, let us see what it means to have face and what it means to lose it.

Examine a series of everyday events that happen only because you have face. You wake up one morning and go about your usual daily activities. You greet your spouse and children, you grouch over breakfast, you rumble into your office bristling with ideas about a new approach to the report you have to present on Friday, you run into one of your best friends during lunch at your favorite restaurant, and so on. People greet you, interact with you, tell a joke you find funny, disagree with one of your ideas, follow an order you give, ask your advice about something, keep you apprised of recent events in the lives of those you know and who know you. Some of the people you see do not know who you are and do not care. Mostly the feeling is mutual.

Now let us enter the twilight zone where you have no face. You are going through your daily routine—make it as glamorous and as exciting as you wish—and no one knows who you are, no one knows your name, no one knows your titles and professional authority, no one recognizes you on any level. No one talks to you, no one listens to you, no one engages in any but the most anonymous interaction with you. You may be able to buy a hot dog from the local stand, but neither the vendor nor any other individual you meet during the day knows who you are. If you go back to the same stand tomorrow, the vendor will not remember having served you today. If he is talking with one of his regular customers, he might well ignore even your human presence.

Now you have no face. You have achieved anonymity and

have become the perfect generic human. You are not invisible—that would be too much fun—but everyone treats you as someone with whom they are not acquainted, who has no status in the community, who is simply a fellow human being who must have a home, friends, and family somewhere, but not here. You have finally gotten down to your bare bones humanity. You are now living a nightmare.

Under these circumstances you would not be going through anything that even resembled your everyday routine. If you wake up one morning in the conjugal bed and your spouse does not recognize you, there will be panic, the police will be called, and you will, at best, be expelled from the house. If you see your children they will ignore you. If you claim any sort of familiarity you will cause them to run away. If you pursue them and act as you normally do with them, you will soon find yourself incarcerated for child abuse or attempted kidnapping. If you walk into your office and no one recognizes you, if your name is not on the list of employees, if you do not have your identity badge, you will be immediately ejected from the building. If you insist, you will be remanded to custody, labeled John Doe, and put back out on the street. This assumes that you have not made too much of a nuisance of yourself.

Nameless and faceless, you will not be able to get a job because no future employer will be able to evaluate your past status or grant you any trust. You will not receive credit, be allowed to rent an apartment, or have any friends you can trust. If you are sufficiently stigmatized the one thing people will know about you is that they must avoid you.

This nightmare scenario is not a drama; there is no plot and there are no characters. It simply shows what it means to lose face. When you have no face you have no recognizable external features, you are not part of any social group, and you have no friends or neighbors, no past or present.

Of course, this is very difficult to imagine, because you would continue to know who you are. The problem is: How long would it take for your knowledge that you are, say, Al to be undermined? Being Al means being vice-president of Consolidated Widget, being married to Sally, having children named Jim and Judy, being best friends with Jack and Steve, being the neighbor of Sol and Betty, and so on. If none of those people recognize you for who you believe you are, it would not take very long before your belief in being Al would become untenable.

Being black in America comes closest to the experience of having no face. But white America also bears a stigma for having produced such conditions and allowing them to persist. This does not in and of itself compromise the achievements of the civilization, but America's continuing difficulty in dealing with its racial problem does diminish her other accomplishments. How then has America tried to give face to her black citizens?

Even though slavery was abolished just after the Civil War, racial segregation continued to be a way of life at least through the middle of the twentieth century. The motor for change was World War II. Black soldiers had fought to defend their nation, and had earned military rank and honors. They returned home to separate facilities and limited prospects; the nation failed to recognize their achievement. White America was shamed by its treatment of these veterans; arguably this motivated the first movement to dismantle segregation: President Harry Truman's order desegregating the military.

The next crucial event in the civil rights struggle was the Supreme Court's *Brown v. Board of Education* decision in 1954 outlawing separate-but-equal schooling. With the support of the national government the civil rights movement sought to integrate Southern schools: Central High in Little Rock and the University of Mississippi. These were followed by escalating sit-ins and nonviolent protest marches.

Throughout this phase of the movement white America was disgraced by the behavior of its law enforcement officers and civil authorities. Using cattle prods and fire hoses on peaceful demonstrators contradicted our sense of who we were. The comparison between the quiet dignity of the black protesters and the vicious brutality of the white segregationists shamed the nation and produced a consensus in favor of civil rights.

This phase of the civil rights struggle was embodied in the figure of Martin Luther King, Jr. He was, as Andrew Hacker noted, "safe and respectable," favoring integration and peaceful change.[26] His approach produced considerable progress and ought not to be demeaned because whites approved. Building a national consensus in favor of racial harmony was a great achievement. Giving face to blacks would not happen at the expense of whites; in fact, it would allow whites to maintain their own self-respect.

But even before King's assassination, the movement was slipping into a different mode, one of violent confrontation and demands for black power. Instead of shaming white society into changing itself, more and more blacks adopted the ways and means of guilt culture. In Hacker's words: "As liberals see it, the erosion of the interracial alliance did not come about from a decline in white commitment. Rather, blacks turned from building bridges to shriller forms of politics that seem to indict all whites."[27] How did it come about that the consensus in favor of civil rights was broken?

The watershed event, Hacker wrote, was the race riots in Watts, Detroit, Newark, and other cities in the mid-sixties: "After those disturbances, race relations never returned to their former plane. Whites ceased to identify black protests with a civil rights movement led by students and ministers. Rather, they saw a resentful and rebellious multitude, intent on imposing its presence on the rest of society. . . . Worsening relations between the races were seen as largely due to the behavior of blacks, who had abused the invitations to equal citizenship white America had been tendering."[28]

Many whites did not understand how the riots could occur at a time when liberal government policies were working to abolish segregation. Feeling that they had made significant gestures to overcome racism, whites tended to blame blacks for the riots.

Occurring at the same time as the military escalation in Vietnam, the race riots brought the war home.

The picture of blacks as rioters and criminals etched itself on white minds, to the detriment of further racial progress. One might well decide to grant certain concessions to rioters in order to quiet them down and make them go away. But it is radically impossible for people to reward criminal behavior with gestures of respect. Later, controversies over busing and affirmative action showed that whites had come to believe that the kind of progress civil rights leaders were demanding would occur at their expense. They balked.

The race riots split the nation into opposing and increasingly adversarial camps. Shame had been replaced by guilt, and this produced an important shift. Where whites had felt shame for the condition of blacks, once guilt culture took over, these same whites felt besieged. Accused, berated, indicted, condemned, punished, threatened, they reacted defensively, rejecting the charges and turning away from their black fellow citizens.

The nation polarized on the issue of race. In Hacker's analysis of the situation, liberals were willing to take all guilt on themselves and to pay retribution to blacks for the sins of their fathers and forefathers. Conservatives refused to accept guilt and tended to disclaim any responsibility for what was going on in the nation's ghettos.[29]

Racism became one of the largest elements in the guilt narrative spawned by Vietnam. To justify their rebellion, radicals had to see Vietnam as emblematic of the disease of American civilization; they had to find an original sin and for that, racism, slavery, and segregation served well.

The civil rights struggle became swept up in this larger story; blacks were living proof of the degenerate nature of the entire civilization. Other special interest groups decided that they wanted to be on the same side, in the vanguard of the revolution.

Black Americans assumed leadership in the antiwar movement when Martin Luther King decided to oppose the war. Seeing

Vietnam as a racist act, akin to their own oppression, black leaders too often expressed solidarity with the Viet Cong. Moreover, a racially integrated military seemed to be incompetent. A society that sought to blame Vietnam on the troops, not the leaders, could easily see it as an exemplary instance of why integration was a bad idea.

Obviously, this was only part of the story. Other, less visible blacks continued through the seventies and eighties to make progress within white society. The black middle class grew enormously during this period, but it grew in silence and invisibly.

Instead of showing the reality of the black middle class, civil rights leaders have concentrated on more dramatic images. The urban ghettos, black crime, youth gangs, and drug abuse have been used by some of them to justify their demands on white society. This tactic has not been very successful. Appealing to guilt has not been as effective as Martin Luther King's tactic of shaming white America by actively countering its negative stereotypes.

It may well be that most whites maintain stereotypical images of blacks. These images are not entirely made up out of whole cloth. If blacks choose to present themselves in an intimidating and angry posture, and if blacks have a disproportionately high crime rate, then the fact that whites come away with some measure of fear of blacks does not mean that they are racists.

Nor is it entirely a function of racism that groups of people gain or lose reputation by the behavior patterns they exhibit in public. We often babble about taking each person as a unique individual, but that is impossible. While it is clearly unfair that a successful black does not receive the same acceptance as a successful white because he belongs to a group that has on the whole been less successful, the recognition within any group that it gains or loses reputation by the way all its members behave can be a powerful motivating factor toward civility and success in society.

I do not believe that playing the racism card is the best approach to improve race relations in America. What will you really accomplish if you convince every white person in America that he is an inveterate racist? Will you make him feel that he is responsible for the behavior of his black neighbors? If you do so you will also be telling his black neighbor that he is not responsible for his own behavior. Parsing responsibility this way has much in common with slavery.

The interests of society are best served by the success of all its members. Failure among blacks does reflect badly on the nation as a whole; whites are acutely aware of this, and probably they wish that blacks would succeed more often. It would be better to assume that the minds of whites are inhabited by "original virtue" toward blacks, not the original sin of racism. Whites would still be divided over how much they should do to help the disadvantaged members of society, but this debate would have more to recommend it than one that descends to indictment and defensiveness over racism.

Whites do have a considerable responsibility for the state of black Americans; they are not, however, solely responsible. Leaders in the black community ought to take responsibility for the things that go wrong for the people they lead. They should not take credit for the good and blame others for the bad.

Using the legislatures, the courts, and the criminal justice system to prohibit manifestations of racism produces considerable resentment among whites who see government becoming intrusive in a way that feels coercive and punitive. Provoking conflict and confrontation will never move the nation closer to civil behavior.

The problem is that the civil rights debate became a black-versus-white issue. And, to use the metaphor, people came to see it as a black-and-white question: one was right, the other wrong; one was innocent, the other guilty. Once the sin of racism is invoked as a defining sentiment, there are no gray areas, no possibilities for conciliation and compromise. You cannot be half a racist.

If whites are taken to be racists, they will have to be coerced, threatened, or intimidated into offering respect to blacks. Such respect is a sham, and coercion always provokes people to save face by rebelling, sometimes quietly, sometimes loudly. When blacks are considered to have been hired, promoted, and compensated for a job because of their race, they do not receive the respect of their colleagues. Their hiring tends to be part of the cost of doing business, paying lip service to regulations.

This is the challenge of affirmative action. When affirmative action criteria are invoked there must also be, within a company, objective performance standards known to everyone and accepted by everyone.[30] Promotion, compensation, and corporate responsibility must be based on accepted standards, otherwise the titles and achievements of black Americans will be devalued. Having a two-track system where a tacit understanding defines black success differently than white is patronizing: you did well, for people like you.

Some have argued that American norms are indigenous to white Eurocentric culture and therefore should not apply to blacks.[31] This approach seems generally to be the practice in our best universities; it holds a special appeal to adolescent minds. The results are hardly encouraging.

As Arthur Schlesinger argued in *The Disuniting of America*, pride and self-respect are not necessarily based on ethnic pride.[32] So long as different ethnic groups share a common national identity, common political and cultural institutions, common rituals and ceremonies, they share the pride that comes about when those institutions function effectively to promote the well-being of the people. America has been the world leader in showing that civic pride and identity can be based on other than ethnic grounds.

Schlesinger attempted to recover the old liberal consensus for civil rights. He did so by denouncing educational institutions that fail to teach the values, principles, and institutions of America, and, more especially, fail to hold blacks to the same standards as whites.

Schlesinger addressed the consequences of the way affirmative action has been practiced in universities. Christopher Jencks saw the attendant loss of self-respect producing a subculture that promoted different standards for different students: "Policies that put blacks in situations where they cannot perform as well as most whites may also have significant psychological costs for blacks. Most of us will do almost anything to preserve our self-respect. This means we avoid competitions in which we expect to do badly. If we are poor athletes, we avoid sports. If we are poor students, we often quit school. . . . Colleges that admit large numbers of academically marginal black students should not, therefore, be surprised when these students create a subculture in which working hard is devalued."[33]

What if this subculture then claims equal status with the dominant culture? The effect of the influence of "ethnic ideologues" was described by Schlesinger: "They have made a certain progress in transforming the United States into a more segregated society. They have done their best to turn a college generation against Europe and the Western tradition. They have imposed ethnocentric, Afrocentric, and bilingual curricula on public schools, well designed to hold minority children out of American society. They have told young people from minority groups that the Western democratic tradition is not for them. They have encouraged minorities to see themselves as victims and to live by alibis rather than to claim the opportunities opened for them by the potent combination of black protest and white guilt. They have filled the air with recrimination and rancor and have remarkably advanced the fragmentation of American life."[34]

Here we have affirmative action run amok. In the name of self-esteem these educational policies have made it impossible for many minority group members to fail—or to succeed according to any objective standards. Since these courses of study tend toward self-involved meditation on one's own experience, they do not prepare students for participation in the workplace.

High self-esteem coupled with low skills is a formula for bitterness and resentment. If the best-paying jobs in the future will be granted to those with the highest level of scientific and technical skills, we must ask how well ethnocentric studies are preparing people for these jobs. Sometimes it appears that they prepare people to cope with not getting the jobs. Learning the best ways to protest does not prepare anyone to function effectively in the marketplace.

Schlesinger's book, among others, points out the serious flaws in the educational approach to affirmative action. It raises the question of whether the university should be the institutional "role model" for further efforts at repairing the legacy of racial discrimination. And if it is not, what other institution could serve as a better model?

People agree generally that the institution that has made the greatest progress in providing opportunity and respect for black Americans is the armed forces. Military institutions are repositories of the values of shame cultures: they prescribe the systematic practice of respect through ceremony and ritual, and they function according to unimpeachable principles of fairness. The military is the organization most apt to institute respect.

Military service demonstrates the highest level of patriotism; a man who serves in the military offers the best of himself to his nation. Under normal circumstances his nation will seek to show its gratitude.

People have made a great mistake in comparing the G.I. Bill to social welfare programs. A grateful nation repays soldiers for their positive contributions to the common good. This has nothing to do with the effort to justify welfare on the grounds that we ought to feel guilty for the plight of the downtrodden. No one disputes offering a helping hand to a victim. And yet, a victim of the system does not have the same claim to its largesse as someone who has fought for it, sacrificed for it, contributed to it.

Military organizations respect hierarchy; they promote uniform obeisance to the rituals of the nation. They value civic responsibility, duty, and pride. And when they discover problems, they solve them. During the Vietnam War there were important instances of racial conflict in the military services. By the Gulf

War these problems had been solved. In a sense they had to be solved; the risks were simply too high to tolerate them.

Regrettably, civil rights leaders have tended to express categorical opposition to military organizations. In part this derives from the fact that blacks who served well in Vietnam were poorly treated upon returning home—though this was not reserved only for blacks—and in part from the idea that military spending takes food out of the mouths of the ghetto poor, an us-versus-them argument. Also, most civil rights leaders have come from the clergy, and religious leaders usually promote peace, not war.

This opposition has had a price. It has actively undermined black Americans' sense of belonging to the nation.

The antimilitary attitude of black leaders needs to be reconsidered. An institution that has done well by blacks—a great deal better than most—deserves clear support. To argue, as some civil rights leaders did during the Gulf War, that the success of blacks in the military was a symptom of society's failure to offer them better opportunities undermines the sense of contributing to an honorable nation. Had the black leadership been more foresighted and supportive of the military effort it could have presented the war as a testimony to the success of affirmative action programs and to racial integration.

The leadership of any group must be held responsible for building a sense of community. Only the sense of a cohesive community can control the antisocial behaviors—teenage and out-of-wedlock pregnancy, gang violence, soaring crime rates—that are destroying the urban underclass. No society can long rely on the criminal justice system to produce acceptable social behavior. To curb the epidemic of antisocial behavior, leaders must state unequivocally that such behaviors are unacceptable and that those who indulge in them will not be welcomed into the community. They cannot rationalize crime as an acceptable response to pervasive racism, nor can they justify rioting as an acceptable tactic to gain political ends.

Jencks has pointed in a constructive direction: "But the oppressed are not just innocent victims. They make choices that help shape their lives, just as everyone else does. If people make these choices on narrowly self-interested grounds, their communities begin to unravel. . . . Censoriousness and blame are their principal weapons in this struggle: blame for teenage boys who steal from their neighbors, blame for drunken men who beat up their wives, blame for young women who have babies they cannot offer a 'decent home,' blame for young men who say a four-dollar-an-hour job is not worth the bother, blame for everyone who acts as if society owes them more than they owe society."[35] If we substitute "shame" for "blame," which renders, I believe, the meaning Jencks intends, we have a good definition of the right kind of leadership for minority groups.

Have black Americans been given face by white America? While we agree that not enough has been done, we would also hold that *some* progress has been made; for some citizens this has been a positive achievement, for others it has clearly been inadequate. Should the nation build on its success or pick itself apart because it has not gone far enough?

There are no simple answers. Legislation has been required to open up opportunities to blacks; still, it ought not to feel coercive to whites either. There are strict limits to what can be accomplished by legislation. Granting rights has little to do with granting respect.

Anyone who wishes to function within a society must adhere to the principles of its social contract. Doubtless people who have been systematically stigmatized will have more difficulty accepting the rules of their oppressors. But in a sense, that is the only viable response to discrimination. The fact that oppression existed in the past does not mean that it exists in the present. Accepting the social contract means playing by the same rules as everyone else, maintaining allegiance to the company or the nation, participating in the rituals and ceremonies that establish group cohesion, and conforming to the behavior codes that apply to everyone.

Such principles work in the army; there is no reason they cannot work in the rest of America.

Also, as the experience of universities shows, blacks should not be placed in positions where they cannot compete effectively, where their pattern of failure can only convince them that the game is rigged against them and that the rules are unfair and unjust. Such policies produce the undesirable effect of convincing whites that blacks are fundamentally inferior.[36]

Failure, wrote columnist Joe Klein, should be placed with the leadership of the black community. Its obsession with entitlement and inequality has masked its "refusal to confront the social pathologies—except racism—that are at the heart of the disparities: crime, chronic welfare dependency, sexual irresponsibility." Some things cannot be solved through legislation. Family unity cannot be manufactured by government programs. In Klein's words: "those African-Americans born and raised in intact families, regardless of income, have a better chance of graduating, finding work and succeeding than those raised in disrupted homes."[37]

As always the test of leadership is humility. When there is a riot in a black community or a series of violent crimes produced by blacks, do the leaders of the community stand up and blame white racism, or do they step forward and express their shame?

Which brings us to Clarence Thomas and Anita Hill. Few events presented the Great American Cultural Revolution so starkly. A man accused of criminal activity faced off against a woman asserting that she herself was sexually harassed. A man proclaiming himself to be the victim of a smear was fighting against a woman defending her obligation to tell the truth. Rallying to the defense of the woman were those who believed that men were engaged in systematic harassment of women to keep them out of the workplace. And defending the man were those who held that even if the charges were true, this simply represented everyday behavior within the black community.

Two prominent beneficiaries of affirmative action programs, who had risen from poverty and segregation to occupy positions of dignity, had their respect stripped away unceremoniously by a panel of aging white males. And presiding over it all was a president who had nominated to the Supreme Court someone whose primary qualifications seemed to be his race and his adherence to principles that the president considered to be politically correct.

Would any of this have happened if Clarence Thomas and Anita Hill were white? We cannot answer that question, any more than we will ever know what really happened between these two antagonists. And yet, we do know that it did happen to black Americans, and that it did, therefore, intentionally or not, rip off the scabs that had been covering the wounds of slavery and segregation.

On another level, were these hearings the indirect consequence of the fact that black Americans had assumed a role of moral leadership in the American Cultural Revolution? Blacks had become morally empowered as the most disadvantaged group in America; they were admired for setting a standard for public behavior that rejected the tired customs of the discredited Anglo-American power structure. Both Clarence Thomas and Anita Hill were idolized for their performances in something that most people considered a sordid and demeaning exercise.

Face-saving compromise was unthinkable. The opponents of Clarence Thomas declared that they would do anything and everything to block his nomination to the Supreme Court. The White House made the mistake of joining the battle on those terms. We do not know who was telling the truth; we do know that everyone was diminished.

When dignity and decency are not respected, everyone loses. The person who lost the most was George Bush. Bush was widely perceived as having sullied a sacred American institution by using his nominating authority to play the politics of division. The president could have withdrawn the nomination to save the nation the pain of the public hearings; the same option could have been exercised by either antagonist. Everyone would have been better off had none of it happened.

This event pitted shame against guilt in a public battle that exposed the underside of race relations in America. In addition, the judiciary committee hearings brought public attention to a war that had been going on in the workplace between men and women.

Some people believe that airing such dirty linen in public is salutary; everyone then has an opportunity to examine his or her own feelings about sexual harassment.

But this is clearly not what happened. The nation did not reach any consensus about what did and did not constitute sexual harassment. One side felt compelled to defend itself against unjust charges; the other side felt compelled to testify to being victimized on the job. The process only exacerbated division. The pious denunciations of sexual harassment made paying lip service into an art form. No one really believed that senators were traumatized by their first exposure to foul language.

Certainly, they were disturbed by what they perceived as a degradation of an honorable ceremony. For years Senate confirmations had been diminished by partisanship; with the Hill-Thomas hearings, for the first time, sexual behavior was openly discussed in the legislative process. The Cultural Revolution had come to contaminate government. Everyone was fascinated by the destructive power of the event; few ever wanted to see it again.

The hearings divided the nation into warring camps, especially among whites. Those whites who were opposed to empowering women could find solace in the idea that women were not trustworthy. Those whites who believed that sexual harassment in the workplace was preventing women from receiving the recognition due them found confirmation for the correctness of their views. Since only two people knew the truth of what happened, the hearings created more problems than they solved.

Another question: Did the hearings make it more or less likely that American business would hire blacks in greater numbers with the confidence that it was hiring people who could do the job and who would not be promoting another agenda that could easily come into conflict with corporate loyalty? What image of blacks in positions of authority did the hearings present through the behavior of their best and brightest?

The hearings also revived the images of blacks enslaved, of black men lynched, of black women raped and molested. Black women saw something of their own experience in Anita Hill and turned away from it to avoid facing shame.

All these points have some validity. When face-saving compromise is impossible, people take sides in a battle over guilt and innocence. When this happens the calculus of shame becomes so complicated that there will be no good and decent solution to the rift that has been created.

The conflict between Clarence Thomas and Anita Hill damaged many reputations; it went beyond responsible debate within a legislative process.

The Senate hearings were a sordid episode in the history of that institution, and institutions always tend to behave unkindly toward individuals who make them look bad. The Thomas-Hill hearings could not have advanced the cause of civil inclusion for American blacks. They turned legislative deliberation into an exercise in public theater.

For many the Thomas-Hill hearings highlighted the fact that blacks are not held to the same standards as white Americans. No one could remember such a degarding public spectacle featuring white protagonists.

Of course, newcomers to any organization are always judged more strictly than those who have long been members. People who have faithfully served an organization for decades earn the goodwill of the group. For having proved themselves trustworthy and reliable, they have built psychological capital and have a generous line of credit. No newcomer has the same advantage; he will always be tested and will often have to go out of his way to show himself to be someone who fits in, who will fully participate in the routines that constitute the group.

Moreover, the longtime member's psychological capital and line of credit are transferrable to other members of his family. They are part of the legacy he leaves to his children. When these children join the organization they have an advantage over a rank novice. The advantage is compounded by the fact that they have been raised in the customs and traditions of the group; by the time they attain membership, behaving properly has become second nature.

Obviously, the situation is unfair to newcomers. Yet it allows for assimilation over time. Many different ethnic groups in America have undergone this process of assimilation in the past; inevitably black Americans will succeed at it in the future.

Folding the civil rights debate into the categories of guilt culture has produced considerable problems. Ellis Cose isolated this point: "It may very well be that the civil rights debate has been so distorted by strategies designed to engender guilt that many whites, as a form of self-defense, have come to define any act of decency toward blacks as an act of expiation." [38]

The American Cultural Revolution did not just bring the war home; it brought the war into the home. One of the most conspicuous effects of this Revolution was the breakdown of the institution of marriage.

The post-Vietnam era saw more than a doubling of the divorce rate, a vast increase of single-parent homes, the feminization of poverty, and a large number of other social problems associated with the breakdown of the American family.

The family is everyone's primary social group. It forms the basis for the Confucian system and for any shame culture. Losing one's moorings in the family undermines one's sense of identity and integrity.

My next topic will be the family. Few institutions are more

critical to the functioning of society. While the legitimacy of American government does not require a defense, the family does. While most people in our society simply want to see the government function better, many intelligent people question whether the family can function at all, what its purpose is, and whether it is worth saving. At a time when such a large number of our citizens live within family structures that have little or no resemblance to what was classically considered as a family, their own experience tells them that perhaps the family is not something that we need to protect and save.

4

Family Secrets

We have all heard the alarms. America is falling behind in education. The future American work force will not have the skills to compete in the global economy. American schoolchildren score well below students in the rest of the industrialized world in science and math.[1] The nation's future hangs in the balance.

Proposed solutions abound: we need to spend more money on education; children's education must become a national priority; children should spend more time in school; teachers should be better paid; national achievement standards must be implemented; the school year must be lengthened; parents must be more involved.

These proposed solutions address one part of the problem. We need to ask how much our society values the education of its children. In the Far East social values promote education. Paul Kennedy, along with many others, credits the "Confucian traditions of competitive examinations and respect for learning," and adds that these are "reinforced daily by the mother of the family, who complements what is taught at school."[2]

The habits and discipline required to use school time effectively cannot be inculcated solely by teachers. They must come from the home and from the family. And they are best transmitted when the home is harmonious, when the family is intact, when authority is respected. A child whose family life is unstable and insecure will not be able to learn effectively.

These are the lessons we draw from the great global tribes. The Japanese, the overseas Chinese, the Anglo-Americans, the Jews, and the overseas Indians have succeeded because they value family harmony and education.[3] They continue to be successful because they place great store in transmitting their collective wisdom to their children. These children are required to be industrious, well behaved, motivated, respectful, and successful.[4]

In recent years America has been falling behind on these terms. To cover this failure, the nation has redefined its educational priorities. It has sought to value self-fulfillment over responsibility to others, creativity over rote learning, rebelliousness over respect for authority. Our nation has increasingly elevated creative endeavor, personal experience, and the quest to become a more interesting personality into proper educational goals. This is hardly the best way to teach mathematics and science.

In many ways the American educational system is the best in the world. We offer more and better higher education than anyone else. But the global tribes succeed because they provide education to all members of their group, not just to those at the top. You cannot distribute authority, goods, and respect if you do not also ensure that members know enough to exercise them judiciously.

The education of children does not exist in a vacuum. If Johnny can't learn, this seems primarily to be a symptom of the much ballyhooed breakdown of the American family, only secondarily the failure of the overburdened educational establishment. When teachers have to function as surrogate parents the business of learning becomes secondary.

Some have touted the revolutionary changes that have recently taken place within the American family. But we should not revel in being world leaders in divorce and out-of-wedlock births. We should not take pride in having discovered that all families are dysfunctional. Ripping the veil off the harmonious family to reveal a festering swamp of lurid behavior will not cure what ails the family. Some problems are best dealt with in private. Public exposure often makes difficult problems insoluble.

In a time of social turmoil, when institutions lose their credibility and when the authority of parents is undermined, children may have little choice but to develop more creative individual talents. Often people make the best of a bad situation, but that does not mean that we ought to be satisfied with the continuation of a bad situation.

American society will not maintain its position in the world without restoring the family. To take some distance from the current mania about dysfunctional families, I will focus on the functional family, how it works and how it can restore itself when faced with trauma.

Beyond the ceremonial and ritual acts that make families function, family members are bound by something else: the intimacy that occurs when members of a group share their privacy and their secrets. To function, a family requires both prescribed rituals and common secrets.

Family members must know how to keep secrets. A family hides its shame from public view. All members agree to present the best possible public face. The face you save is never just your own.

A family cultivates a collective reputation. Parents owe it to the parents from whom they received it and to the children to whom they will pass it down to maintain it.

We tend to think of traumas like child abuse as being of the essence of family secrets. But any breach of privacy devalues the family's achievements. We err in thinking that family secrets serve merely to cover up crime. The salient paradigm concerns hiding details of private life that would compromise decorous public presentation: for example, telling the world that your spouse often belches at the dinner table.

No one should act in public without regard for how his actions will reflect on the rest of his family. Keeping private matters private means acting with decorum outside the home, presenting a serene public face. Anyone who reveals family secrets in public or who acts in such a way as to lead people to think less of the family has betrayed a sacred trust.

The veil of secrecy thrown over private matters does not mean that any behavior is acceptable once the door of the household is locked. Bad habits learned at home will eventually make themselves known in public by the most vulnerable and susceptible family members—children.

The protection of the home allows the young to rehearse their future public roles in situations where their partially formed character will not be subjected to public scrutiny. Thus errors are more easily corrected because they do not compromise the rest of the family.

Secrecy should never be used to rationalize license. Parents act with propriety at home to teach their children by moral example: they teach decorum, respect for the privacy of others, good manners, responsibility, and obligation.

The basic questions are these: How are families organized, how are roles divided, who bears which responsibilities? The more strict shame cultures offer a basic paradigm that maintains two types of authority and responsibility. The mother cares for and brings up the children. The father protects and provides for the rest of the family. The children must demonstrate filial piety; they are taught to respect parental authority and acknowledge their debt to their parents and ancestors for love, life, education, material comforts, and the family's good name.

As the mother usually represents the values of home—and in some cultures, like that in Japan, she exercises almost complete authority in decisions that relate to the home[5]—the father presents the family's public face. Thereby women and men maintain separate spheres of authority. A similar practice existed during the first half of the nineteenth century in the northern United States.[6]

Sumiko Iwao offers a Japanese perspective that shows how a woman's role is valorized in Japanese culture: "Japanese traditionally associate home and family with warmth and comfort while the outside world is viewed as cold and often indifferent; this gives the family great intrinsic importance in the eyes of Japanese, especially women. The society is intensely competitive and achievement-oriented, for children and young people in the academic realm and for adults in their professional lives. It is widely believed that unless individuals are part of a family that is stable, they cannot fulfill their full potential, whatever their chosen pursuit. Since family members can ultimately bring back to the family the best rewards society has to offer, maintaining the home as a solid, nurturing base is an occupation that can offer great material as well as personal fulfillment, as women long engaged in this profession can attest."[7]

There is a logic to this way of separating spheres of authority. It may be outmoded and unsatisfying, but it is nonetheless logical.

This logic concerns the consequences of the biology of reproduction. Perhaps this should not be decisive; perhaps in the future it will not be. But we will gain by examining a venerable human institution as something other than a criminal conspiracy.

First, we note that it is far easier for a man to repudiate the consequences of his sexual acts than it is for a woman. Thus was created a kind of bargain that attempted to avoid a problem that has come to infect contemporary America—the deadbeat dad.

Traditional cultures adopted a simple strategy to accomplish this: first, female chastity would guarantee to a man that a woman's offspring were his; second, through the marriage contract, a man would swear publicly to take responsibility for his children. Failing to fulfill this contract causes severe public shame.

Note that women have been held to a standard that concerns

private behavior and is very difficult to verify. Men have been judged by a public standard that is easily confirmed.

The contract does not permit men unlimited access to sexual partners. Men may have the biological capacity to father countless children, but if they attempt do so they will have to spend a considerable amount of time fighting off male rivals.[8] This is not an economical way to run a society. Also, very few men can protect and provide for a slew of children from different mothers.

Since men have never been the primary caregivers for children, they were granted the role of representing the family outside the home; they were simply more available for this task. As Richard Posner argued, men are not incapacitated by pregnancy or needed for lactation.[9] And since men are, by and large, physically stronger and more aggressive they have the skills required for success in a competitive arena, whether it is hunting or warfare. In any event, men are universally socialized toward action in the world outside the home. Women have been taxed with caring for small children because they have the greater investment of time and effort in any pregnancy.

Given these roles and responsibilities there are two obvious ways for parents to fail. A father who cannot protect or provide for his family and a mother who neglects or abandons her children would experience shame under this system.

But what happens when a father cannot provide for his family because of the state of the general economy? In contemporary America one salary rarely suffices to support a family. If this condition forces a mother to go to work, thus to spend less time with her children than she would wish, should she be judged harshly for accommodating an economic necessity?

Here we have a situation where, by traditional standards, both parents are failing their obligations somewhat, but through no fault of their own. Do they experience shame for knowing that the mother's career is necessary for the family to maintain its standard of living? Or do they modify family roles to allow everyone to save some face?

Compare this with Japanese practice. Sumiko Iwao emphasizes that while Japanese women have recently entered the work force in increasingly large numbers, they do not take jobs out of economic necessity. The Japanese husband continues to support his family. But this also means that a woman's work must take second place to her familial responsibilities: "If [women] work, the majority choose and go about their work as much as possible at their family's convenience. If their employment should prove detrimental to family or home life, it quickly becomes the object of reconsideration, even if the work itself is appealing or rewarding."[10]

Americans have dealt with their new economic circumstances by asserting that women gain more self-fulfillment from work than from changing diapers and mopping floors. One would have great difficulty contesting the point. But note well that a woman's "choice" to work absolves both husband and wife. Are they facing or masking shame?

Effectively, they are doing both. Most people know that denouncing a man as inadequate will put severe strains on a marriage. At the same time, since raising children does not occupy all of a woman's life, her ability to pursue other interests will free her from an existence that would constrain her within limits determined by her biology.

Fathers fail their families in other, more blatant, ways. The deadbeat dad masks his inadequacy by walking away from his obligations to his wife and children. The less he thinks about them and sees them, the less he feels that he has failed them.

And then there is the case of the abusive father: instead of protecting his wife and children against those who would do them harm, he himself becomes the one who harms them. Often he believes that he is asserting his manly authority; in fact, he is masking his shame with an obscene caricature of the paternal role.

The most extreme failure occurs when a man's home and family are destroyed by some outside invader. A man who does not fight to protect his family suffers great shame. If your country is overrun by marauding barbarians who burn your home, destroy your property, rape your wife, and murder your children, you will feel the most profound sense of having failed to protect them. And this beyond the pain you feel over loss. If a man's wife dies, he will experience grief but not shame.

It should hardly be surprising that such major failures discredit the patriarchal social order. This pertains even when there is nothing that the man could reasonably have done differently given the circumstances, and when the aggressor was a tyrant. The logic of shame is implacable.

Being a victim does not eliminate feelings of shame, nor does obtaining justice against a criminal. The fact that the protector himself becomes, along with his family, a victim, only aggravates the shame.

To examine this situation in its most extreme form let us look at one of the greatest traumas of our times, an event that so surpasses the bounds of what we consider to be human that it can only be considered demonic or sacred. I wish to examine here the way Jewish survivors have dealt with the Holocaust.

Most especially, but not entirely, I want to look at how survivors have dealt with their trauma within their families. How can such a trauma be dealt with as a family secret? Can it be dealt with otherwise? What does it mean to face the shame associated with being a victim of the Holocaust? And how can a people that has undergone such an extreme trauma overcome it?

One child of survivors, Helen Epstein, expressed herself as follows: "I did not like talking about my parents or the war, because talk meant accepting that the war had happened and, more than anything else in the world, I wished it had not. The idea that my mother and father had been forced out of their homes and made to live like animals—worse than animals—was too shameful to admit."[11]

According to Hillel Klein, Israeli children of survivors tend to treat this fact about their parents as a family secret; they accent the positive aspects of their parents' lives and do not think about the rest: "They are proud of the active part their parents took during the persecutions and even today as defenders, saviors, or representatives of the persecuted. There is no reference to suffering or to any traumatic situation which occurred to the parents. It seems there is a common denial by the children and the parents who never tell about the suffering and torture they went through in the ghetto or the concentration camp. They handle this memory like a common secret: they negate and deny."[12]

In the parlance of psychotherapy, the concept of "denial" means that they are avoiding their shame. But this raises some difficult questions. How do we know that they are not dealing with their trauma in the right way? Are we confident that we know the best way for children to deal with such an overwhelming experience of parental shame?

In Israel, the strategy used by these children has been adopted in the way the nation's history is taught. One daughter of survivors said, "The most important thing about history as it was taught in Israel . . . was fighting the British and the Arabs. There was something shameful about talking about the Holocaust. Something very degrading."[13] In the early days of Israel, Holocaust survivors were shunned by the rest of the populace. How, their fellow citizens would ask themselves, could they have let this happen to them?

Beyond commemorative ceremonies, which ensure that the Holocaust is not forgotten, Jewish people have dealt with this trauma through the creation of the state of Israel. Israel answers the question of what they would have had to do for the Holocaust not to have happened and not to be repeated.

The Holocaust exposed a major failure of leadership in the European branch of the Jewish tribe. The leaders of the European Jewry failed to protect the members of their community. In some cases the leaders of Jewish councils cooperated with Nazi authorities in a futile effort to mitigate the horror. In others they revolted; in others they simply committed suicide. But certainly in this, one of the more patriarchal cultures in the West, the Holocaust served to discredit paternal authority and leadership. That many members of the post-Holocaust generation distrust such authority is understandable, even if mistaken.

Should one expose or hide such failure, when it is public knowledge? Exposing it works against the strategy that shame cultures always employ to overcome failure: to make people forget failure by producing a consistent pattern of success. Hiding it works against the guilt cultural approach: to continue to bear witness, by one's suffering, to the guilt of one's tormentors. The first approach will dissociate the future from past failure by accentuating past successes and producing future successes. The second approach will attempt to integrate the event as meaningful. Instead of facing shame and moving on, this approach will require community life to be reorganized to avoid future trauma: people will be induced to live in a state of hypervigilance.

Some survivors never escaped the trauma of the camps. Whatever the reason, they made their existence into an inescapable reminder of what for them had become the only reality. The message to others can be summarized: the horror was so great that henceforth nothing can ever again be normal.

In some sense this feels like a reasonable reaction to a sacred horror. And yet, activities that perpetuate the conditions in the camps, even intended as a permanent reminder, grant some measure of credibility to those who believed the worst of Jewish culture.

One child of survivors described her family as dysfunctional: "I don't know if you can understand this, but my family never did anything together. We never sat down at a table together; we never ate together; nothing ever as a family. Food was eaten alone. In the store, my mother would always be the first one. My father always used to say that even in the forest she always took food for herself instead of thinking of other people. She always talked about how hungry she was. . . . There was never a happy moment that I can remember at home. . . . My mother didn't teach me to be proud of myself. She didn't teach me to take care of a household, she never told me about my body, she never *talked* to me, can you understand that. . . . The order of normal life was so confused for them during the war that abnormalities became normalities. People were capable of everything. Anything was permissible in order to live.''[14]

A trauma that was not overcome was fully present all the time in the household of the survivors. It invaded every corner of family life. This mother lived as though she were still hiding out from Nazis, as though the degraded existence imposed on her by the war somehow constituted her character. If that were the case, then the treatment she received or the way of life she was forced to adopt would have represented the truth of her being.

Another way survivors dealt with the trauma through guilt involved learning that the event was perpetrated by their fellow human beings.[15] Therefore, they, as humans themselves, are capable of the same deeds. This cure involved teaching the survivors that they share a common humanity with their persecutors.

The approach is severely flawed. Teaching Holocaust survivors that they had had intentions that corresponded to the deeds of the Nazis tells them that their torment was punishment for their criminal impulses. Also, the people who perpetrated the Holocaust ought not to be welcomed back into any human community. Having disgraced themselves they are forever stigmatized and denoted as monsters, or some other nonhuman term.

Where guilt was eschewed, families concentrated on restoring dignity by building a life that would make people forget what they had been through. They maintained appearances so that their children would not inherit their shame. One man saw his family in this sense: "My parents had come through that ordeal and I had boundless admiration for both of them, for surviving with dignity, for pulling the pieces together and succeeding so beautifully in their new life. I'm very proud of the fact that my father, my uncle, and my cousin, who arrived in this country as penniless refugees, managed to create a highly successful business instead of succumbing to despair. I never thought of my parents going through indignity or humiliation. I don't remember ever being angry at them or ashamed of them because of what they went through.''[16]

Significantly, they regained their pride. In Epstein's words: ''Families had reputations to maintain. Success was measured not only in property but in the continued adhesion of children to tradition. Much of the community life centered around *shul*, and a rich pattern of weddings, engagement parties, circumcisions, and religious festivals.''[17]

Are these people living in ''denial''? Or would it be more accurate to say that they have come to terms with the shame of the Holocaust privately, in their own ways, and have redoubled their efforts to build a community? The fact that we do not know how these survivors faced their shame does not mean that they have denied it.

Like the Jews, the other global tribes produce group coherence with ceremony and ritual, whether it be the family dinner or community square dance. Now we want to examine what this looks like under normal circumstances.

What does it mean to belong to a family, and how does this influence a child's motivation when he first confronts the world of education? How does a family socialize its youngest members?

A child is going to school. Upon his small shoulders he carries the weight of his family tradition. As he enters into a social environment outside the home, he knows that his eventual success will redound to the credit of his family, his teachers, his community, and his ancestors. His mind is concentrated on the work at hand. The price for failure is so high, for him and his, that he has little choice but to work to do well.

He has learned this at home by interacting with his parents and imitating their behavior. He has also heard of the success of other family members. And beyond that he has learned to learn.

School does not emphasize the child's development into a well-rounded personality. It is not another nursery; it does not provide the comforts of home. The child goes to school to learn to compete in a marketplace; he is training for the examinations he will take many years later and that will determine his future. Courses that allow the clearest distinction of merit are the most valued: science, mathematics, technical subjects.

The child's success will bring honor to his ancestors and to his family name. It will show proper respect for his elders. For now, the best way he can demonstrate filial piety is to do well at school.

If he fails there is precious little his family can do for him, and even less that it would wish to do for him. Failure is unthinkable; if other family members have failed they are not discussed at the dinner table. Shameful subjects are hidden from view; they are not belabored or publicly acknowledged.

Such an ambiance will produce a child who will excel at school. These motivations will propel him to work harder and longer than other children. The system here described corresponds to the Confucian way; it is practiced in Japan and the Far East, but not only there. It explains why Oriental students in American schools have been successful of late, and why Jewish students have always done so well.

These cultures emphasize hard work because their children do not grow up with a sense of entitlement. No one inherits a title, no one feels entitled, and no one expects to live off the work of others. Education is valued over breeding. Family honor is an irrevocable trust; it must be preserved and protected. Those who fail at this fundamental responsibility have their names removed from the roll call.

Traditionally, the agrarian aristocracy has felt itself to be entitled. Aristocrats in such a system believe that by birth they are better than everyone else; achievement does not matter, and scholastic success has no real importance. They look with contempt on those who toil to earn a living; they sneer at the bourgeoisie. An idle and decadent aristocracy considers work dishonorable and demeaning.

The American Revolution was fought to rid us of the influence of such an aristocracy, but did not prevent it from persisting in the figure of the slave-owning Southern planter. He valued passion over education, emotion over intelligence. He liked the world as it was, he had no need to change it, and he even believed his agrarianism more powerful than Northern industrialism. As W. J. Cash described him: "From first to last, and whether he was a Virginian or a *nouveau*, he did not (typically speaking) think; he felt; and discharging his feelings immediately, he developed no need or desire for intellectual culture in its own right—none, at least, powerful enough to drive him past his taboos to its actual achievement."[18]

In a functional family the family dinner often serves as a ritual affirmation of group membership. It transforms nourishment from a private experience of consumption into an orderly social event. It brings everyone together, allows all to share experience, to garner counsel, and to see that achievements count to the credit of the family. A child who has scored well on an algebra test sees his success celebrated at the dinner table; thereby he understands that his good grade contributes to family pride. Most important, this ritual relieves family members of any sense of being alone. The threat of expulsion from this circle—Go to your room!—has always counted as a way to foster discipline with the sanction of shame.

Without such a ceremonial confirmation, the members of a family will come to function as autonomous individuals; their behavior, their successes, and their failures will only count for themselves personally. They will not have to answer for their bad behavior, and, beyond a wish for self-aggrandizement, they will have little motivation for succeeding.

A family is not a romantic idyll in which solidarity is created by covering everyone with love. A child may receive all the love he could ever deal with and still be harmed by not knowing whether anyone will be there when he comes home from school, by not knowing when and with whom he will be having dinner, or by not knowing whether anyone cares about how well he did on his spelling quiz. Erratic evidence of deep affection will not compensate for the insecurity produced by inconsistent behavior.

Even when families are intact—something that is increasingly uncommon—it often looks as though everyone is running in different directions, each exclusively and uniquely concerned with self-fulfillment. For the child this can only mean that he is surrounded by disorganization. He will become uncertain about his place, his role, and the extent to which he can count on others.

If a child feels that his dinner is a chore for his parents, something that gets in the way of more interesting activities, he will not be able to develop the kind of identity that derives from belonging to a group. A child sitting alone at the kitchen table eating dinner that is served by a distracted parent will experience this treatment as punishment. He may eventually respond with behavior that will force his parents to attend to his concerns.

A functional family requires stability and harmony. Unless open conflict is involved, children prefer that their parents remain together, and thus, that their world not be disrupted, even when their parents are not happy and self-satisfied.

The most serious disruption of family routine is obviously divorce. Her studies of the effect of divorce on children led Judith Wallerstein to conclude that "for most of them, divorce was the single most important cause of enduring pain and anomie in their lives. The young people told us time and again how much they needed a family structure, how much they wanted to be protected, and how much they yearned for clear guidelines for moral behavior. An alarming number of teen-agers felt abandoned, physically and emotionally."[19]

Certainly, there are occasions where a single-parent household provides a more stable environment than an openly violent marriage. Some studies have suggested that the unstable predivorce environment already produces deleterious effects before the actual divorce.[20]

Nevertheless, most studies point in one direction. This led Wallerstein, among others, to find cause for alarm: "For example, one national study of 699 elementary school children carefully compared children six years after their parents' divorce with children from intact families. It found—as we did—that elementary-age boys from divorced families show marked discrepancies in peer relationships, school achievement and social adjustment. Girls in this group, as expected, were hardly distinguishable based on the experience of divorce, but, as we later found out, this would not always hold up. Moreover, our findings are supported by a litany of modern-day statistics. Although one in three children are from divorced families, they account for an inordinately high proportion of children in mental-health treatment, in special-education classes, or referred by teachers to school psychologists."[21]

In England, researcher Sara McLanahan "has shown that children who grow up in single-parent families are more likely to drop out of school, marry during their teens, have a child before marrying and experience a breakdown of their own marriages."[22] A Cambridge psychologist, Martin Richards, concluded that "the chance of a child going to university is halved by a parental divorce. All these effects, incidentally, are either weaker or nonexistent when a father has died."[23]

There may well be other reasons for these findings; divorce often produces a marked reduction in standard of living, and this too may contribute to a child's sense of emotional insufficiency. What does seem to be clear from these studies is that family conflict and a disruption of routine damage children psychologically.

Nor should we be surprised that remarriage is not a cure. If having a place within the family counts as a primary component of identity—a child knows who he is because he knows how he is related to other family members—then remarriage risks producing confusion. Mixed or blended families produce a dizzying collection of half siblings, stepparents, and the like.

Andrew Cherlin articulated the complexity of the issue: "Divorce is bad for children, but not for all children equally. It is very bad for a small group of children, and moderately bad for many more. If the marriage is truly filled with conflict, it may be better to have a divorce. But here in the United States, many marriages that could limp along end because people are bored. I'm not sure that children are harmed in such marriages."[24]

Many marriages probably would not end if there were an effective social sanction against divorce. And yet when large numbers of people have been divorced, the behavior becomes a norm. At that point many people have an investment in the correctness of breaking up a marriage. When this happens, the idea of stigmatizing divorce as deviant behavior loses its force.

A divorce is a public admission of failure. If people understood the shame involved in such events and the cost paid by children, they would make more informed decisions about divorce.

For a fuller analysis of the bases for a functional family we turn to Confucius. Confucius provided one of the best theoretical presentations of the familial basis of shame culture. At a time when personal fulfillment and rebellion against authority are articles of faith, it is good to measure the importance of filial piety.

Confucius's concept of the family focused on rules and roles. In that version of the family, Benjamin Schwartz wrote, "we are dealing with the question of how persons who have reached the age of self-awareness handle their family role relationships."[25] In such cultures children learn through experience how to act within their assigned roles and to play by the rules. But they do not learn such behavior from abstract principles; they learn first by emulating parental models.

Educating by setting an example provides the perfect instance of Confucian values. It diminishes the element of coercion; the child is encouraged but not forced. He sees what is right, not told what is wrong. As Schwartz stated, "To Confucius, it is precisely in the family that humans learn those virtues which redeem the society, for the family is precisely the domain within which authority comes to be accepted and exercised not through reliance on physical coercion but through the binding power of religious, moral sentiments based on kinship ties."[26]

The public practice of active respect for the virtues of others cultivates one's own virtue. Ancestors receive honor for having augmented the capital of the family name. A harmonious human society must actively bind itself through its links with tradition; respect for names, titles, and offices is inculcated by rituals honoring ancestors.

In the Confucian system a child is not being judged against an unattainable ideal. Being held to an example that parents have fulfilled tells the child that virtuous behavior is his birthright.

The logic is simple. A father who orders his child to be disciplined and hardworking cannot at the same time spend his days watching television, eating popcorn, and drinking beer. It is very difficult to say to a child: Work hard at school so you will not become like me. A smaller success may breed a larger success, but a failure will not breed success.

The Confucian family differs significantly from the way we view the institution. It is not organized around the husband/wife dyad, but around the father/son relationship. Thus it devalues romance and values filial piety. As Confucius said, "Give your father and mother no other cause for anxiety than illness."

Numerous examples of filial piety can be found among the Confucian classics. But some ancient tales are properly grotesque, like that of "the eight-year-old boy who allowed mosquitos to 'feed without restraint upon his blood until they were satisfied' in order to prevent them from biting his parents."[27] In a two-thousand-year-old story, a man decided to bury his child because he did not have enough food to feed both his mother and his child. While he was digging the child's grave, however, he discovered a vase filled with gold, a reward for his virtue.[28]

Filial piety has a more pleasing aspect, and it is common to all of the successful tribal cultures. Freud recounted the story of a Jewish man who had demonstrated proper filial behavior toward his dying father: "His father was ill for a long time, and the nursing and treatment had cost him (the son) a lot of money. Yet it was never too much, he was never impatient, he never wished that after all it might soon come to an end. He was proud of his truly Jewish filial piety towards his father, of his strict obedience to Jewish Law."[29]

The ancient Chinese roots of filial piety lay in ancestor worship. As Schwartz described it, "Ancestor worship highlights the kinship group as a paradigm of social order—that is, as a network of intimately related roles."[30] Ancestral spirits are not burdened with individuation; they are not identified by life stories or personal dramas.

If a father's role is to protect and to provide for his family while maintaining the family's good name by acting honorably in all his interactions with others, then he is remembered for that. In contrast to other ancient cultures the Chinese does not have an elaborate mythology[31] containing murders, rapes, incest, theft, mutilation—all the elements that constitute drama and trauma.

In practice, the lack of a significant mythology or respect for any forms of individuality produced a society that achieved spectacular successes but did not know how to right itself when it began to fail. Through the sixteenth century, China was the most advanced civilized country in the world. Once it failed, however, it was like a car running without brakes. It has taken centuries for China to right itself, and even now it remains to be seen whether it can slow down and make turns to avoid disaster.

A kinship system based on filial piety values hierarchy. Schwartz explained, "Since the kinship roles are inevitably and 'naturally' hierarchic, based as they are on ascriptive biological differences between the old and the young and the male and the female (in a patriarchal family), hierarchy and role on this level are an integral aspect of the ultimate frame of things, although I must point out that by its very nature kinship hierarchy is not fixed and unchangeable. Sons become fathers; daughters become mothers and mothers-in-law; and all become ancestors.''[32]

Filial piety produces obedient and disciplined children. It produces children who work assiduously on the tasks set for them by their teachers and by other authority figures in society. In the Orient it has produced some of the best-educated groups of children on earth.

If the teacher is teaching algebra and geography, the attitudes of filial piety contribute to learning; questioning the bases of these disciplines would be debilitating. However, if the teacher chooses to indoctrinate the children in the precepts of Maoism, the same students will apply themselves with equal fervor to learning that.

The traditional practice of filial piety in China was not always benign. Since the linchpin of the system was the father's benevolence, his abuse of his position was always a threat. Historically, coercion often corrupted the system. Jonathan Spence described the reality of the practice in the eighteenth century: ''Within the family structure, fathers committing a given crime against their sons were punished far more lightly than sons who committed the same crime against their fathers, and the same was true of husbands harming their wives, or older relatives their younger ones. In one case in which the father killed his son by burying him alive, the Ministry of Punishments carefully reviewed the facts and concluded that the governor had acted wrongly in sentencing the father to be beaten for the crime. Fathers who killed sons should be beaten only if they had acted 'unreasonably,' argued the ministry. In this case the son had used foul language at his father, an act that deserved the death penalty. . . . The father was acquitted.''[33]

Our horror at such stories is somewhat mitigated by the knowledge that the Puritans who settled Massachusetts had a law in 1648 that prescribed "the death penalty as a punishment for stubborn or rebellious sons over the age of sixteen who refused to obey either their father or mother. The same punishment was also provided for children who struck or cursed their parents. No child was ever executed under this law, but several were fined or whipped by the courts for being rude or abusive to their parents."[34] Doubtless they were inspired by a biblical text: "For every one who curses his father or his mother shall be put to death. . . ." (Leviticus 20:9).

In practice the Chinese system failed to allow for correction. This was known to Tocqueville: "The Chinese, in following the track of their forefathers, had forgotten the reasons by which the latter had been guided. They still used the formula without asking for its meaning; they retained the instrument, but they no longer possessed the art of altering or renewing. The Chinese, then had lost the power of change; for them improvement was impossible."[35]

The Confucian picture of family harmony led to visions of society with each subject in his proper place, knowing his duties and obligations, maintaining attitudes of basic humility and respect, knowing what to do, with whom, and how. Such well-ordered social organizations often provoke ridicule by Americans. Without also appreciating their appeal we will not be able to understand the importance of the family in shame cultures and the reasons why such organizations, having become global tribes, tend to be so successful in socioeconomic competition.

Families are the most durable social institutions. They are ethnically homogeneous; they share the same culture, rituals, and ceremonies. No matter how far you roam you still belong to your family; you can still count on other members of your family to offer you trust, confidence, and even succor.

In a family, membership is a birthright and an obligation; you cannot desire to be a member of a family. It does not matter whether other members of the family like you: you are still relatives. Only the most serious breaches of comportmental norms will lead to exclusion from a family.

The proper attitude of the head of the family is Confucian benevolence or Aristotelian magnanimity. His role is to provide, therefore to give, in humility to others, not to keep things for himself. He holds his position in trust, distributes respect to others, and gives face to the clan. Otherwise he will not be able to govern and will not receive the respect that is his due.

He is humble toward those from whom he has received his trust. The greater his authority the more he must humble himself before the ancestors who have handed down this authority. His ego is effaced; if he leads a sacrifice, he does so to signify that what he possesses he holds on trust. He does not sacrifice to expiate guilt.

Emphasizing the father's role in the family is ultimately misleading. The father stands as a beacon whose moral example induces good behavior in others, but his virtue is evidenced mainly in his actions outside the home. The Confucian father must be emulated from a distance, because he has so little presence in family life.

Clearly, this is a critical social function, not to be discarded blithely. Nevertheless, when we consider hands-on decision making and the kind of interpersonal interaction that must occur within the home, mothers are the ones who exercise authority.

Far from being a servile function, motherhood under these conditions involves making significant family decisions: where and how to live, where the children go to school, how they dress, whether they do their homework, and even how the family income is invested. Such is the case in contemporary Japan, a land of absent fathers.

Women organize home life and keep it functioning: they care for and educate children, they are present to share secrets, they involve themselves directly in the most private and intimate details of their children's lives.

Under such circumstances, which are not entirely foreign to our own society, it is critically important that the person who will make these decisions has a free choice of the partner with whom she will be engaging this life work.

However much we may now take such things for granted, one of the most important reforms in human history was the replacement of arranged with companionate marriage. Clearly, this was not the last word in respecting women, but it must count as crucial. We may find it insufficient because it reforms what has always been a woman's role, but effective reform usually builds on what has worked in the past; it does not destroy the past in favor of a utopian vision that has never been.

Even if men's relations with other men maintain all the basic principles of shame culture, whenever women are not trusted, when they are coerced, threatened, intimidated, and tortured into submission, a society will contain at its core an element of guilt culture.

Under those circumstances, oppression is not limited to what men do to women. While her father and husband make the decision that "arranges" a young woman's future, the agent of her oppression on a day-to-day basis is more often another woman.

In eighteenth-century China, women were not merely subjected to the whims of their husbands. When a woman was married to a man she barely knew, she entered his family household as daughter-in-law, dominated by the often implacable will of her mother-in-law.[36] In a culture that saw the role of wife and the romantic attachment of a married couple as a threat to filial obligations, a tyrannical version of filial piety was practiced in the home. This must be counted as the most significant flaw in the practice of the Chinese family.

Is the historical oppression of women an aberration or does it inhere in the structure of the family? How we answer this question will bear heavily on how we see the family and whether we think it is worth saving.

Some have argued recently that abuse is the salient aspect of a woman's experience under male dominance, and that the best way to remedy this situation is through exposure, indictment, prosecution, and punishment. Those who seek to use the law to solve all problems will attempt to punish all crimes. And lately they have seen families as conspiracies of silence designed to protect fathers.

If that is true, family secrets merely serve to cover up criminal actions. The image of a woman who says nothing while her husband is molesting her daughter counts today as one of the paradigms for family secrets.

Privacy may be abused in order to protect improper actions, but its primary social function is to produce bonds of trust between members of a family and to extend such bonds to friends in different degrees. It includes some people and excludes others; intimacy is meaningless without selection.

That the privacy of the home may become so important that a family member will refuse to disclose the criminal activities of another strikes us as unjust. And yet we do understand a woman's moral dilemma when she is forced to choose between turning her husband in and keeping silent to hold her family together. Our legal system declares that private conversation between spouses is privileged in the same sense as attorney-client or priest-penitent communication. Interestingly, parent-child communication is not privileged.

Guilt culture holds generally that anything that has to be hidden from the public must be criminal. It demands continual public exposure to cleanse the system. And yet, when exposure becomes a way of life, the sanction of shame loses its force. This will produce more bad behavior, with only the police and courts left to control it.

The guilt culture approach poses a difficulty I have already alluded to: the more you expose abuse the more it becomes the social norm; the more abuse becomes normal the more people will feel an obligation to conform to the norm. The worst forms of abuse of women—foot binding in imperial China and genital mutilation in contemporary Africa—were hardly secrets. Known to everyone, they were most often accepted without a second thought. When they were criticized by outsiders, they were defended as part of a cultural tradition outsiders did not understand.

Let us examine an extremely pervasive form of child abuse, foot binding in imperial China. Not only was this not a secret; it was a source of great pride. And while no woman exposed her crippled feet to just anyone's eyes—since they were made into the ultimate private parts—no one was unaware of the existence of the practice.

The practice of foot binding reveals the dark underside of the family in imperial China. It bespeaks a culture that evolved historically in the direction of pervasive decadence. The Chinese bound women's feet because it enhanced sexual pleasure.

The practice also highlights a significant theoretical failure. Confucian philosophy demeaned any number of activities that traditionally have been the repositories for masculine values. Confucius was opposed to the military, to commerce, to trade, to industry, and to merchandising. Those who accepted these values could hardly compete successfully in the marketplace or the battlefield; they took out their frustrations on their families.

There is nothing magical about good ideas; their fate depends on who put them into practice and under what conditions.

Within the Chinese Empire uncritical acceptance of all aspects of Confucian teaching produced a cult to the Sage. This form of idealization required people to force reality to fit the model proposed by ideas: in much the same way, if I may speculate, that the Chinese forced women's feet into an unnatural appearance that suited their fantasies.

How did it happen that the Chinese bound so many women's feet for such a long period of time?[37] How did such abuse continue unchecked?

Practiced by mothers on their daughters for the pleasure of their future husbands, this mutilation began during the Song dynasty around the tenth century and lasted until the overthrow of the Qing dynasty at the beginning of the twentieth century.

For one thousand years Chinese men abrogated a central function of paternal authority by disregarding the pain and suffering that was entailed in foot binding.

Does a father feel protective toward a six-year-old daughter? Does he seek to shelter her from the cruelties of the world and to make her existence as pleasant as possible? If so, what are we to make of the fact that girls of this age in increasingly large numbers—some have estimated that between 50 percent and 80 percent of Chinese girls had their feet bound by the end of the nineteenth century—had their bones broken, day after day, by bandages that tightened around their growing feet like a slow but inexorable vise?

These girls lived in constant pain; their cries were sometimes muffled, but at other times screams or whimpers of pain must have filled the home. What could their fathers have had in mind as they listened to the effects of this torture? Where was their sense of shame?

And what were the mothers thinking? Did foot binding begin when some ladies of the court decided that they wished to emulate a clubfooted empress or imperial favorite? What does it mean when a culture promotes the emulation of deformity? Did the women who crippled their daughters simply believe they were the repositories of an ancestral rite that needed to be respected? Did they so fear punishment that they dared not refuse? To what extent does complicity involve responsibility?

Here is the way it was at the end of the nineteenth century: "In those days, when a woman was married, the first thing the bridegroom's family did was to examine her feet. Large feet, meaning normal feet, were considered to bring shame on the husband's household. The mother-in-law would lift the hem of the bride's long skirt, and if the feet were more than about four inches long, she would throw down the skirt in a demonstrative gesture of contempt and stalk off, leaving the bride to the critical gaze of the wedding guests, who would stare at her feet and insultingly mutter their disdain. Sometimes a mother would take pity on her daughter and remove the binding cloth; but when the child grew up and had to endure the contempt of her husband's family and the disapproval of society, she would blame her mother for having been too weak."[38]

Foot binding was a sign of social decadence. Its purpose was to promote sexual pleasure. Chinese men found feet that looked like "three-inch golden lilies" to be irresistible. Tiny feet indicated delicacy and femininity. Women who walked on bound feet were said to move with a lilting gait that Chinese men found to be erotically appealing. Clearly, bound feet became the primary fetish of Chinese male sexuality.

Also, the Chinese had discovered that when a woman walked on stumps this would exercise muscles whose increased development enhanced sexual pleasure for both parties in sexual congress. There was, effectively, no limit that was allowed to stand in the way of enhanced sexual gratification. Chinese men's pride in their women's feet became a way of asserting their competitive advantage in some imaginary competition over sexual achievement.

A culture that so valued pleasure must have functioned by means of extensive taboos. Moreover, it must have believed that physical pain and suffering would be redeemed by physical pleasure. Such a practice defied Confucian teaching.

This remains, however, one of the most stark instances of male tyranny where the power of men was based on the stigmatization of women. Men ruled, but the only way they could pretend to have any self-respect was at the expense of their women.

It is impossible to imagine that a woman living under such a system would offer respect for her husband or her ancestors freely. Not only was she coerced into obedience, but she became a living witness to the price of disobedience.

Foot binding was eliminated from China in 1911. It had been banned on Taiwan by its Japanese occupiers in the last years of the nineteenth century. To the Japanese the practice represented servility and was a public disgrace. Chinese public opinion turned against it because China opened up to the outside world. With that the shameful nature of this practice became clear and China stopped torturing young girls. What had been considered normal was revealed to be shameful.

What effect did this practice have on family life? The women who were hobbling around on bound stumps still had responsibility for bringing up the next generation of the emperor's subjects. Do you seriously imagine that these mothers taught their children genuine respect for authority?

Foot binding was only one sign of decadence. The ruling mandarin bureaucrats may well have represented the flower of Confucian philosophy, but their social practice defied it. Writing at the beginning of this century, Max Weber called them "aesthetically cultivated *literati* and polished salon conversationalists rather than politicians."[39] And they were not alone in their decadence. In his *Sidelights on Chinese Life*, written around the same time, John MacGowan described the Chinese as inveterate gamblers, opium addicts, wife beaters, people prone to torrents of obscene language and content to act like slaves.

MacGowan estimated that around 60 percent of Chinese men beat their wives. He recounted a story of a man who was mocked by his neighbors for not beating his wife. In order to restore his self-esteem, the man beat his wife to death.[40] Not only women were beaten in imperial China; beatings were a central element of the penal and educational systems.[41]

Chinese men were decidedly not very good at protecting their homes and providing for their families. They spent centuries fighting and losing wars to outside invaders; they lived under occupation and enslavement. Between the sixteenth century and the late twentieth century they turned the greatest civilization in the world into one of the most backward and impoverished.

To mask their shame they brutalized their wives and children. Unable to cripple their enemies, they crippled their wives and daughters and coerced their sons into absolute and unquestioning obedience.

Dealing with such problems within an enclosed group is extremely difficult. But then again, no family, no community, no clan or tribe can long function alone. A family interacts and forms alliances with other families. When something is wrong within a family, other families will have a vested interest in correcting it. Problems in a small group are usually solved by referring to a larger and stronger group.

In extreme cases certain practices need to be outlawed, by outsiders, regardless of one's respect for community traditions. This is a difficult moral issue. Do we not believe that the current practice of genital mutilation of women in Africa ought to be stopped, and that if the communities that practice it cannot do so, that it ought to be stopped by outsiders? We may not like the fact that the Japanese took over Taiwan at the end of the nineteenth century, but we are not offended by the edict that put an end to foot binding. Not all community standards are created equal; not all of them deserve the same respect.

Community standards change for the better when a group notices that it is losing out to another group that maintains different standards. The ones that should prevail are those that produce a group that is most effective and most efficient, one that excels at protecting and providing. Decadence and oppression are poor positions from which to compete economically and militarily.

A group can only recognize that it is dysfunctional in comparison to another group that is more functional. Economic and military competition causes nations and societies to modify their standards in order to succeed better. Anything else will feel like an imposition and will not generate the social consensus that supports genuine change.

Relying on a human propensity for virtue is hardly a failproof system. It is, however, generally superior to what is required to police behavior universally. No one can intervene in the affairs of a neighbor—be it a family or a nation—unless the egregiousness of the fault has had a direct impact on outsiders.

The strict separation of public and private in shame cultures serves to allow people to reform bad behavior before it becomes a public nuisance; but it should not be understood as offering license to behave any way one pleases within the confines of the home.

A sincere man, Confucius said, does not take advantage of a darkened room. He meant that people should not abuse privacy to cultivate bad habits. While it is true that no one needs to know what goes on in the privacy of your home, making a habit of disrespectful behavior at home will eventually lead to your exploiting others in the public world. To say that the division of public and private encourages abusive relationships in the home is like saying that when an actor always gets his lines wrong in rehearsal this will have no effect on his public performance. There may not be a necessary connection between poor rehearsal and poor performance, but it is reasonable to believe that in time of stress the actor will revert to rehearsal form.

Some forms of disrespect appear with a pleasing countenance. First among them is the idealization of women. This is often considered, not without reason, to be a mask for abuse. Taken as a point of pride, it has never been hidden from public knowledge.

One American version of the ideal woman was found in the Southern belle of the pre–Civil War period. Her domestic splendor, however, was purchased by the labor of female slaves. The strict division of domestic labor made the Southern belle a pampered creature whose status degraded the value of work. Slave-owning society considered work beneath its dignity.

Slavery was clearly not a secret. With it, socially deviant behavior became a way of life. Southerners believed in their way of life, they sought to defend it through force of arms, they considered themselves to be acting in the best interests of *everyone* concerned. The loss of a sense of shame produced a society where the decadence of an idle aristocracy became a badge of honor.

However much his book has been disputed,[42] W. J. Cash's *The Mind of the South* offers a valuable picture of this culture and its people. Even though Cash has been challenged for seeing the antebellum South as a guilt rather than a shame culture, he offered a subtle analysis: he saw that paying lip service to honor and decency does not produce a shame culture. When the word "honor" is used to provoke fights and conflicts, it masks a failure to act honorably. And when "decency" is used to justify slavery, it masks indecency.

Cash described the Southern character as a great parody of decency. As romantic individualists Southerners were vain and contemptuous of industrious Northerners.[43] As faux aristocrats, they never quite got courtesy right. Cash described the "planter manner" as "subjected to grotesque exaggeration. Its beauty vanished under such pomposity, such insistent and extravagant lady-and-gentleman grandness as one expects to find only in the pages of some servant-girl romance; or, lacking this, in a preciousness so simpering and so nice or, again so loftily supercilious that one might decline to believe in it if it had not been set down by the soberest observers."[44]

The Southern attitude toward women was split. On the one side the Southern planter sexually exploited his African slaves; on the other he idealized his wife to the point of idolatry. Both were systematically humiliated; such practices belie a guilt rather than a shame culture.

The treatment of the female slave is an ugly chapter of a dark time. Deprived of her dignity, the female slave was considered to be a sexual being, depraved to the point of always wanting sexual relations, lacking any discretion or discernment about choosing sexual partners.[45]

Prey to the sexual appetite of slave owners, she had no say that would count as a refusal of relations or an accusation of rape. And she could not be defended by her man. Since the male slave's dignity was compromised by the way his woman was treated, he had little interest in drawing attention to her and his shame.[46]

Obviously, such activities could not be covered over entirely. Cash captured well the feelings of the slave owner's wife: "Yet if such a woman knew that the maid in her kitchen was in reality half-sister to her own daughter, if she suspected that her husband sometimes slipped away from her bed to the arms of a mulatto wench, or even if she only knew or suspected these things of her sons or some other male of her family, why, of course she was being cruelly wounded in the sentiments she held most sacred."[47] And, she could do nothing about it. To mask her shame she denied the evidence of her senses.

Physical resemblance between planters and their racially mixed children made it impossible to ignore what was going on. These children, to the slave-owning families, were a permanent stigma, something that could not be kept secret and therefore had to be kept separate.

Civil War–era diarist Mary Chesnut rendered the extent to which women would go to retain the appearance of dignity: "Like the patriarchs of old our men live in one house with their wives and their concubines, and the mulattoes one sees in every family exactly resemble the white children—and every lady tells you who is the father of all the mulatto children in everyone's household, but those in her own she seems to think drop from the clouds."[48]

Coupled with the systematic abuse of slave women was the idealized picture of the honor of Southern white women. "She was the South's Palladium, this Southern woman—the shield-bearing Athena gleaming whitely in the clouds, the standard for its rallying, the mystic symbol of its nationality in face of the foe. She was the lily-pure maid of Astolat and the hunting goddess of the Boeotian hill. And—she was the pitiful Mother of God."[49]

Show instead of substance, ego in place of pride: the antebellum South created an extraordinary mockery of self-respect, decency, and humility. Romantic and hedonistic, prone to violence and passion, too quick to take offense, too slow to accept its own shame, this region became a disgrace to the Union, a deviant subgroup that needed to be brought back into line by force of arms.

For all the talk of honor, the antebellum South really understood one thing—force. According to the Southern codes of mock honor there was only one way to defend honor. That was violence: "These men of the South would go on growing in their practice of violence in one form or another, not only because of the reasons at which we have already looked but also because of the feeling, fixed by social example, that it was the only quite correct, the only really decent, relief for wounded honor—the only one which did not imply some subtle derogation, some dulling and retracting of the fine edge of pride, some indefinable but intolerable loss of caste and manly face."[50]

Instead of employing courtesy and etiquette to avoid conflict by finding face-saving compromise, this culture parodied these rules to produce conflict, as though strife were a fundamental good. Southerners made violence a first, rather than a last, resort.

Originally settled by Royalist refugees from the English civil war, the South represented an idea of honor based on an idle aristocratic class. This was the concept of honor that America, according to Tocqueville, had been founded to change. The Virginia planter had slaves to free him from honest labor so that he could indulge in the rarefied pursuits proper to a mandarin class.

No one, however, exemplified idleness better than Southern belles. They were hardly adept at keeping house: "Heat, dust, and ever-worrisome insects sometimes undermined household resolve to make even spacious dwellings presentable. Neither slave nor mistress took pride in keeping good order. . . . There was too much to do and little to show for the effort once things were done. Instead it was easier to immunize oneself with the distractions of talk and drink for the men, seeing friends for the women."[51]

Yet, these women owed their pampered condition to slave labor. Married to men who held human beings as property, they were obliged to suffer the indignities of their own roles and the consequences of their husbands' action in silence.[52]

While these women were present to indulge their children, the female moral center of their homes often became "the ubiquitous mammies" who were there "to give succor and nourishment." William Faulkner, "like generations of Southern men before him, declared his loyalty to the memory of his 'Mammie,' " Callie Barr. In Faulkner's words, she gave to his family "a fidelity without stint or calculation or recompense. . . ." He described her as "brave, generous, gentle, and honest. . . ."[53]

Did the black mammie produce the ultimate indignity of the Southern belle? Was her presence a constant reproach against the ethereal ladyhood of a woman whose life was supposedly given over to "honor" but who could not be a mother to her children or make a home for her family?

Elizabeth Fox-Genovese has isolated the key to this family structure in the fact that in the antebellum South the family was the center of both reproduction and production. Men and women did not hold home and work as separate spheres of authority.

As a representative American individualist, the Southern male tyrannized both his workers and his home. His world was enclosed within itself; it had only the most superficial concern with market forces and did not care how it appeared in the eyes of outsiders.[54]

History could provide many other examples of the degeneration of the family. Piling up evidence will not answer the central question: Is the family corrupt or corruptible; are the people degenerates, or have they all been misled; is tradition a useful guide to action, or should it be jettisoned completely?

A functional family may contain a deviant element without forasmuch becoming dysfunctional. Keeping the deviance secret maximizes the chances for continuing the family as a coherent and ethical social unit. Only under extreme circumstances can we properly declare that the institution of the family has become corrupt throughout a society.

The family is a functional social unity that has proved itself throughout history; as with any group, it is subject to degradation. This does not mean that the family will be or should be as it was; as a human institution it has undergone change and improvement through trial and error. Its form and practice are neither fixed immutably nor subject to infinite variation.

Far too often idealistic political thinkers promote the destruction of the family without having any idea of what that would entail or what would come to take its place. Some have set out to destroy capitalism by undermining the family. Others have decided that shame culture is the ultimate enemy, and that it must be destroyed. Perhaps the best course is to abolish filial piety.

Much of this has already been tried in our time, so at least we have something that can serve as a reality check. No one in the twentieth century pursued these ends with more zeal than Mao Zedong. Mao believed that China had been ruined by the classes who practiced shame culture and that shame culture was intrinsically corrupt. Thus he sought to eradicate all forms of propriety in order to promote conflict and guilt. The Maoist revolution had to reach into the heart of the family, to eradicate filial piety, respect for the past, and the residues of Confucianism. What it did in fact was to restore and amplify the tyranny of imperial government.

Thus was created the Great Proletarian Cultural Revolution. Mao sought to overthrow the practice of filial piety by empowering students and allowing them to persecute their parents and all other authority figures in the society. And as with other totalitarian regimes, Mao encouraged children to denounce their parents as spies and counterrevolutionaries.

Wishing to promote conflict, Mao explicitly opposed the principles of "personal loyalty, propriety, and harmony."[55] He stated that it was bad to avoid arguments "for the sake of peace and cordiality," or with someone because "he is an old friend, a fellow villager, a fellow student, a close friend, someone beloved, an old colleague, or an old subordinate."[56]

Mao began his effort to break down the vestiges of shame culture by discreetly submitting the élites to a process of brain-washing, or "thought reform." At first this process occurred within prisons; later, the Cultural Revolution made it a way of life.

Thought reform inverted filial piety by inducing people to betray friends and family and, ultimately, to denounce their fathers. A sense of identity based on social ties and family loyalty was destroyed. A new one based on belief in a cause was put in its place.

Attempting to make this work for all society produced the Cultural Revolution. Instead of isolating people in prison, it began by destroying the ties that bound them in groups. Recounting her experience as a member of the Red Guards, Jung Chang said, "I had been brought up to be courteous and respectful to anyone older than I, but now to be revolutionary meant being aggressive and militant. . . . Over the years of the Cultural Revolution, I was to witness people being attacked for saying 'thank you' too often, which was branded as 'bourgeois hypocrisy'; courtesy was on the brink of extinction."[57]

Jung Chang also described how she learned guilt as an adolescent during the Cultural Revolution. In place of filial respect, children were indoctrinated into mindless idealization for Mao. Since Mao was perfect, all failures were the fault of others. "One day in 1965, we were suddenly told to go out and start removing all the grass from the lawns. Mao had instructed that grass, flowers, and pets were bourgeois habits and were to be eliminated. . . . I was extremely sad to see the lovely plants go. But I did not resent Mao. On the contrary, I hated myself for feeling miserable. By then I had grown into the habit of 'self-criticism' and automatically blamed myself for any instincts that went against Mao's instructions. In fact, such feelings frightened me. It was out of the question to discuss them with anyone. Instead, I tried to suppress them and acquire the correct way of thinking. I lived in a state of constant self-accusation."[58]

Breaking down the authority of fathers, mothers, and teachers led to tyranny. The radical individualism produced by the elimination of respect made young people prey to the commands of the totalitarian state. Like a Great Mother goddess, the state promises to care for everyone, especially after people have been rendered fully infantile and asocial. In place of the many fathers who give face to the members of their families, the mother state is ruled by a tyrant who has no shame and grants no respect to anyone.

Other aspects of the Chinese Cultural Revolution sound strangely like ideals espoused by our own cultural revolutionaries. Beneath the monstrous images of Mao, everyone basked in a unisex egalitarianism. Men and women worked together as equals and even wore the same drab clothes; military personnel removed the insignia from their uniforms. Eventually, China descended into a frenzy of public trials and executions, causing the economy to grind to an ignominious halt.

The Cultural Revolution ended in a bloodbath. To restore order out of the chaos he had created, Mao ordered his army to suppress the Red Guards. The ensuing slaughter put an end to a great social experiment.

Both the Chinese and the American Cultural Revolutions showed in different ways that destroying the institution of the family by discrediting parental authority leads to social horrors. Systematic exposure of each and every flaw in each and every family exacerbates the very difficulties it purports to solve.

But how then should a society counter abuses that exist within the privacy of the home? When dealing with domestic violence our goal should be, wherever possible, to preserve the family while putting an end to the violence.

If deviant behavior can only be stopped by the restoration of a sense of shame, then making it appear that violence pervades all families can only worsen the difficulty. Large numbers of people confessing their dirty secrets in public creates the wrong impression. Restoring shame means first reconstituting the normative image of the functional family. Rather than take the fifties family as an illusion, we ought to consider it to be real.

Excessive public exposure normalizes deviant behavior and makes it something that one need not feel ashamed of. If every family is dysfunctional or if all men are abusive, then your own dysfunctional family or wife-beating husband counts as normal. If you assert that there is no abuse within your family, you are in "denial"; made to feel abnormal, you will be excluded from the group of those who have learned to deal with their repressed traumas. You may become prey to psychotherapists who believe that you have repressed the memories of your abuse and now must recover them in order to denounce your family convincingly. But public denunciation harms everyone, and you might find that you have destroyed a mildly dysfunctional family instead of repairing it.

When the traumatic event is not public knowledge, when privacy can be maintained, people do best to face shame in private. When a man stands up in front of an Al-Anon meeting and reveals that his alcoholic father had sexually molested his sister, he is effectively learning to feel shame and to overcome his guilt. His previous silence does not make him a co-conspirator.

Those present at such meetings note clearly the broken countenance that accompanies the violation of a sacred family trust. Even when the hidden secret is a criminal deed, people still retain a strong sense of propriety. Even when secrecy has been used to cover up a crime it still remains a primary social virtue.

Someone who is facing shame will show it on his face. The trembling visage, the choked expression, the terror of decomposition, these are present in anyone who faces his shame in front of a group. If the group is an Al-Anon meeting, then it does not count as public exposure but as a private facing of shame. The emotion suggests that private does not mean cost-free.

While the man needs to face his own shame in private, he does not want to expose the secret publicly because it may well be something his sister has forgotten and overcome or made peace with. What good would it do to make her remember it again, or to allow others to visualize her being molested? And would she ever forgive him?

If, however, the molestation is currently occurring, one is obligated to intervene. Failure to do so produces shame. Many localities today require therapists who know about child abuse to notify the proper authorities. Thus the law harmonizes with an extralegal moral duty.

Today in America we are suffering from overexposure, and this has, perhaps paradoxically, made it increasingly difficult for the culture to stamp out familial abuse.

We become numb to horror and often require even worse horrors to feel anything. But there is an increasing recognition of the dangers of overexposure and of the potential for a loss of a sense of shame.

New York Times columnist Anna Quindlen stated this well: "But while ignorance can make you insensitive, familiarity can also numb. Entering the second half-century of an information age, our cumulative knowledge has changed the level of what appalls, what stuns, what shocks. Someone calls a reporter and says, 'I have this foster child and he's going to be returned to his biological mother and I'm afraid she'll kill him.' And part of your mind registers that this is a kid at risk and part thinks, oh, the old foster-kid-and-abusive-mother story.

"We have the opposite of silence now; we are awash in the revealed world, talking of things that for so long were adjudged unspeakable. Events that are merely tragic must yield space on the page for those that are truly terrible. Gang rapes instead of rapes. Pre-adolescent killers instead of teen-age ones. It is a sliding scale, and sometimes you have to wonder where and when the slide will end."[59]

How can a society go about preventing such things from happening in the first place?

If one man in the neighborhood is exposed as a child molester, he—and his family—will be ostracized by the community. His fate will serve as a deterrent to others who have similar ideas.

What would happen if the accused tries to defend himself on the grounds that his neighbors all wish to do the same thing, and that their outrage reveals only their own repressed feelings? Would this tend to promote shame or guilt?

If all men are child molesters, they can form their own deviant subgroup, and their habits will become the norm for the group. They will no longer be deterred by shaming. In fact, as we saw in imperial China, a group of wife beaters can band together and threaten to ostracize the one member of the community who does not beat his wife.

How does a community deal with deviant behavior according to shame culture? Public opinion must be galvanized, and the social consensus that holds that child abuse is deviant and exceptional must be maintained.

One way to do so is exemplified by what the state of New Jersey has called Megan's Law. A community thereby has the right to know when a convicted child molester, released from prison, has settled in its midst. Thus the community may choose to ostracize the person, not only asserting that he is unwelcome but also that it will not tolerate such behavior.

Extensive legal wrangling has wrapped itself around this law. Is ostracism cruel and unusual punishment? If so, this tells us that shaming is a more powerful deterrent than a few years in a penitentiary. Are the privacy rights of the molester being violated? Only the most peculiar notion of privacy would suggest that the results of a public trial must be protected from public view.

Forcing convicted child molesters to register with local police departments represents an effort to forestall the possibility that a released sexual predator hide behind a veil of anonymity to circulate undisturbed in a community where his past is unknown. Thereby, many state governments have attempted to apply in the larger community a sanction that would normally be applied in a smaller community.

The released criminal may well have paid his debt to society, but this fact, in and of itself, does not reconstitute his good name and reputation. In a small community functioning as a shame culture the criminal who has shown remorse has volunteered to be identified in front of his neighbors as a criminal. He does not try to hide behind a mask of anonymity.

Failure to offer a public apology may well be counted as an intention to commit the same crime again. Does the community in that case have the right to coerce the molester into being publicly identified? I believe it does.

The situations that function the least well as deterrents involve dramatic encounters between abuser and victim. Most of these concern spousal abuse. Did Lorena Bobbit's mutilation of her husband deter men from sexually abusing their wives? Did it empower women? Did the endless exposure of this sad incident make it less frightening or more of a sick joke for the late-night talk shows?

When individuals feel they must take the law into their own hands the community has lost its moral consensus about what constitutes unacceptable behavior.

Thus the case of Francine Hughes, however compelling and frightening, could not really serve to deter domestic violence. This case formed the basis for Faith McNulty's book *The Burning Bed.*

On March 9, 1977, Francine Hughes was subjected to a torrent of abuse by her ex-husband, Mickey. She was beaten, cursed at, humiliated, and raped, as she had been for twelve years. That night, as her husband slept, she poured gasoline on the floor of the bedroom and lit a match. Mickey Hughes was incinerated, and Francine faced a charge of first-degree murder. Eventually she was acquitted by reason of temporary insanity.[60]

To the extent that this example inhibits, it does so by intimidation. Francine Hughes may well have been right to have done what she did; her action, and especially its attendant publicity, will not reduce the amount of domestic violence in America.

It empowers women, but the example it sets is too extreme

to serve as a model for an effective response by a battered woman. If women feel that the choice is between accepting abuse and murdering their abusers, many will choose the former. While this case appears to empower women, it disempowers them by removing the intermediate choices between acceptance and murder. In order for a case to function as a model deterrent, the perpetrator must be socially respectable, must have received society's honors, must be a role model and subject to emulation by others. He must also accept his shame and offer a public apology. Once the model is established at the top it is easier to apply it to others.

The recent case of Judge Sol Wachtler fulfills these requirements well. Chief judge of the New York State Court of Appeals, the highest court in New York State, Judge Wachtler had been considered a viable candidate for the United States Supreme Court and for the governorship of New York State.

Judge Wachtler did not beat his wife. His behavior did not occur within his own immediate family. His case concerns another form of criminal abuse of a woman. Despairing for having been rejected by his former mistress, Joy Silverman, Judge Wachtler decided to make her believe that she was being subjected to blackmail threats and that her daughter might be kidnapped.

He wrote to Silverman (and her daughter) that he possessed photographs of her engaged in sexual acts and would expose them publicly if he did not receive $200,000. He believed that if she thought she was in danger, she would turn to him for help.

Extorting money, threatening to harm a child, sending an obscene message to a teenage girl, these were Judge Wachtler's crimes. The public did not react as it did to cases like that of Francine Hughes. There was no division of public opinion. In this case public exposure was a punishment in and of itself. The trial was almost irrelevant in comparison to the loss of an otherwise sterling reputation. The case demonstrates that shaming produces a consensus over both the immorality of the act and identity of the responsible party.

Finally, Judge Sol Wachtler resigned his position and offered a public apology before the Federal District Court in Trenton, New Jersey, on March 31, 1993: "I know, Your Honor, that my behavior from late 1991 to late 1992 was foreign to my 62 years on Earth. I am deeply ashamed and sorry for what I have done to others—Ms. Silverman, my family and those who entrusted New York State's court system to my care. I know that I cannot ever make up for those acts."[61]

Would the Wachtler case deter deviant behavior toward women? Will other men see reflections of some of their own behavior and recognize it now as shameful? A single, local example can influence behavior only when there are other examples. And other community leaders must set an example for propriety in their treatment of women. When the nation elects notorious womanizers to high public office, it shows acceptance of men who humiliate their wives.

To footnote Judge Wachtler's story I offer a comment he wrote to a law student months before his disgrace: "I cannot escape the feeling that I could enjoy life a bit more if I didn't care quite as much about what others thought of me. Unfortunately, the strictures of a civilized and easily scandalized society have kept me from the ultimate happiness of saying or doing whatever I wanted at any given time."

How did such an eminent jurist get himself into such a position? His words offer an answer: he had overcome his sense of shame in order to find "the ultimate happiness."

Obviously, filial piety has everything to do with sexual behavior. A group has a direct interest in the sexual behavior of its members. It will regulate that behavior either by shaming those who deviate from the norm or by punishing those who transgress any one of a number of prohibitions.

Under normal circumstances each family member has a filial obligation to perpetuate the family by reproducing. Societies do not survive if they do not encourage this enterprise. And they look askance at those who do not fulfill this primary social obligation.

People who are single or who are childless or whose children are born outside the proper channels are subjected to some degree of ostracism by those who live more traditional lives. Exceptions are often made for those who lead a religious life, because their vocation serves the interests of society. Their ministry contributes to the community by perpetuating its values; they engage themselves actively in socially valuable functions like education.

Clearly, group survival depends on reproduction. Social conventions honor ties that serve the group, and cast dishonor on those that threaten its survival. Not because an act in itself threatens the group, but because everyone's practicing it would. Mother-son incest is more taboo than father-daughter incest because the connection between a younger man and an older woman is reproductively inefficient. Perverse sexual acts that are practiced to the exclusion of heterosexual coitus are considered more degrading than those that accompany the reproductive act. Extramarital sexual relations are condemned because their offspring will have no family to care for them, thus they will become wards of the state.

Groups have an interest in the consequences of sexual behavior. Different cultures, however, employ different strategies to ensure the continuation of the group. Some opt for numerical strength; they worship fertility and believe that people should produce many offspring, the better to guarantee survival, and even dominance, over less efficient groups. They often make extensive use of sexual taboos to heighten and encourage sexual desire.

Other groups emphasize maintaining the culture, its attitudes, its values, its traditions. Providing for a few offspring responsibly is more important than producing a slew of them. Groups that practice this policy recognize that overpopulation is as much a threat to family honor as underpopulation. These groups tend to see sex as a normal part of everyday life—subject to neither excessive prohibition nor permissiveness.

These two approaches are practiced, respectively, by guilt and shame cultures. The first sacrifices its respect for tradition to the fear that some disaster might eradicate the group. The second sacrifices unwieldy families to a process that ensures that the family name will be continued by responsible and well-educated people.

Each will adopt different attitudes toward sexuality. In a guilt culture sexuality will be identified with fertility. Other ways of obtaining sexual pleasure will be prohibited as an offense against a fertility god. Individuals will be defined and identified by their sexuality. Since private behavior has a significant influence over what the society perceives to be moral character, the group will attempt to regulate what people do in the privacy of their bedrooms. The group needs to know if anyone is practicing nonprocreative sexuality, and takes appropriate action to limit the waste of reproductive potential.

In shame culture the practice of respect requires that sexuality be hidden and that people be judged by their public conduct, regardless of what they do in private. Reproduction is clearly a filial obligation, but this does not require an obsessive interest in sexuality. Other ways of obtaining sexual pleasure discreetly are accepted because they function as a kind of contraception. Since taboos make sex more important, these cultures do not emphasize them.

People cast a blind or indulgent eye on "perversions" because they do not believe sex to be an important indicator of character. Character concerns how you bring up the children you have, not how you experience pleasure.

How then do cultures deal with sexual deviance within the family? Take the example of male homosexuality.[62] Many cultures reserve a special condemnation for male homosexuality, especially the passive male homosexual, because, of all the many kinds of sexual behavior, his position makes him least likely to reproduce. An active male homosexual can more easily exchange a female for a male partner.

Most, if not all, human societies are organized as male hierarchies. Since men perform most public functions, their ability to fulfill their roles has been taken as critically important to social order.

In shame cultures male homosexuality tends to be overlooked as long as the man in question is either married and a father or a celibate minister. Certain homosexual activities have often been accepted in military and athletic cultures, as long as they remain private acts performed under abnormal conditions. If a soldier in a garrison under siege beds down with another soldier, this will not bother anyone unduly. Many cultures do not have a concept of homosexual identity, only of homosexual acts committed by solid citizens under stress.

The passive homosexual position is associated with effeminacy and seems to be contrary to the warrior mentality; therefore, it is repudiated in military and militaristic cultures. These same cultures have less difficulty accepting homosexual acts performed by a man who remains in the masculine position. They seem to hold that a man who adopts a feminine position, in public or in private, will be less apt to fulfill his manly responsibilities than will a man who maintains a consistently masculine posture. Among homosexuals, male and female, the passive male homosexual is the only one whose organ of sexual satisfaction is not proper to his gender.

There is little doubt that all cultures are especially interested in the erectile capacity of the male sexual organ. The phallus is a source of pride even among young boys: when little Johnny has his first erection, he is likely to show it off to his mother.

Shame cultures take the phallic function to be primarily symbolic and social; the phallus is only secondarily fertilizing.

In male homosexual encounters, what matters is whose phallus is actively involved; that partner has the dominant or masculine position. This division ought to correspond to the social status of the participants. If an older man, for example, mounts a younger man, this affirms the social order: each is in his proper place. If the roles are reversed, the older man is disgraced for occupying an inferior position in relation to someone who is socially inferior to him.

Writing of classical Greece, David Halperin stated, "Sex was a manifestation of public status, a declaration of social identity; it did not so much express an individual's unique 'sexuality' as it served to position social actors in the places assigned to them (by virtue of their political standing) in the hierarchical structure of the Athenian polity."[63]

Guilt cultures reject such phallocentrism. They privilege the fertilizing capacity of the male organ; ejaculating semen, a man serves the purposes of female fertility. Guilt cultures condemn the phallus to glorify its seed and to worship fertility.

Practices like abortion and even contraception are considered to be violations of the law of a fertility god, and are severely condemned by guilt cultures. The same goes for masturbation, oral and anal sex, all homosexual acts, and the use of pornography that portrays deviant behavior. It makes no difference whether these acts take place in private; anyone who commits them is as guilty as he would be if they were committed in public.

People whose sexual behavior intrinsically precludes procreation are labeled as evil; they are often counted among the damned. Worse are those who desecrate seminal fluid by casting it into the gutter. While the greater shame lay in the receptive homosexual position, the greater guilt lies in the active homosexual position.

In guilt cultures homosexuals have been hunted down and persecuted, as though society had to rid itself of a corrupting influence.

Since homosexuals do not reproduce themselves, and since the formation of a homosexual community requires the continual "enlistment" of members from the heterosexual community, guilt cultures imagine that homosexuals are predatory, continually on the lookout for straights they can convert to their ways. These cultures make of homosexuality a danger that must be controlled. Keeping it secret makes it more dangerous and seductive.

In regard to family secrets, two questions are relevant. The first concerns the homosexual's decision about revealing his sexual orientation to other members of his immediate family; such an act does not require public exposure. The second concerns whether the homosexual should announce his orientation to the rest of the community.

Most homosexuals have traditionally preferred to keep their sexual orientation to themselves. Families who suspect, or even know that members are homosexual, do not advertise the fact publicly. At times they do not even allow themselves to think it.

Current biomedical research suggests that people do not choose to be homosexual. And yet, since homosexuals are not identifiable as a group in the way that genders and races are, each individual has something of a choice about whether he wants anyone to know that he is homosexual. In shame cultures people do not condemn homosexuals for being homosexual, but rather for publicizing the fact. These cultures do not identify people by their sexual activity; therefore anyone who publicly calls attention to his sexual acts is considered deficient in shame.

Of late an important social problem has arisen in this regard. Male homosexuals who have had no intention of coming out are being brought into public view and being identified according to their sexual practice by the outward manifestations of AIDS—this through no choice of their own. Evidently, this challenges society's ability to tolerate those it has traditionally considered to be deviant.

The shame culture attitude toward male homosexuality requires discretion and dissimulation. Homosexuals have functioned effectively at all levels of American society and have done so with distinction. And yet they have been forced to live a lie.

Many homosexual authors seem to believe that the shame culture approach is superior, if for no other reason than it shows more respect for privacy. And yet, its crux is the requirement that homosexuals remain in the closet, and many homosexuals today have found that to be an unjust burden. Moreover, in the age of AIDS that has increasingly become impossible.

Homosexuals are certainly integrated into American society. Some work effectively in the straight world at the cost of hiding their sexual orientation. Otherwise they have tended to gravitate toward professions and communities where they make up the majority of the members. Whether the society can integrate open homosexuals without this split remains to be seen.

It may be counted as a dubious achievement to have written a chapter on the family without having mentioned love, romance, or connubial bliss. I have chosen to begin with the family as institution, and later to discuss the anatomy of human intimacy within (and without) this institution. My purpose is simple: intimacy supplements the ties that bind people together in families (and in clubs, friendships, or collegial circumstances); it cannot work as a substitute for institutional ties.

Intimacy questions implicate women more directly than men, and the way society addresses them bears heavily on how it offers respect to women. Different societies approach this differently. The American way, inherited from the Puritans, is to grant a woman a choice about how she conducts her life, and how she chooses a mate. The more a woman has a choice in these matters, the more she can rightfully be held accountable for the success or failure of her future conduct.

In Tocqueville's words: "In a country in which a woman is always free to exercise her choice and where education has prepared her to choose rightly, public opinion is inexorable to her faults. The rigor of the Americans arises in part from this cause. They consider marriage as a covenant which is often onerous, but every condition of which the parties are strictly bound to fulfill because they knew all those conditions beforehand and were perfectly free not to have contracted them."[64]

But also, adding a woman's concerns to the institution of marriage made it that marriage could never again simply be an arrangement or a social convenience. As David Fischer wrote, "The Puritans cherished true love, and insisted that it was a prerequisite of a happy marriage."[65]

Replacing arranged marriage with companionate marriage based on love and romance has been a great Western achievement, one that allows women to make free choices, to be held responsible for their actions, and to exercise a decisive influence on the institution of marriage.[66] It has also required the invention of a new set of social practices where men, for a change, have not dominated. These are called courtship; they define the world of love and romance.

5

Love and Marriage

If there were no boundaries between public and private domains there would be no shame. Since shame occurs when private matters are exposed in public, shame cultures are mobilized to ensure that such a breach does not occur.

These two domains are represented by the home and the marketplace: the one an area of peace and harmony, the other an area of competitive striving. These places have different rules and different values, and in principle they ought to complement each other, not be engaged in a battle for supremacy. The man who competes vigorously on the job may also show kindness to his wife and children.

Shame cultures seek to maintain the boundaries; guilt cultures wish to eliminate them. Shame cultures believe that public propriety promotes respectful behavior in private; guilt cultures hold to the contrary, that good behavior in public screens private abuse. Shame culture produces romance by a modulated play of exposure and concealment; guilt culture sees desire in the dramatic conflict between male aggression and feminine deception.

Finally, shame culture sees love sustained by marriage; guilt culture feeds sexual desire by making it conflict with society's interests.

In shame culture even romance requires people to maintain face. Greater intimacy increases vulnerability; this makes it even more important for people to respect the feelings of others. In interpersonal communication saving face means not hurting the feelings of the other person. Shame culture does not believe that conflict is inevitable or that it needs to be cultivated to enhance passion. It takes sexual attraction to be natural, enhanced by adornment and play.

Guilt culture, on the contrary, poses an ideal communication where people are completely open about their own feelings, no matter what effect it produces on others. Worse yet, it has convinced people that their nastiest thoughts are the most truthful and that failing to share them makes a relationship superficial. Guilt culture turns face inside out and upside down.

Still, ugly thoughts do cross everyone's mind, and human society does not expect that these will never get an airing. Thus, alongside the decorum of the marketplace and the sanctity of the home, it has created profane spaces where such thoughts can be ventilated without counting for anything.

In bars, nightclubs, and bordellos you can act in ways that would in more orderly spaces subject you to opprobrium. All who participate in such exercises know that what occurs is not meaningful, that it should not be taken personally, and that its confidentiality must remain inviolate.

When the boundary between public and private is systematically breached, institutions are threatened. The moral authority of those who direct and represent such institutions is based on their strictly maintaining face. How seriously can you take the general's stars if his fly is open or if his daughter was Playmate of the Month? How much confidence will you have in his leadership if you are thinking about his sexual peccadilloes?

When shame culture degenerates, the boundaries blur. What

had hitherto been a private matter now becomes public knowledge. Efforts to publicize privacy are pronounced a good thing; they lift repression and free the human spirit. Expression and exposure become moral virtues; those who assert that some matters are not fit for public discussion are denounced as hypocritical and repressive. Civic life becomes filled with gossip, government and corporate secrets are commonly revealed in the press, and the explicit representation of sexual matters becomes family entertainment.

In the mad pursuit of free expression people lose track of the reasons for maintaining boundaries between public and private. And psychology has encouraged these activities by pronouncing repression bad and expression good.

If there are feelings you would discuss freely with an intimate, but not at all with a mere acquaintance, does that mean that you are repressing your feelings when you are talking with an acquaintance? The closer you are and the more you have in common with someone, the more freely you can express yourself without fear of giving offense. Such confidence must be earned. Not exposing sexual fantasies to someone you just met is not repression; it is considerate. Stifling an insulting expression shows respect, not repression. Insisting on sharing your misery often masks an attempt to force intimacy.

Face-saving techniques are commonly used to parry undesirable romantic overtures. A man or a woman who is the object of unwanted attention will usually not reject the other person outright, but say that he or she is not ready to be involved. People normally refuse unwanted invitations by declaring themselves to be very busy with previous engagements.[1]

Most people know that frank rejection threatens the other person, and may even provoke anger and retaliation. This dynamic bears a strong resemblance to the common tactic of Japanese businessmen who refuse to say no to an offered deal, preferring to declare themselves interested but needing time to think things over.

Is this a correct approach, or should people in these circumstances learn to be more truthful? If we consider the face-saving solution to be normative, they ought not. Undesired attention is simply a misunderstanding, and ought to be taken as such. Civilized communication requires that one avoid threatening the other person's face.

Failure to respect face produces serious psychological damage. Someone who has lost face will often become depressed. A pervasive sense of failure and worthlessness characterizes that condition; it manifests itself in sleep disturbances, loss of appetite, and diminished libido. The depressed withdraw from normal social interaction, including romantic attachments.

Normally, treatment requires the individual to restore self-respect, but an alternative is proposed by guilt culture. Most commonly it seeks to manufacture desire artificially by promoting envy and anger. These emotions can serve as powerful aphrodisiacs for the depressed. And they manage to serve society: the world, as Shakespeare said, must be peopled.

If we ask what purpose is served when American men and women express so much hostility toward one another, the answer is: to mask depression by promoting a self-esteem based on romantic passion. The price, however, is far too high. Making men angry and women envious may produce an artificial desire, but the cost in suffering ought to dissuade us from seeing this approach as other than what it is: an effort to solve a problem by pretending it does not exist.

The post-Vietnam period saw a revolution in American gender relations. Traditional masculine and feminine roles no longer seemed to be viable; at times they were inverted, at other times confused. Some suggested that this was the price we would have to pay to accomplish the next step in the expansion of civility: respecting women beyond their traditional roles in family and romance.

The point most often missed was that the woman's revolution was accompanied by the decline of the American male.

Throughout the course of human history groups of men have lost wars; some have even ducked fights. Few, however, have ever involved themselves in a large-scale military campaign without intending to win. And few have gone to such lengths to mask their shame. For American men this began their decline.

It was based on guilt. Some believed that we should have withdrawn from Vietnam; others that we should have pulverized it. Out of these two rejected policy options arose two versions of a new American male. Basically, he was two-faced. The sensitive, caring type, fully in touch with his feminine side, stood back to back with an ill-mannered lout who was quick to anger, eager to beat up anyone who was defenseless. These two are connected because the man who cannot show sufficient anger when it is justified is likely to show excessive anger when it is not.

Eventually, things evolved to the point where we were regaled with the picture of grown men out in the woods pounding on drums, getting in touch with their inner wild man, and learning to cry. Truly, they had lost all sense of shame.

Instead of cultivating discipline, honor, and self-respect—the better to compete at work—young American men were out getting their ears pierced, their chests shaved, and their queues braided.

Is it any wonder that women believe that *they* should take charge? Manhood became subject to withering criticism by women and others, and precious few men sought to defend themselves. Criticism in itself is not damning; failure to respond is. Those few who did defend themselves were neither the best nor the brightest.

For the most part men hunkered down: they allowed women to walk down the corridors of power, but they rarely gave them real authority. They paid lip service to the idea of sharing domestic responsibility and then were nowhere to be found. They welcomed women's increased sexual assertiveness and then got headaches as soon as their partners took a sexual initiative. The term ''passive-aggressive'' became an important diagnostic description in psychiatry.

Other men lashed out at women. They stifled their anger at the disruption of their all-male workplace and then went out and beat their girlfriends. They came to believe that since women want sex as much as men, a refusal was a personal insult requiring revenge. Forcing women to have sex became prevalent in ways that it had never been. Previously young men and women had engaged in an intricate dance about how far they would go; the rules were clear, the limits were understood by both parties. In our revolutionary times this dance lost its playful quality; no one knew what the boundaries or the subtleties were. Sex became a battle, not a dance.

For a nation that had decided that racism was its original sin, sexism became public enemy number two. This brought sin directly into the home and the bedroom. Sexism means that relations between the sexes are defined by male hostility toward women. Men seek to subjugate, dominate, and abuse women. Men's thoughts and fantasies, the institutions they have invented, are based on their hatred of women. Whatever men have accomplished has been achieved at the expense of women. Statements asserting men and women to be different were denounced as discriminatory—unless they declared women to be superior.

Men were told they ought to feel guilt; they needed to atone by relinquishing all vestiges of male authority. Some did; some did not. But one of the masculine roles that too many men did give up was the one that obliged them to protect women. Women were asking for independence and autonomy; too many men saw that as meaning that they could do what they pleased to women without fear of sanction. Men are less afraid of the law than they used to be of a woman's father or older brother.

Throughout human history men have abused women: we are not lacking in grotesque examples of sexual violence or oppression on the basis of gender. But is this the truth about relations between the sexes? Is marriage a criminal conspiracy invented by men in order to keep women in a subservient position? Was it created out of fear of the power of women?

If all men are sexists and if their impulses toward women are predatory and oppressive, the only solution is for them to feel guilt, atone for it, and renounce traditional masculine roles. In practice this makes men either overly inhibited or overly violent toward women. It does not create anything resembling a harmony in the everyday home life of citizens.

Men function best in relation to women when they know the rules and see other men following them. Being part of a group of men in which courtesy toward women is the rule motivates men in the best direction. Since male human beings have hormonally determined aggressive tendencies, society in its wisdom has decided that it is better that men not act according to impulse, that they not follow their feelings.

Some have proposed, as a way to diminish male violence toward women, that men get in touch with their feminine side. This is roughly equivalent to teaching them how to cross-dress in order to let them know how it feels to be a woman—a notion, incidentally, that shows considerable disrespect for women.

Aside from falsifying who they are and subjecting them to potential ridicule this policy dispenses with the sense of obligation that inheres in male bonding. When men do not know how to behave around women they will either be inhibited or will express themselves with greater, not lesser, hostility.

Most women who have succeeded in getting a man to reveal his true feelings have lived to regret it.

The evolution of gender roles has made some strides beyond the constrictions imposed by guilt cultural thinking. Many writers have preferred reform to revolution and have contributed to our understanding of the nature of relations between the sexes. To promote such a reform we need to see masculine and feminine as other than synonyms for criminal and victim.

Evidently, human societies have identified private spaces with women. By placing a sacred trust in the roles of wife and mother, society has circumscribed women's roles by the requirement to embody the private domain. The fact that this responsibility has often been coerced does not mean that women would never choose it.

The word "embody" is not simply a metaphor here; it refers to the fact that the female body is held by most societies to represent the private domain.

The division of public and private is often associated with the division of the sexes. The public domain, i.e., business and government, tends, with great consistency, to be dominated by men; the private domain, i.e., the home, relationships, and romance, tends to be dominated by women. This division is so pervasive that no one, to my knowledge, has shown a functioning social organization in which the public sphere is dominated by women and where the functions associated with the home—child rearing, homemaking—are dominated by men.

Government, business, and commerce are for all intents and purposes, a man's world. Whatever the reasons, the values represented by that world seem mostly to be manifested by men. Men have made the rules, men have played the game, and these are arranged to affirm masculine identity.

Nevertheless, the marketplace also contains many occupations that are identified as women's work. Certainly, there are more now than there were in the past. But as a rule these occupations are considered to be supportive, even subordinate to the real business at hand.

Of late many women have vigorously disputed the identification of women with home. Wishing to undermine the idea that a woman's place was in the home they have rejected, even at times stigmatized, the role of housewife. The message: if a woman works merely as wife and mother, she is nothing.

Stigmatizing the role of wife created its own problems. If a married woman is not a wife, then what is she? Does she have a place in the home? Does she have authority and responsibility there?

If societies are organized by roles and rules, then each member of an organized unit like a family will have a role comporting duties and obligations. Thus is the family hierarchized and domestic labor divided.

Men can be sons, fathers, husbands, or brothers; women can be daughters, mothers, wives, or sisters. Aunts, uncles, grandmothers, grandfathers, are extensions of these basic roles.

Parent/child relations establish hierarchy; they are defined by responsibility to care for and protect, balanced by an obligation to respect and obey. Brother/sister and husband/wife relations involve cooperation and separate spheres of authority.

Roles define responsibility. Without this definition endless haggling often occurs over who is to make dinner, who is to wash the dishes, who is to pick up the children, who is to wash the car. If there are no roles, failing to rake the leaves does not label anyone as irresponsible but becomes an occasion for a dispute over who is at fault. When tasks are performed adequately in a situation where roles are not defined, the person performing them does not receive credit for fulfilling a responsibility. A man may even use his achievement to berate his wife for not doing some other task whose responsibility has not been defined.

The coldly analytic quality of these definitions seems to leave little place for romance. It may have been misguided to see family organization as oppressing women, but such a highly structured environment cannot place great value on love, romance, and intimacy. After all, true love is never conventional. Bringing the system of rules and roles into balance with the needs for romance and intimacy is a worthy goal. Deciding to crush the former in the interest of the latter introduces an imbalance that serves no one's interests.

Having liberated themselves from the role of housewife, women came to assert more positive values of femininity: personal relationships are more important than competition for status; connecting with people is more important than social duties; knowing one's feelings is more important than mindlessly following rules; romance and desire are more important than ceremony and ritual.

Men participate in this private sphere under the domination of women. Their role is subordinate and supportive, though generally it is best that they not know it. No one seriously believes that men have authority when it comes to being in touch with feelings. A situation which does not have well-defined rules and roles exists in alien territory for men. And perhaps that is as it should be.

Other aspects of women's traditional roles in society have excluded men. Childbirth and child rearing, housekeeping and other domestic chores have tended to be dominated by women. Women join together in groups to share their experiences, to commiserate about their difficulties, to transmit the wisdom they have gained. The experience of female solidarity involves connection based on sensitivity and empathy. Since the experiences involved are proper to women, men are usually not welcome in such groups.

The interests of men and women ought rightly to harmonize in society. When the division of public and private breaks down, as happened in our own Cultural Revolution, the home becomes an arena of conflict, and the business world becomes more touchy-feely. Instead of having a set of rules proper to each space, the two sets of rules compete for hegemony. Men want the home to be run like a business; women want business to be run like a home.

Since shame culture uses business and the military as its paradigms it is hardly surprising that its values should sustain a masculine ethos. Does this mean that an ethos more attuned to women's issues should be based on guilt culture and that relationships existing outside the marketplace should repudiate everything that the marketplace stands for?

The more correct assessment is that in a shame culture the division of the sexes is held with great strictness; the sacred boundary between public and private translates into an equally clear boundary between the worlds of men and women. Social harmony and community consensus are fostered by granting respect to each in his or her proper sphere of authority.

In guilt culture things are different. Guilt knows no boundaries and seeks to break down artificial divisions between public and private. Struggles for power within both worlds produce more heat between the sexes; anger maintains disharmony, and disharmony sustains passion. For guilt culture, social convention represses and feeds desire.

The pursuit of private passion seems to conflict with the values associated with the family and marriage. We commonly believe that someone we love is irreplaceable. Don't we love people for what is unique about them rather than what is common? Love within a happy marriage differs from the love that is formed when two people make their romance into a reproach against that institution. The latter is more exciting, the former more durable.

The greatest love stories in Western civilization defy convention, violate propriety, and break the rules. Romeo and Juliet, Tristan and Isolde, Abélard and Héloïse, Phaedra and Hippolytus—all these lovers engage their passion in defiance of their families and society at large. They are individuals, lost and alone, clinging desperately to each other as sole means of social support. Of course, all these stories end tragically, and often there is a macabre beauty to the lovers' fate, as though, in death, they had gained a final victory against all those who sought to keep them apart. Legend has it that when the grave of Peter Abélard was opened to receive Héloïse's corpse, Abélard's ghost rose up to embrace her. The eternal thus triumphs over the temporal. Failure on earth must mean success later on.

Some young lovers were clearly challenging the practice of arranged marriage. Eventually the institution would respond by allowing and even encouraging marriage based on love. Thus humans came to recognize that romantic love was not necessarily the enemy of social institutions. The fact that two people made a good match from society's point of view did not preclude their falling in love. Society's approval could sustain love over time. Society's disapproval produced more intense momentary states of passion.

Romantic love could coexist with propriety, decorum, and general good manners. Eschewing the passionate extremes indulged by youth, this love could grow over time to produce an intimacy that would harmonize with socially beneficial goals.

Romance would simmer, not boil; the sexes would be partners, not adversaries. The more each partner demonstrated trust, loyalty, and reliability, the more they would forge sustaining bonds of intimacy. Whatever momentary jolt a romance could receive from envy, jealousy, and mistrust would ultimately be mitigated by the confidence forged by years of harmonious transactions.

In the past, it appears, men and women knew how to get along. This skill has long since fallen into disuse. To establish a way for men and women to overcome the war between the sexes in order to live in domestic harmony is an old and a new challenge.

To get a handle on these issues we shall review some contemporary thinking about the division of the sexes. One book stands out from the rest, not only for its general excellence, but because its commercial success has made it a cultural phenomenon in its own right. I am thinking of Deborah Tannen's *You Just Don't Understand.*

For Tannen, men and women fail to communicate across a large cultural divide. Beyond the idea that we need to understand gender differences—most people know exactly what the differences are—she addresses a contemporary condition that I would call the alienation of the sexes. Each sex has hunkered down to defend its own turf and to promote its own mode of functioning as the standard by which the other sex ought to operate. Neither is seeking conciliation, but hegemony. In this breach Tannen proposes respect for the way the sexes differ in their patterns of communication.

As she has emphasized, men speak of the world, women speak of themselves; men communicate information, women communicate their feelings. Whereas men tend to present themselves in the best possible light as actors in the public arena, women express their private suffering, placing value on their ability to connect with others by sharing secrets and caring for other people's misfortunes.

Men assert prestige by presenting themselves according to where they stand in a male hierarchy. When a woman wishes to communicate something of who she is, she will expose her personal feelings about an issue.

I would add this: When a woman speaks of togetherness, she is referring to an experience that two people undergo in the same way, and about which they share their feelings in confidence. When a man speaks of togetherness, he is referring to two people being at the same place at the same time, participating in the same event, regardless of whether they communicate anything at all.

Nothing is gained by judging either sex with standards that apply to the other. When this happens, men consider women to be whiny complainers and women see men as insensitive ghouls.

But are the differences really so stark? We do not want to make masculinity and femininity into moral absolutes that remain the same no matter what the circumstances. If men and women are distinguished too strictly, they risk becoming caricatures of ideal types. There is more to human communication than asserting gender. No one acts the same way with all people all the time. Surely we know that men do not use the same language in speaking with their wives and mothers as they do when they are trading stories in a barroom. Nor do women share confidences with men in the same way they communicate with other women.

Not all men come home from work and lecture their wives on their achievements. They do not all attempt to impart extensive information about their business, paying no attention to what their wives find important. Similarly, not all women fill the atmosphere with litanies of complaints, recounting all the day's travails, no matter what their husbands think.

Ordinarily men do not seek from women what they have with other men, and women do not seek from men the kinds of relationships they have with other women. Nor ought either to do so.

Under better circumstances people accommodate each other. Most men understand what they can expect from a relationship with a woman and what they ought not to set their hearts on. Idem for women.

Men function within a world where status counts; their efforts are directed to showing their place in the hierarchy; they are constantly jockeying for position. Generally, wives have been known to accommodate these tendencies, if only because they have a direct stake in their husbands' status. For their part, men have usually been willing to accommodate their wives' concerns and predilections. They do not do so because they know what it feels like to be a woman but precisely because they do not.

Women have difficulty accepting a man who comes home from working on chemical engineering and who then imagines that his opinions about the conduct of the household and the upbringing of the children should stand as an absolute authority. This "lord of the manor" attitude shows disrespect for the woman's efforts to maintain a home and for her extensive practical experience in the area. Similarly, a wife who assumes that her moral superiority gives her a special insight into how her husband should conduct his business will be perceived as meddling in areas she does not understand.

When a man confides his troubles in a woman he is looking for a cheerleader. When a woman confides her troubles in a man she is looking for moral support, thus sympathy and understanding.

If, as Tannen suggests, men and women represent two different cultures[2]—which is certainly the way it has appeared lately

—then they will inevitably either speak at cross-purposes or come into conflict. If, on the other hand, it is understood, as part of the marital contract, that each partner has a different sphere of authority, then the two ought not to come into conflict.

If a woman allows a man to have the upper hand—or at least to think that he does—this is because locating herself in a hierarchy of competing aggressive beings is not the way she gains self-respect. And if a man refrains from interfering in decisions that concern home and family, the realm of private and intimate matters, this is because his self-respect does not depend on forming connections in this way.

Tannen's thesis contains some truths. Nevertheless she errs in seeing men as inveterate individualists. Men connect with other men but not in the way women connect with other women. Men do not share confidences, offer sympathy, tell their troubles, recount endless stories; they do not, in other words, seek to forge a connection based on shared feelings.

The connections men establish are determined by the groups they belong to; the link is defined by the roles, rules, and titles that constitute the group. Men form groups to compete and perform at optimal efficiency; they avoid discussing what went wrong because this reduces morale.

Given the stakes in the game, they must solve problems as quickly as possible; belaboring failure will waste time and effort. Victory in battle goes to those who correct mistakes quickly and decisively. Sharing feelings inhibits action.

Male bonding depends on maintaining the group's appearance of harmony and efficiency; trust and loyalty are primary values. For a man to get along with men he must first know what not to talk about. In such a group everyone sinks or swims together; asserting personal needs becomes counterproductive because cooperation succeeds only when group interest is given primacy over individual concerns. The value of the individual lies in his contribution to a collective endeavor.

Competition among men does not produce winners and losers; it establishes the hierarchical order. The team that loses the Super Bowl is not a loser: it is the second best team in football for that year. Competition in a shame culture should never be an all or nothing proposition.

One might even argue that men are more highly socialized, women more highly individualized. Compare the uniformity of men's dress with the individuality of most women's fashion. A man who is not dressed like other men will feel embarrassed; a woman who is dressed like other women will similarly feel embarrassed.

Among women, degrees of intimacy are established according to the extent of secrets shared. Each woman contributes something personal that represents her as an individual; these contributions harmonize and resonate together. Women validate their identity as they come to know that their experiences as women are not uniquely theirs.

I will venture the following analogy: a woman relates to other women by attuning herself to the emotional tonality she is receiving, roughly like tuning an instrument with the aid of a tuning fork. An older woman becomes the emotional standard against which others tune themselves to attain connection.

This method comports risks. If a woman feels drawn sympathetically to someone who has suffered extreme abuse, she may attune herself to the other woman's pain and come to believe that she has experienced a comparable trauma.

According to Tannen, women in groups value cooperation, consensus, expression of personal feelings, conciliation, conversation, storytelling, and so on. This assertion must be qualified: women do these things in order to establish common feeling and shared intimacy, not to go out and compete on a football field. And whereas on a football team each player will have a very different role to play, in a women's group each woman will receive recognition for the uniqueness of her own experience. A group of women contains equal individuals; a group of men consists of guards, tackles, linebackers, tight ends, coaches, and owners.

Besides, any male culture that values "face" will prefer reconciliation over conflict. Saving face is the way men form consensus and conciliate differences in order to cooperate as a collective unit seeking to achieve a specific goal.

Once a woman's vulnerability has been exposed, for example, by confessing her deepest secret to her best friend, she has an important interest in avoiding conflict and confrontation. Women compete with other women—sometimes for men, sometimes over the relative success of their children—but they do not ordinarily form groups to compete with other groups or to transact business. The satisfaction of having a best friend or a close circle of female friends takes place on a different and more intimate level.

When men in business situations conciliate differences, they avoid intimacy and allow each man to maintain the appearance of having won something. Everyone must have some face, and be treated with the proper respect according to the rules that define the organizational hierarchy.

Women among themselves will attempt to protect each other's emotional vulnerability and to ensure that everyone feels liked and accepted. The performance of ritual and ceremonial gestures of respect, which gives face in a male organization, is of less importance than an open, honest, and genuine sharing of feelings.

Men and women represent two sides of face. A man must defend his title and status, sacrifice his personal happiness to the good of the team, and make every effort to avoid any reference to fault or failure. For a man, "loss" means losing status, or being a loser.

For a woman, self-respect is more directly tied to her body. Face, for a woman, does not stop at the neck. Thus emotion is valued because it shows more of the person; emotion would make a man more diffuse, less concentrated, a weaker competitor. Understanding your opponent's state of mind may grant you a competitive advantage; feeling bad for the loss you want to inflict on him will not.

In more common parlance, a woman's honor has usually referred to her sexual behavior; honor among women has been identified with chaste behavior. People today say that a woman who behaves promiscuously does not respect herself. Also, a woman's self-esteem has often been defined by how attractive she appears to men. The issue of how one is seen by others has always divided the sexes. While the uniformity of male dress draws attention away from the body, the diversity of female dress highlights and emphasizes a woman's body.

A woman's face is both a socially identifying feature and an instrument of erotic attractiveness. To maintain the latter a woman will from time to time modify her appearance with a new haircut or new makeup. She uses masquerade to signify that she does not belong fully to the public sphere, but that she represents another, more private place, one that is less consistent and more mysterious.

Women's issues in today's politics—freedom of reproductive choice, child care, and sexual harassment—directly concern the female body. The feminist agenda seeks to reclaim a woman's control over what happens to her body. But it has also, at times, repudiated those aspects of the feminine masquerade that women have deployed to create romance. Thereby it has addressed a difficult issue: How can a woman have a social identity in the workplace and still be the embodiment of feminine mystery, if she should so choose?

Avoiding the trappings of feminine beauty has always been a social option for women; it signifies lack of interest in the erotic mating dance. If we wish to change the social codes through which the sexes seek to attract each other, we must keep in mind that those codes allow some people to signal a wish not to be engaged.

When a woman wishes to be involved with men but decides

not to employ the feminine masquerade, she risks having her signals misinterpreted. If she compensates by becoming more explicit about her intentions, she may find that men feel she is sending mixed messages and cannot be trusted.

Confused signals also produce unwanted and inappropriate attention, most clearly in the workplace. The issue of sexual harassment shows the vulnerability of a woman's position in the business world. Directly linked to her bodily existence, it is most evident when a woman is working at a traditionally male job. On the job, a woman will take overt references to her sexual role as demeaning. Endearing terms place a woman outside the corporate world. And yet, she may feel some regret that no one notices how good she looks one day, and may even lose confidence in her attractiveness.

Does a woman therefore feel that the more she works within a male world, seeking prestige and status in the hierarchy, the more she will lose touch with her body?

Author Judith Posner suggested that when a woman considers whether her work has become too important, she will pay special heed to the messages her body is sending. "A woman who rejected a compulsive work ethic years ago, and has always been in touch with her body and its cycles, concluded very matter-of-factly: 'When I work too hard my blessed body puts a stop to it.' "[3] Another woman, discussing her decision to leave her job, said, "It's like I couldn't leave until I had no choice. Finally, it was my body which wouldn't let me stay. My body was screaming."[4]

A woman attunes herself to her own and other people's feelings because her authority and credibility, her ability to understand and to be understood, her human connections, will depend on it. No one gives up an advantage willingly. And this is so even if she seeks status in the more masculine world of business and commerce.

The difficulties faced by women who exist in two worlds—home and workplace—are most often discussed in terms of the demands of motherhood. Only women are mothers, and mothers have primary responsibility for bringing up children.

The description of women's communication offered by Tannen and many others fits quite well with the requirements of motherhood. The person charged with caring for an infant must be more attuned to nonverbal communications, must be more empathic with the needs of a helpless being, must be able to form connections in circumstances where titles and ranks do not matter. And the relationship between mother and child is certainly intimate. If children function outside adult shame culture, they must be brought up by someone whose being can be grounded on something other than competitive striving for hierarchical position.

Men and women now compete for the same promotions and the same accounts. Regrettably, they have brought the same spirit of competition into the home, fouling their conjugal relations.

The different roles of men and women in a traditional marriage complement each other, but only as long as each party can respect the integrity of a role that differs from his or her own. There is a significant difference between the idealistic and, for the most part, impractical solution of having husband and wife share all responsibilities equally and the more obvious situation of having each party respect the validity of the other's contribution to a marriage.

The marriage contract is based on mutual respect for ''face'' and for the integrity of the couple as a social unit with common interests. Such a contract requires that people follow some basic rules. As Aaron Beck wrote, ''It is a given that one spouse is expected to do nothing to diminish the other's social image. Thus, in public, the spouse should be concerned, helpful, respectful, and should avoid being callous, uncooperative, and disparaging. Finally, rules regarding the financial security of the family, such as not overspending, are vital to its existence. These rules are quite reasonable [but] if people treat them as absolutes and inviolable, and if infractions are regarded as warranting punishment, a conflict is inevitable.''[5]

In almost all cultures a married couple has a shared identity; the achievements and honors of the one are shared by the other. Having a stake in her husband's success, a wife would have little interest in challenging it; her own success would rest more in how well her home functions and in how well her family coheres.

The issue cannot be whether or not women should work outside the home. Women always have worked outside the home, and people have rarely given it a second thought. The idea of women who do not have to work outside the home derives from aristocratic practices.

Does a woman's having a career imply that she rejects the idea of shared pride and common interests? This might make her a competitor and therefore not a trustworthy partner. Is her career an explicit or implicit criticism of her husband's role of breadwinner? Men who oppose their wives working see it as a criticism of their ability to support their families and to bring honor to others beyond themselves. If a woman decides that she does not want to associate herself with her husband's "face," this counts for many men as a rejection.

A man will be more concerned with how it looks to others that his wife, for example, is too busy to accompany him to a corporate function, while a woman will place greater value on the quality of communication the couple achieves while they are alone together. These are not competing priorities, but clearly each partner must accommodate the other's need to maintain a different kind of face.

The absence of women from the home has produced one set of difficulties. The presence of women in male-dominated professions has produced another. Pervasive sexual harassment is part of the problem, but not all of it. The larger issue concerns the fact that girls have not in the past been socialized to the kinds of rules and games that exist in the workplace.

The skills that Tannen considers to be proper for women can often come into conflict with the requirements of career advancement. Women grant greater authority to their feelings than to a set of abstract rules and obligations, and this makes it far more difficult for them to overlook flaws and errors in the interest of presenting the best public face. At the risk of generalizing, women are taught to be truthful—true to their feelings, true to their friends, true to their love. If the marketplace is defined by the necessity to maintain the appearance of propriety, the home will represent truths that are hidden from public view.

Moreover, an executive whose actions are determined by clear policy directives is far easier to follow than one who allows himself to change course when things do not feel right. Since feelings are private, it is very difficult for others to know where they will lead.

Certainly, women have not been welcomed into the corporate world with open arms. No matter how well they have been socialized to the rules of business conduct, women are usually treated like alien creatures invading a male domain. Even once inside, they are often excluded, not treated as members of the team, not asked to join in the various bonding rituals that constitute group solidarity.

Evidently these exclusions give women the impression that they are being punished for reasons that solely concern their gender, but it also reinforces an impression that something is being hidden from them. And if this something is honorable, why would anyone have to hide it? Women are held in suspicion and come to be suspicious themselves.

Women who join the work force are often astonished that things are not at all what they seemed, that unethical practices occur commonly, that men tend to cover up for each other, that they prefer to hide rather than reveal faults.[6] Being a team player and sacrificing personal truth in the interest of the team's competitive performance are not values that generally prevail among women. Relationships among women value truthfulness and the ability to reveal secrets and vulnerabilities.

Some women propose to reform the workplace by introducing values with which they feel more comfortable. In some cases this may be useful, in others not. The bottom line in business, however, is the bottom line. And the reforms instituted to accommodate more women on the job will have to produce results that are equal to the results that were produced in the old, male-dominant world.

Some jobs are so demanding, and the competition so fierce, that it is nearly impossible to have a "life" outside of work. The condition of associates at the major New York law firms comes immediately to mind. These jobs were created for people who had wives at home. Either everyone will have to work less, or else women will be required to make sacrifices that their male colleagues do not have to make.

Most often, however, a woman will leave her company before the company becomes feminized. Women leave jobs where masculine values dominate, particularly large bureaucratic organizations, to move into smaller businesses, where creativity and individual effort count more than existing within a rigid hierarchy. The marketplace has been offering more and more opportunities for women to work in careers of their choice. Where this choice is free, women find some work environments congenial and others unappealing. Idem for men.

At times introducing women into some workplaces has reduced worker morale. This problem was recently isolated by sociologists in a study of the effect of introducing people who are different from others into a work group. In their report, "Being Different: Relational Demography and Organizational Attachment,"[7] Professors Anne Tsui, Terri Egan, and Charles O'Reilly III, offer what they claim is one of the first studies of what happens to the majority of workers when people different from the norm are introduced. They demonstrate that when work groups lose their homogeneity, the male majority shows diminished commitment and loyalty to the group, increased absenteeism, and general dissatisfaction.

Why should this be so? A job that tends to be dominated by men will provide a sense of masculine identity for those who hold it. The more women there are, the less the occupation will provide a masculine identity. Eventually, it will become associated with femininity and lose status. Moreover, in a sexually mixed workplace the different modes of communication will necessarily produce more misunderstanding and require more time to rectify the ensuing difficulties.

Tsui et al. report that morale loss has also been evident when other "low-status" individuals, especially blacks, are introduced into an otherwise homogeneous group.

Thomas Sowell has described well the difficulties inherent in diverse workplace environments: "intergroup incompatibilities can raise production costs, whether through interruptions of work by arguments or fights, through mistakes in communication because of the workers' misunderstanding of each other's language, or because an atmosphere of tension in the workplace lowers morale in general or causes a firm to lose its best workers, who are more likely to have job alternatives available elsewhere, in less tense surroundings."[8]

Of course, one fundamental difference only appears when sex is in question. I will call it the locker room complex. If a group of same-sexed individuals is in a locker room, the introduction of a member of the opposite sex will produce an immediate sense of shame. At that point they will all know that they are naked. They may cover their sex; they may expel the unwanted intruder; or they may become extremely self-conscious of their behavior, lest they offend their visitor. Finally, they may seek to harass the intruder by mockery; they are in uniform, the intruding individual is not.

If, on the other hand, a same-sexed representative of a different racial or ethnic group were to enter, the people in the locker room would not become immediately conscious of their nakedness.

In her study of conflict resolution in Japan, Susan Pharr emphasized the importance of homogeneity: "Homogeneity (based on shared experience, attitudes, language, and so forth) operates to insure that superiors understand the vantage point of inferiors and take their position into account.''[9]

Mixing ethnic groups normally upsets the homogeneity of the workplace. Women, of course, are not an ethnic group; they are an indispensable part of any culture. Their presence in the work force poses a complex problem: they represent different priorities from the male group, and they belong to the same culture as the dominant males.

Traditionally, women have tended to gravitate toward ''women's work,'' attaining to a status that corresponds to their status within the family. This has not caused problems.

Nontraditionally, women have recently begun entering male occupations in increasing numbers and have pursued careers that are in conflict with their traditional roles.

This has posed its own set of difficulties. The women who are competing with men on the job are often also seeking to have a romantic life with men outside the workplace. Obviously, ethnic groups can live separately in ways that men and women often cannot.

The entry of women into male-dominant professions has placed great strains on marriages; the more a woman sees her career as more important than family, the more a man risks losing face.

Cleverly, men have adopted new ways to save face under the new social conditions. A very successful man will assert that his professionally accomplished wife adds to his stature because it shows him to good advantage. But only so long as the man's success outdistances that of the woman. Media magnate Ted Turner married the highly accomplished Jane Fonda. Senator Robert Dole's wife, Elizabeth, has had a distinguished career without anyone's thinking that the senator's face was threatened.

A man will rarely choose a woman who is more successful than he is, because this will make him look bad in the eyes of other men. And if his woman's career is relatively equal to his own, a man will save face by subtly disparaging her career: it pays less well, it is women's work, she's great with the children, she got the job because of her gender, she still has beautiful skin. A successful woman will feel that she can offer more love to a man because she does not need to rely on his income. Her motivations are clear: she does not wish to compete or contest his status as breadwinner; she simply wants to offer the kind of pure love whose acceptance would be face-saving for her.

For women, liberation often promises that economic independence and social autonomy allow for a free and unadulterated offer of love. And yet, this means that a woman professional will have a different agenda from her male colleague.

If a woman in the workplace does not compete with male co-workers who have similar ambitions, she will be placing herself at a disadvantage.

The best we can say is that we are only beginning to face the complexity of these issues. Certainly, they are often played out in ways that largely escape what legislation and litigation can control.

Beyond overt sexual harassment, there are subtle forms of disregard that discomfort working women by producing an environment that is neither conducive to cooperation nor overtly hostile. I am thinking of the small, almost imperceptible gestures that fall well short of outright harassment: the animated conversation between men that abruptly ends once a woman appears, the failure to offer gratitude to women workers, the glance that is averted so that a woman is neither seen nor acknowledged when she is walking down the hall, the blank expression when a woman speaks up at a meeting. Then there are the minor slights, like failing to invite a woman to after-work drinks, ignoring her suggestions, speaking ill of her behind her back. None of this constitutes criminal activity; it cannot be policed with the means now available. Yet, it does exist, and it does reflect attitudes that often remain unacknowledged.

Were a woman included in men's conversations, the nature

of the conversations would necessarily change—similarly, for two women talking when a man appears. If the conversation concerns experiences outside work, two men will have more in common than will a man and a woman. And if there is no place where men can get together and discuss their experiences as men, they will feel repressed by society and will react with hostility to those they hold responsible.

Another kind of male solidarity is based on traditional views of the sexual division of labor. If John's friend Paul is disconsolate because he does not have a job, John is not likely to look kindly at the fact that Paul has been replaced by Sally. If Paul was John's supervisor, and if Sally now holds that post, John may very well find himself less capable of following the directions Sally gives, not because they are worse, but because he has trouble taking orders from a woman.

All men first encounter women as mothers; they recall a time when the person who knew them at their most vulnerable was a woman. When a man believes that women see his posturing as a façade, he will recoil from situations where women have authority over him.

The other problem concerns leading by setting an example. If a manager sets the mood of a workplace by his behavior, his manners, his decorum, as well as by the orders he gives, he exercises leadership by providing an example for others to emulate. And people often emulate their betters unconsciously. Among the reasons that a man will not want a female superior is this: he risks adopting feminine habits that will cause him to be ridiculed in the world of men. While a male employee might feel it a point of honor to dispute the authority of a female manager, a female employee may feel that she has more to gain than to lose for being under the authority of a male manager.

A woman may well adopt masculine traits unconsciously by emulating a male boss. Society, however, shows less prejudice toward this form of cross-identification than it does toward male effeminacy.

For the woman herself, society's tolerance may not suffice to compensate for the fact that the more she adopts masculine traits the less romantic attention she receives from men. Masculine cues are evidently not designed to attract men.

In some cases women react by placing an undue emphasis on the outward signs of femininity, sometimes pursuing beauty to extreme ends. Often to little avail. When the cues concern tone of voice, gestures, attitude, and movement, these are not affected by a new lipstick or a face-lift.

Of late, perceptions about relations between the sexes have been dominated by extreme cases: the abusive wife beater, the child-molesting father, the sexually predatory teenage boy, the hysteric, the witch. These are compelling dramatic images; they speak to a pervasive feeling that the sexes no longer maintain even the pretense of getting along. To remedy the situation we will need to recognize that extremes are not the rule: if they were, the problems would be insoluble and sexual differences would be irreconcilable. Examine first sexual harassment.

We recognize that there are degrees of sexual harassment; if penalties are imposed on those who engage in such activities, then the penalties must concord with the severity of the offense. Men who force female subordinates into sexual acts, men who make women run a gauntlet of clawing hands, and men who propose exchanging promotion for sexual favors are at an extreme where severe sanctions are warranted.

On the other side, men who tell an off-color joke in a woman's presence, who admire a woman's appearance, or who use a derogatory word in speaking about women ought to be subject to less severe sanctions. As always it is better to appeal to a sense of decency than to a fear of punishment.

If society decides that all forms of sexual harassment are equivalent to felonious rape, it will be impossible to form a viable social consensus against the more egregious forms of this offense. A woman's accusation will be taken less seriously if it does not correspond to a society's version of what does and does not constitute a criminal infraction. Also, social custom defines what is and is not harassment. What counts as offensive behavior in one social group might be considered joking around in another.

Making sexual harassment into the norm that defines relations between the sexes has had a devastating effect on such relations outside the workplace. Teaching people to fear each other—as though there were no other way to show respect—distorts relationships. The more energy you spend defending yourself against real and imaginary dangers the less effort you will invest in finding ways to get closer.

Seasoned adults know that their language must be modified to fit their relationships with their interlocutors. Young people do not draw such subtle distinctions, even less so today since no one seems especially concerned with teaching courteous ways for the sexes to relate.

Shame culture promotes reform rather than punishment, education rather than stigmatization, conciliation rather than litigation. Cases of harassment ought, whenever possible, to be resolved in private. A man who oversteps the bounds of propriety ought to have the opportunity to apologize and mend his ways. Our goal should be to eliminate sexual harassment, not necessarily to inflict bodily punishment on every man who has ever done it.

A more general issue can be addressed here. Some of what constitutes sexual harassment is supposed to represent "normal behavior" in what are called male-bonding rituals: derogatory remarks about women, fantasies that are less than kind and gentle, leering and shouting at certain vulgar displays of the female body, and so on.

We should reflect before accepting this stereotype as typical of male behavior. Men have been much maligned recently, and they have, regrettably, fought back in ways that tend to confirm the worst judgments of their behavior. The truth is that adult men do not seek to bond with others of their kind so they can make stupid remarks about women, nor do they look at every female who crosses their path as a potential sexual conquest, nor do all their thoughts and fantasies involve criminal enterprise. Stereotyping men as sexual predators does not make them courteous and considerate toward women.

Young men especially are the most hormonally challenged. They have strong sexual impulses and respond quickly to sexual stimuli in the environment. If they are unmarried or unattached their sexuality has not been socialized; thus, they have not been accepted publicly by women as sexually competent beings. The more stimuli they are exposed to the more they may feel the need to process their reactions by acknowledging them before others who share them.

Why then do they need to do so in such repulsive terms? Responding to such stimuli places men in a vulnerable position; they use deprecating humor to pretend that they are in charge when they are not. Tender expressions of care among men count as weakness and vulnerability, causing the man who makes them to lose stature.

A second difficulty concerns the way men interpret sexual stimuli. When a woman passes a group of men wearing an outfit that is sexually enticing, no member of the group believes that she is attempting to seduce him. When each man reacts to the stimuli he must be able to assert that it is acceptable to have a male response but that it is not acceptable to believe that the woman's signals are addressed to any one of them in particular. Strangely enough, sharing the response makes it less likely that any one of them misinterprets the signal.

Perhaps this stretches the point. And yet, if the attractively dressed woman were your friend's wife, sharing your feelings of sexual excitement in vulgar terms would not be appropriate.

Married men, for example, rarely engage in adolescent banter about female anatomy. If they possess a minimal sense of dignity they do not brag about their sexual experiences with their wives. To derogate one's wife is to derogate oneself.

The absolutist position on sexual harassment says that any discourteous remark must be condemned, no matter where it is made. This leads to a wish to police all male behavior, even if it requires extensive invasion of privacy. The shame culture position holds that what men say among themselves in private is of no one's concern; how they behave toward women in their lives is subject to sanction when it becomes noxious.

But are they not then, to recall the words of Confucius, taking advantage of a darkened room, thus cultivating a bad habit that risks manifesting itself in other forms of behavior? No more than the habit of undressing at home would lead you to undress on a street corner. In fact, they are following the rules that pertain within a profane space like a bar or a bordello. Feelings that are ventilated in such spaces are presumed to be proper to the space but no others. The men who are drinking and cursing are effectively repudiating thoughts that might well have been planted in their minds but with which they choose to dissociate themselves. When the news showers us with so many violent and erotic images, how else are we to process and discard them?

It commonly happens that two men will make jokes at each other's expense, without this being taken as a reflection of the feelings of each for the other. And self-deprecating humor is commonly understood as a sign of humility, not a sign of tendencies toward self-objectification.

Men who are involved in occupations that require high degrees of aggressiveness tend to believe that the presence of a woman will take away their edge. They believe that their own tendencies toward courtesy and protection will make them less fierce competitors. Are they right or wrong, and how much of a risk should we take?

Consider a recent example. When Mikhail Gorbachev was the leader of the Soviet Union, his wife, Raisa, wanted to inspect a submarine, despite the fact that Soviet naval personnel maintained a prejudice that if a woman sets foot on a submarine, that vessel is "jinxed." Thinking this to be irrational, Mrs. Gorbachev undertook the inspection. In the aftermath no one from the Soviet navy would go back onto the submarine and it had to be decommissioned.

Here we are clearly dealing with an irrational opinion. But if that irrational opinion produces a military calamity, ought one still to disregard it?[10]

Societies change their sexual policies, as ours has recently, which is all to the good. At present people seem to evaluate these changes according to whether they feel happier as individuals. But this is shortsighted. In the long run society will appraise the changes in terms of whether they produce increased economic growth and social harmony.

Sexual policies will be judged in the economic marketplace that produces and distributes goods and services. If the new policy is accompanied by economic decline or social chaos, people will turn against it. Personal satisfaction will be overruled by the general misery that accompanies social disintegration, and society will eventually come to believe that certain types of individual happiness are nothing more than a way of learning to enjoy being a loser.

To exit guilt cultural thinking about the division of the sexes, we must agree that the division is not the consequence of a worldwide trans-historical conspiracy inflicted by men on women.

Men do not seek to exploit women; they did not invent marriage to prevent women from fulfilling their potential. As a social convention, marriage has a very long history, during most of which it has followed roughly the same form. As such it deserves respect for its durability; it serves a social purpose and has done so better than any other formula available to date. It is also subject to modification as the conditions of human life change.

The increased longevity of human beings makes it such that a woman will spend a relatively smaller proportion of her adult life dealing with child care; thus the need to make a substantive place for women in the workplace takes on greater urgency.

Any modifications of the social contract must be held to some standards of objective evaluation. The old contract was designed to allow men to concentrate their attentions more fully on the marketplace and to permit women to focus their energies on the task of raising children. Any new contract must be judged by its ability to fulfill these socially valuable functions.

The myth of a male conspiracy to oppress women is part of the guilt narrative that formed in the nation after Vietnam. This narrative resulted from the failure of American males on the field of battle. Women saw themselves suffering the consequences of Vietnam without having had very much say in the conduct of policy. It was like taxation without representation. But it also meant that women were not guilty of what happened in Vietnam; thus they were well placed to claim a moral high ground in opposition to the military-industrial complex.

The sexual side of the post-Vietnam guilt narrative has shown women breaking free from their deadening marriages, fighting abusive husbands, and rejecting the life society set out for them in favor of alternate lifestyles. Women saw themselves as morally obligated to rebel against the male-dominant culture and to free themselves from its failures. Thus they could lead men out of the wilderness of patriarchy and into the light of redemptive equality.

Intellectuals contributed mightily to the formation of this narrative. By promoting the value of women's literature they asserted that men had failed because of their inability to hear different voices. The anti-pornography movement seemed to hold that sex between men and women is fundamentally abusive of women. Susan Brownmiller's *Against Our Will* argued that a male will to rape women lies beneath the surface of all heterosexual intercourse.

Real events, most often public trials, have also fed the narrative. The Clarence Thomas–Anita Hill hearings showed many women that they too had been sexually harassed. Their outrage filled the airwaves. Well-publicized trials, like the McMartin Pre-School case in California, made it appear that the sexual abuse of children was rampant in our society.

These cases are supposed to demonstrate that the two sexes are moral absolutes. Men and women are engaged in a battle and cannot coexist harmoniously. In the extreme versions, a woman's depending on a man for financial support makes her an indentured servant, and a man's paying for a woman's dinner invites her to prostitute herself.

No narrative ought to be the basis for social policies. Fictions enact and embody dilemmas; any solutions they offer are as fictional as the characters who play them out.

When translated into policy, narratives produce contradictions. How can society encourage men to spend more time parenting when the media are saturated with horror stories of men who sexually abuse their children? What sense does it make to deconstruct the role of breadwinner and then call for the prosecution of deadbeat dads?

Obviously the problems are real. But rather than take men to be potential sexual deviants, why not grant them virtuous tendencies that social practices can cultivate? When men object to the revolutionary changes society is undergoing, perhaps they deserve a serious hearing.

Second, we need to recognize that women are not always innocent. Usually men produce the most visually compelling forms of abuse, but it is not excluded that a woman shows great hostility toward a man by rejecting him emotionally, insulting and mocking his efforts, or otherwise undermining his confidence in his own abilities.

If men have failed to show proper respect for women, we should also acknowledge that many women have refused to allow men to use the traditional gestures that signify it.

Part of the solution concerns the general behavior of men toward women through decorum and courtesy. Men who open doors for women, who hold their chairs, help them with their coats, treat them to dinner, and practice traditional etiquette are promoting respect by setting a public example of proper behavior.

Admittedly, a relationship governed by courtesy is less passionate, less spontaneous, less surprising, than one that jettisons decorum in favor of desire.

Some would say that courtesy is demeaning because it seeks to keep women in their place by treating them as weak and feeble. They see these gestures as signifying that women cannot take the initiative, be independent, or care for themselves. Clearly, this is a false alternative. The fact that a man holds a door for a woman does not mean that either of them believes that she is incapable of opening a door. If he holds her coat for her, this does not mean that either of them believes that she does not know how to dress herself.

These behaviors simply allow respect to function publicly in relations between the sexes. They decrease aggression and violence, even at the cost of diminished passion. Also, customs are always subject to modification. If society decides that it no longer wishes to have people bow and curtsy, or that it no longer wishes to have men open doors for women, it is no great loss. The problem arises when no new customs are produced to replace the ones that have been discarded.

The post-Vietnam era in America saw an increasing concern with women's issues and with the values traditionally associated with femininity. A society producing a guilt narrative will direct its attention more toward women's experience. To mask the shame of failing at war, many Americans sought to belittle the masculine ethos and to esteem those members of society whose identity has nothing to do with martial values.

Incapable of facing the shame of failure, men retreated into worlds of fiction and feeling. Identifying with those who were not responsible for a trauma allowed many men to proclaim their innocence and occupy a moral ground from which they could denounce the culpable parties.

In Western culture the final form of guilt narratives is redemptive. For someone who has failed, guilt narratives make a seductive offer. They tell the failed businessman that the system is itself corrupt. His failing is a sign of virtue; he was incapable of playing and winning in an evil world. Thus his failure stands as a sign of his transcendent goodness; his true fault was losing touch with his capacity to love. Then he can rediscover his love for his wife and children, qualities he had overlooked while he was pursuing filthy lucre. Instead of thinking that he has lost everything, he discovers that he has regained his soul. He may even find new friends, change his party affiliation, and join a cult. Out of his failure will be born a new identity, a new group membership, and a new happiness.

Some men try to make their lives accord with a guilt narrative by renouncing public obligation in favor of decadent pleasures. In place of the man's man, who dominates in shame cultures, these new men will be ladies' men. They will exude charisma; they will charm and seduce. Attuned to women's feelings they will excel at winning women's love, ultimately to reject it because it is all they are capable of winning.

A culture in which the traditional view of family duty breaks down will replace it with various forms of passionate attachment. It will model relationships on adolescent infatuation: two young people who have few obligations forge an exclusive connection through the power of their love.

But how does romantic desire derive from guilt culture? Essentially, by default. Since shame culture avoids open discussion of sexual matters, guilt culture has been able to colonize the field and assert pride of ownership. It does so, putatively, to protect individuals from abusive authority figures. Since authority is subject to abuse, guilt culture declares that all authority is abusive and that another culture must be created beyond its reach. Nothing is further beyond its reach than the sanctum sanctorum of a woman's boudoir.

Guilt culture pretends to support social order by subjecting sexuality to taboos. To the extent that such taboos are coercive they produce sexual desire, and attempt to make it the defining experience of a new culture.

Shame culture sees normal sexual activity taking place within marriage, regulated by the concept of reciprocal conjugal duty. Guilt culture declares that this rule oppresses women; it proposes a more exciting and satisfying sexuality under the banner of defiance and rebellion. It offers a new culture in which women are in control.

The dominance of romance is based on two master narratives: one says that human institutions are the enemy of individual fulfillment through love. Being in love makes people rebel; their love threatens the social order; its representatives will try to destroy them; ultimately, love will triumph. The other sees men racked by their criminal sexual impulses, tempted to exercise them, and learning to control them by developing a conscience and by engaging in other forms of self-castigation. The process requires the mediation of a good woman. A man will learn to emulate her virtue and reject traditional masculine values in favor of redemption.

Whether Dante's Beatrice or Raskolnikov's Sonya, the love of a woman shows the way. The salutary power of a feminine balm resolves the conflict that the guilt narrative has produced. Justice favors love over duty.

Guilt culture neither mediates nor reconciles; it attempts to sharpen differences in the hope that their dialectical friction will produce erotic love. We recall that Plato's myth of the creation of Eros involves an act of female-dominant copulation between two characters named Poverty and Plenty, lack and excess. The story is told in *The Symposium.*

In this myth the female character, Poverty, exercises power over her reluctant male partner, Plenty. As the story goes, Poverty seduces Plenty by getting him inebriated to the point that he can no longer resist her charms. Once he is completely drunk, she has her way with him; as a result she gives birth to Eros.

Another version of this myth produced the medieval practice of courtly love. Ladies left waiting in their castles while their lords were off fighting the Crusades evolved a romantic practice of seducing the adolescent youths who were working for them. These youths became poets and troubadours: they showered their female masters with adulation and expressions of affection; they offered to undergo any trial to prove the sincerity of their love. The woman's gift of *merci* would resolve the narrative tension and redeem the youth's travails . . . for a time.

Perhaps women must dominate the realm of desire because they have a greater stake in its outcome. Women are certainly more at home with feelings of love. Plato's Poverty is more comfortable with exposing her vulnerability. The male Plenty must be ''coaxed'' into such self-exposure. Only an adolescent male who has little status can place himself in such a vulnerable position in relation to a woman; for him it is an apprenticeship, thus he risks little.

The importance of desire in guilt narratives gives the impression that guilt culture owns romance and that shame culture would cause it to wither and dry up. What then does love have to do with face?

The power women exercise in romance has everything to do with the way they present (and hide) face. From the most extreme case of wearing a veil to the more moderate cases of changing hairstyles and makeup, social practice has almost universally required a woman's face to be camouflaged. As with the female body, a woman's face has often been defined by an interplay of exposure and concealment.

Traditional feminine attire supposedly works to entice, induce, and seduce. A man is lured through partial revelation promising further discoveries. Whatever exists behind the veil must never be exposed in public. Such exposure would make it into a commodity.

Clearly, sexual attraction between men and women is promoted by modesty. Constant exposure of nakedness is anti-erotic.

The same also applies to the exposure of all emotions and secrets. Complete concealment of the body also thwarts desire. A woman who never reveals any of her emotions is choosing to avoid erotic attachments.

At one extreme, the nun's habit signifies that the game of seduction is not being played; at the other, the tramp's public display makes seduction into a business transaction.

Under normal circumstances romance must avoid both extremes. But note the following problem. A woman who dresses up for a party is not doing it for the attention of each man who sees her. Partially exposed, she is vulnerable, and will be obliged to use various gestures to select the person to whom she is addressing what appears to be a public display. This is the specific vulnerability of her position and role.

She deals with this vulnerability by disguising her face and dissimulating her identity through the use of cosmetics and the like.

Others who see her may believe that she wishes to attract them, and they are usually disabused of this assumption by signals that tell them their suppositions are unfounded. She may take the arm of the man she is with, display a wedding band, refer conspicuously to one man in conversation—these gestures signal that romantic approaches from others are unwelcome.

Seduction requires face-saving compromises, but these cannot be compared to those achieved in the marketplace, because men and women are not using the same currency. One is presenting the signs of public status and position, the other the values of privacy, the home, and intimacy. Thus, face saving in these circumstances requires each partner to respect the fact that the other has different priorities and a different role in their erotic dance.

In one type of seduction, a woman will play to a man's sense of his own self-importance by asking him to inform her of the fascinating work he does and of his many successes in it. She will play to a typically male propensity. She will seduce him by showing that she sees him as a man. He in turn will respond with flattery, gifts, and the kind of romantic words that he believes she wants to hear. He will tell her how unique and special she is, how beautiful she looks—in order to make her feel that he values her as an individual woman. He will play to her confidence in the goodness of her soul, the richness of her inner life. In seduction, as in friendship, people see others at their best.

If she prizes romance, a woman does not present herself as she is, but as how he wishes she were. Her compensation is the satisfaction of exercising her creative faculties in constructing a public persona.

A budding romance requires dissimulation and mutual deception. Since face is not yet involved, the relationship is unstable. It may glow in the dark, but eventually it will have to present itself in the light of day. The social being of each party requires this transition. As soon as two lovers are socially recognized as a couple in their respective worlds, face will be involved.

Young love retains its charm only for a short period of time. As happens at *A Masked Ball* of operatic fame, when the clock strikes and the convives remove their masks, he discovers that she is not who he thought she was, and she discovers that he is not who she thought he was. That is when the true challenge begins.

In romantic love the requirements of propriety and conformity take second place to those of mystery and intimacy. Within a shame culture courtship is not an end in itself, but a prelude to something else. The attraction between two people will be enhanced by the discovery that it need not conflict with duty. This is the precondition for a comic outcome. If love is a mystery, it must find a resolution.

Romance is the one instance in which what is masked is not shame but face. That is why a woman's face offers the most apt representation of this game. When women dispense with the feminine masquerade, the game of romance falls flat.

Desire can only be sustained within a social context; it may not have the fiery quality of a mad passion, but for lack of that quality it will have a far better chance of enduring over time. A woman who knows how to organize a home need not abandon the qualities of surprise and unpredictability that make for romance in marriage. It is one thing to be late, quite another to be unreliable.

Examine the workings of seduction from this perspective. If a woman arrives late for a dinner date, her failure to adhere strictly to ceremonial form serves a specific romantic purpose. It surrounds her with an air of mystery and allure, enhances her presence, and makes it appear that she is not too anxious, that she has other things to do, that she is not too available, and that she must be won. If she were a man, and if the dinner were a business meeting, her lateness would give offense.

As with any breach of etiquette, this one calls forth various narratives to account for the disrupted routine. The man who is nervously sipping his second drink will normally imagine stories that account for her tardiness. They will range from her having been held up at the office to her having been involved in an accident. His initial expectations about the sight of her entering the restaurant and the content of their conversation will have already been thrown into question.

The woman's absence creates a mystery, and the man will invent different fictional solutions. A studied use of impropriety attracts by transforming the frustration of being kept waiting into a sign of romantic interest.

A woman's lateness ought to produce a reaction in her companion; preferably he will interpret his mix of fantasy and frustration as a sign of his own romantic interest rather than as a sign of her being unreliable.

Here the rules are stretched and bent but not broken. This is allowable because the lovers are acting from behind masks; they are not dealing with each other face to face. They are trying to convince themselves that each one is someone else, someone who corresponds to the image that each is looking for.

The greatest seducer is a chameleon. Camouflage protects it

from predators at the same time that it lures victims into striking range without their becoming suspicious.

Since women seem to have a larger stake in these matters, the task of maintaining the romance in relationships usually falls to them. Women are more apt to make adjustments in their appearance to fulfill male images of desirable partners than are men. This happens because women represent the private domain in public. Male dress does not signify sexual desirability, but professional accomplishment.

Nowadays women are almost obliged to be two-faced. They function within the public domain as members of the work force: there the rules of face apply to them as much as they apply to men. But in the world of romance women must function from behind a mask. At times this even involves masking professional achievements.

Women represent privacy, the home, even the sacred; they control romance because they represent things that are mysterious, indecipherable, subject to interpretation. What is private ought rightly to remain hidden; it loses something whenever it suffers public exposure.

Usually men respect a woman's privacy. No man ever really wants to know everything a woman is thinking or feeling; he prefers to remain intrigued, fascinated, infatuated.

Nothing is more intimate and private to a woman than her love. And yet this private activity also has a public face. A woman is often judged according to how well she provides a home for her family and an upbringing for her children. At other times she is given credit for her husband's successes and blame for his failures.

Romance is another story; to make it work a woman must never allow men to forget, upon meeting her, that she is "in costume" and that she has been sent out into a public domain as an emissary from another world.

A woman's self-respect is defined by her ability to maintain that balance, to uphold the importance of privacy, home, and even romance. In recent years women have gained additional self-respect through their achievements in the workplace. Regrettably, this new self-respect has been attained with a corresponding loss of confidence in the ability to attract men.

If women feel especially insecure about their feminine charms, this must reflect either their knowledge or their anxiety that these charms are losing some of their power. When a woman decides to postpone marriage, she will perhaps need greater confirmation of her romantic appeal—especially if she has undergone more romantic traumas than has another woman who married her first love out of college.

The larger lesson is that a woman's gain of self-respect for mastering the game of management consulting does not permute into the kind of self-respect gained by being the master of the game of love. Men ought to respect women's professional achievements. If a man is related to a woman, he ought to take pride in her achievements, just as she would in his. Beyond that, most men do not find a woman's achievements to be sexually enticing. Very few women have ever seduced a man by showing off their M.B.A.s or Ph.D.s. We would make some modest progress if men did not allow such achievements to dampen their ardor.

All of this sounds quaint and outdated, at best. While the traditional woman's role tended toward making women homebound and excessively modest, to the point of being mysterious to themselves, the new roles for women have gone too far in the opposite direction. Today women are overexposed.

The truths about women's lives and experiences have, more often than not, been shrouded in mystery. Under the influence of the American Cultural Revolution our society seems to have decided that rendering women into a sacred mystery was a sign of systematic repression.

Repression theorists concluded that the failure to speak publicly about women's experience was detrimental to everyone's well-being and that only full disclosure could remedy the situation. Thus many people tried to lift the repression by exposing each and every aspect of feminine experience.

Confessional and highly personal articles, books, films, to say nothing of everyday conversation, lifted a veil that society had thrown over various aspects of women's experience. Pornographers exploited the situation to their own benefit, and the advertising profession used television to expose products that concern the most intimate aspects of women's experience. Television advertising today commonly portrays menstruation, yeast infections, women's bladder control problems, douching, mammograms, and feminine hygiene deodorants, with no embarrassment.

The news media have followed suit. Beyond the frank discussion of women's health issues, journalists found that viewers were fascinated by endless discussions of what it feels like to have been abused, traumatized, raped, molested. The habit of self-exposure often tells people more than they ever wanted to know. It may provide useful information to the voting public, but, still and all, one has to wonder how the public weal was served by televising the William Kennedy Smith trial. Was any purpose served by providing viewers a graphic description of an alleged rape, accompanied by scenes of the jurors passing the alleged victim's underwear from hand to hand?

Women have also claimed the right to expose their own sexuality in ways that make sense to them. Now women speak in their own voices, of their own experiences. Whether through *The Hite Report on Feminine Sexuality* and Erica Jong's *Fear of Flying*, at the beginning of this movement, or, more recently, a book called *The Erotic Silence of the American Wife*, women have claimed possession of their own sexuality. If women were simply communicating with other women, there would be no problem here. The problem arises because these communications are in the public domain.

But how do women take back their sexuality when they are exposing it in public? How can a woman feel that there is something mysterious about her when some version of everything she has ever felt is public knowledge? How can she feel that she has something special she can offer to a man and that he can only find with her when the same thing, or a reasonable facsimile, is available everywhere?

The most compelling contemporary clinical manifestation of the overexposure of the female body exists in those young women who are obsessed with weight. Dieting fads, self-induced vomiting, constant exercise, time spent searching for flaws in the mirror, the quest for the perfect body—these are obsessive preoccupations for far too many young women in our culture.

Beginning in the seventies, eating disorders became a near epidemic, persisting through the eighties and into the nineties. Women suffering from them act as though they are bearing a stigma, a sense of being constantly exposed to public view, judged wanting, and rejected.

Some women attempt to control their weight by making eating a crime. The binge-purge syndrome corresponds well to the transgression-punishment dyad. And, as always, this does not deal with shame.

Bearing a stigma means having nowhere to hide; nothing can conceal the least bodily flaw. Surprisingly, these women do not believe that fashion and cosmetics can cover defects. They despair of creating a minimal sense of mystery or an aura of seduction, and if they do, they are convinced that someone will discover that the mystery conceals some ugly truth. Perhaps they are suffering because they have lost faith in the feminine masquerade.

Having overcome shame, women with eating disorders have fallen into guilt culture. What they are seeking, often desperately, is a secret, something that is intimate to them, some way in which they can feel mysterious and alluring, even if only to a mental health professional.

How can we go about solving some of the problems that have befallen relations between the sexes in the post-Vietnam era? If we do so by reviving a sense of shame, here that means restoring the division between public and private.

In the home the values associated with intimacy, caring, and relating must be granted pride of place. These are the values that define a woman's self-respect. Intimacy is the other side of face, the private rather than the public side. It concerns those aspects of one's personality that one shares only with a small number of people. If known by the public, these things compromise one's ability to command respect in a public position.

Since everyone, ultimately, is naked beneath the uniform, and since that nakedness will be known by some people, the ability to consecrate private spaces and to confide in people who are worthy of trust is critically important. The ethical virtues implied in the position of intimacy involve loyalty, reliability, and responsibility, and to these must be added silence and the ability to keep secrets.

Maintaining intimacy also involves the ability to tell lies in order to avoid offending other people or hurting their feelings. Keeping up appearances is essential to a functional marriage, even when one is obliged to hide some things from one's spouse. People need to overcome the idea that the best way to relate to each other is through truth-telling, self-exposure, and carping criticism. If you do not have confidence in your spouse's abilities and character, your own judgment of a mate is subject to serious doubt. And if you cannot express encouragement and support when you have some doubt, then you are actively engaged in undermining the other person.

Everyone who has surpassed the age of adult reason knows that if you want your lover to do better at lovemaking it is better to offer praise than blame. Blame undermines self-confidence and makes future sexual encounters into tests that will either prove or disprove the validity of the criticism, always with a nasty edge.

Human erotic history tells us that sexual attraction is not sufficient grounds for matrimony. By and large, a good marriage is based on a myriad of factors concerning compatibility, mutuality of interests, friendship, common values, and so on; these need not be possessed by the best sexual partner you have ever had.

In the not so distant past people knew how to do these things. They maintained harmonious marriages that lasted for decades. And I doubt that these marriages were all lacking in affection and romance.

For many people today the choice is between full and open expression of every complaint and a more decided effort to dissimulate in the interest of preserving a marriage. If we get beyond the silly belief that dissimulation constitutes repression and if we learn to honor and respect those with whom we are most intimately involved, then perhaps we will have a better chance of recovering the secrets of durable relationships, even in marriage. We might also learn a few new things about love.

6

The New Face of Psychotherapy

A victorious army returns home in formation. Crowds line the streets; the troops are showered with confetti. All pass in review before the commanders and a grateful public; their success is celebrated. Everyone shares in the gain of pride and prestige. Such was the case with World War II and with the Gulf War.

Defeated soldiers return home alone. No one parades up the avenue; no one dances in the street. Just as the soldiers look within themselves to find the psychological reserves that will allow them to construct a new life, so does the populace retire to the bosom of home to commiserate.

If the leaders are punished or if they accept the shame of defeat, the individual soldiers will have an easier time rebuilding their self-respect. If not, they will question themselves, search their souls, try to discover what they did wrong and why they were defeated. Many will blame themselves and find the means to suffer an added punishment.

If the institutions in which they placed their trust have betrayed them, they will not be able to repair to those same institutions for solace. Each individual soldier will effectively be on his own, with his own feelings, his own memories, his own sense of diminished self-worth.

Despairing of saving face, each will turn inward in an effort to save his soul. How can he save face by affirming his standing in a discredited group?

Traditionally, religion has provided a refuge from social turmoil. Religion ministers to individuals, but it also provides membership in a group that was not involved in the failed military effort. Religion transforms wounds that do not serve as badges of honor into indictments of society. Its business is saving individuals.

The first elected American president in the post-Vietnam period publicly identified himself as a born-again Christian. His two successors were elected with considerable support from the religious right.

While Clinton and Gore seemed to have only the most tenuous relationship with religion, they displayed their personal emotional scars at the 1992 Democratic Convention as a qualification that would count in an Oprah-fied world. Each presented himself as someone who had known personal trauma, had overcome it, and had learned a valuable lesson from it. It resembled the theology of the "fortunate fall," or felix culpa: it was good that mankind fell into sin because that provided the occasion to receive redemptive love.

Clinton spoke of having been born without a father present, of having been abandoned by his mother, of standing up to an abusive and alcoholic stepfather. Gore shared the pain of nursing his injured son back to health, and told how the experience taught him to hate the internal combustion engine.

Just as psychoanalysis has always required its practitioners to undergo personal analysis, so now public office encourages candidates to demonstrate an experience of therapeutic catharsis. Thus has psychotherapy invaded our culture. Soulfulness has triumphed in a secular form. Instead of leading by example, these new leaders assert that they are human just like everyone else.

President Clinton overcame two stigmas that normally would have disqualified him for the presidency: first, he actively avoided the draft; second, he was publicly identified by his extramarital sexual activities. Active avoidance of civic duty would normally count as presumptive cowardice; exposure of sexual behavior would compromise the dignity of public office.

In a shame culture an individual qualifies for public office by concealing his psychological flaws. Knowledge of their existence undermines the leader's ability to command respect. Behavior in a crisis, experience, judgment, and maturity as demonstrated by relevant professional experience qualify a person for leadership. A candidate shows off his stripes and his medals; he does not expose his doubts, his failings, or his vulnerability.

After America was humiliated in Vietnam many of its citizens mistook their shame for guilt. Nothing obliges people to face shame; often they interpret their feelings as guilt. They then attempt to numb their guilt by confession, self-criticism, and self-castigation. This reduces the pain while providing a certain amount of pleasure.

Instead of discarding a mistake through apology, the individual will seek to add it to his psychic furniture. He does not see his mistake as an aberration requiring active repudiation, but a meaningful statement of who he is, requiring his private embrace and atonement.

Often patients attempt to use psychotherapy to such an end. Normally, therapy should lead a person to become a contributing member of a functioning group whose achievements he can take pride in. It should neither collude with the individual's conviction that no such groups exist, nor allow him to validate himself in defiance of all groups.

Thus, there are two forms of psychotherapy: the one teaches the individual to regain his sense of shame and to identify as a member of a group. The other teaches the individual that his pain is guilt and that he must incorporate his sinful impulses, thereby to develop his creative potential and full humanity.

The first is adaptive, the second rebellious. The first seeks to make people into functioning members of society; the second to make them believers in a religion or ideology.

The use of one or the other depends first on the nature of the group. A nation that has been humiliated and whose leaders have been held accountable may restore its national honor through the work of its citizens. It will seek to recover its dignity by making people forget its humiliation.

The more often the nation has been humiliated the more difficult it is to sustain the idea that an aberration has occurred. Losing a war is one thing, losing many wars quite another. France has lost most of the wars it has fought during the last century or so; thus it has been difficult for that nation to restore national honor without sounding arrogant. Psychotherapy in France has tended to reject the goal of adapting to social norms. Different nations with different histories make different uses of psychotherapy and religion.

Should those of us who practice psychotherapy emphasize the individual soul or the importance of belonging to a group? Should we lead patients to experience their traumas within a paradigm of guilt and innocence, punishment and expiation, or should we allow them to face their shame, even when that shame derives from their having been a victim?

The first solution appeals to our sense of justice and fairness, and yet the second is more effective therapeutically. But there are no easy solutions, and even someone who chooses to make self-respect through socialization the keystone of his practice will still have to deal with the transgressions, both real and imagined, that the patient has committed and suffered. Also he cannot ignore the fact that the patient, before coming to psychotherapy, has developed his own ways of dealing with his personal trauma . . . usually along the paths proposed by guilt culture.

Ask yourself this question: Is human existence a series of traumas, failures, and disasters punctuated by an occasional apparent success whose purpose is to sustain dramatic tension?

Does a human being have the fullest experience of his individuality when he submits to a destiny that guarantees the continual repetition of the same traumas, failures, and disasters, with enough different characters and plot twists to trick him into thinking that he has experienced something new?

Can you remove yourself from this nightmare when you learn that by suffering you are paying for your sins—of word, thought, and deed? Must you believe that you have brought suffering on yourself and can only be released from it by atoning, doing penance, making a fit sacrifice, and accepting an offer of love? Or should you declare that whoever has caused you to suffer is himself the true criminal, and that you will be released from the pain of your existence only when he is truly punished?

In a shame culture the child does not lurch from trauma to failure, but experiences a series of successes—he learns to walk, to talk, to eat, to love, and to work. He grows as he acquires significant social behaviors: from toilet training to table manners to doing his homework to earning a living. The child's successes extend to getting a good grade on a spelling test, winning a dance contest, being part of a sports team, and attending a school that wins the county championship.

All of these experiences are real and formative. The influence of our religious tradition has caused many of us to overlook their importance.

That tradition will retort to this list by saying that if little Tommy has merely been properly socialized, he will not become enough of an individual.

How much of an individual do we really want him to be? If Tommy was molested by his uncle, his shame will make him feel separated from all the groups he belongs to. Guilt culture will treat the trauma by teaching that this experience shows Tommy the fundamental truth that he is alone in the world, that he can count on no one, that he should respect no authority: the pain of betrayal is not worth the risk of extending trust.

It will tell him these things to make him feel better; it wants to protect him from shame by calling his bad feelings guilt and by offering to purge them. It will teach him how to integrate the trauma by finding an advantage to having lived it. Guilt culture uses trauma as something that protects people from becoming too absorbed in the teeming mass of society.

Why would Tommy not achieve any individuation by becoming the star halfback, or by getting good grades in school, or by being Jamie's friend?

Within a group personal achievements and commitments to others serve to individuate. They do not spare Tommy from all trauma or ostracism or isolation. Children in shame cultures know shame, and they know it very well. The cultures use it, however, to socialize, not to isolate, individuals.

A child may experience shame, withdraw for a time, and then return to the group. Tommy is standing in the corner of the classroom with his back to the students. His shame is unbearable; he will never put gum in Sally's hair again. Beyond learning the price of discourtesy, he must also learn that his bad behavior is a sign of insufficient social skills. His teacher will show him the correct way to behave in a group. Tommy will apologize to Sally and take some lessons in elementary courtesy.

If he grows up and gets angry at a woman, he will not think that this is the inevitable result of being punished for putting gum in Sally's hair. He does not think to revolt against the injustice of his punishment by abusing someone else. Nor does he imagine that he hurt Sally because he has hostile feelings toward girls. He does not spend his time keeping such hostility in check because he does not feel it in the first place.

People always compare and contrast new acquaintances and situations with those they have known in the past. They also invoke historical precedents to provide guidelines for their personal decisions.

Does this mean that we are all enslaved to the past and doomed to repeat it, or does it allow us to follow good examples and repudiate bad ones?

When you as an individual decide to take a job, your decision is influenced by your past experience and your knowledge of the experience of others. Your choice will depend on whose opinion you respect and whose you mistrust. If you follow your guides carefully and make the best decision you can, does that involve your individuality? Certainly it does. But now you have become an individual within a group, not an individual whose sense of self depends on being isolated from all groups, incapable of profiting from the lessons of the past and doomed to repeat the same mistakes over and over again.

Shame culture sees individuality in terms of face. Quite literally the face is each person's most prominent identifying feature; it makes you noticeably different from others. By providing your public identity, it defines you as a member of certain groups with titles and obligations to those groups. An individual cut off from a group in a shame culture is identified by his stigma instead of his face.

Guilt culture sees individuals as having something called a psychology. The Greek word *psychē* means soul. The individual's uniqueness is not put on public display; it is hidden in the depths of the soul. Psychologists minister to individual souls, they care about how individuals develop, and they see groups as collections of individuals.

Western religion has made the individual into something sacred. As Emile Durkheim wrote, "Because we have an immortal soul in us, a spark of divinity, we must now be sacred to ourselves. We belong completely to no temporal being because we are kin to God."[1]

If the individual is sacred, so are his rights. He needs to exercise those rights in order to gain his ultimate freedom and perfectibility. Since this concept places the individual above all temporal authorities, it makes him prey to those who would represent divine authorities.

Identifying yourself by face requires that you rely on others. A real individual, however, does not like to rely on anyone other than himself. He will prefer to identify himself by how he feels about himself. You and only you are the final authority on how and what you feel.

Shame culture posits the individual as player of games or participant in the marketplace. The individual is neither an actor in a drama nor its author. He does not create himself ex nihilo, but engages himself in a space defined by rules and he acts by moving symbols on a game board. His moves reflect his intelligence; they do not express anything that is specifically and uniquely his. A move becomes his when it responds effectively to a configuration that has never existed before. One might say that discovering an original strategy in a chess game requires creativity, but it is hardly the same as a work of art with a style and signature that allow people to recognize its author as clearly as they would his face.

Western religious tradition is the source of the concept of the asocial individual. The soul of Western man is judged according to whether he sins or is sinned against, what he believes and disbelieves, not on what other members of his family do. Your place in heaven has nothing to do with whether your team wins or loses.

Each person is responsible for his own soul; he may seek the intermediary of a church or the ministrations of one of its representatives, but when the time comes for him to answer for his moral being, he will do it alone. And God will want to know more than whether he did the right thing; God will be even more interested in his motivations and intentions, the state of his soul. Western God has always been well versed in psychology.

Western religions lead people to reflect on their fears and hopes; they bring people together into a community of those who hold similar beliefs. Their introspective meditations are designed to accomplish two things: first, to convert people to the system of beliefs that constitutes the religion; second, to provide answers to the largest metaphysical questions (life and death, the meaning of human existence) and the most basic moral issues (how to conduct one's life in order to ensure happiness and peace, here and in the hereafter). Western religions focus the individual on issues that take him beyond secular community. In psychological terms they seek to produce a well-rounded personality with depth of feeling, breadth of understanding, creative self-expression, and compassion for others. What anyone does with such a personality has often remained obscure.

Zen Buddhism, in a shame culture, does not interest itself in teaching theories and beliefs; it attempts to produce actions that are simple, direct, self-denying, and automatic.[2] Connected in Japan with the code of the warrior, called Bushido, it emphasizes dignity, loyalty, filial piety, and moral asceticism.[3] Rather than allowing its subjects to ponder the meaning of life or death, Zen tells warriors that they must always be ready to die. Rather than fear death as a final punishment or seek it as an ultimate reward, they must accept it as something to be desired.

The warrior is most effective when he rids his mind of all thoughts of motivation, intention, and desire in order to perform actions that are automatic, spontaneous, and proper to the occasion.

Ruth Benedict emphasized the importance in Japan of a cult of ''expertness'' that she associated with the practice of Zen: ''The description of this state of expertness is that it denotes those experiences, whether secular or religious, when 'there is no break, not even the thickness of a hair' between a man's will and his act. A discharge of electricity passes directly from the positive to the negative pole. In people who have not attained expertness, there is, as it were, a non-conducting screen which stands between the will and the act. They call this the 'observing self,' the 'interfering self,' and when this has been removed by special kinds of training the expert loses all sense that 'I am doing it.' ''[4]

The action here cannot be just any spontaneous outburst. Having overcome self-consciousness, the expert must do the right thing at the right time in the right way.

The Zen state converges with the idea that you never see your face directly. By attaining this state you become so involved with what you are doing that you do not think about it while you are doing it. Athletes call this being in a groove; movements feel harmonious and automatic; they provide the satisfaction of public achievement.

As applied to swordsmanship, the credo of Zen may be summarized: he who thinks is lost. The Zen moment occurs when your adversary is thrusting his sword at you. There you have no time to deliberate about your desires, to think of victory or defeat, to plan strategy, to think of the consequences of your action, to entertain doubt, to get in touch with your insecurity. Any thought causing the mind to reflect on itself or to imagine potential trauma would be fatal. The warrior can neither ponder the trauma he may incur nor the trauma he wishes to inflict on his opponent.

The goal in many ways is the contrary of the idea of being psychologically self-aware. As Suzuki described, "As long as [the warrior] is *conscious* of holding the sword and standing opposed to an object and is *trying to make use* of all the technique of swordplay he has *learned* he is not the perfect player."[5]

But there is more to life than swordplay. And the warrior ethos is not offered to everyone in the culture. And yet the values represented by Zen are easily translated into actions that may occur within the home. To ensure the serenity of private space the Japanese engage in something called a tea ceremony. From the purity of the water to the absence of decoration, this ceremony seeks to cleanse the soul of distraction, doubt, and worry.

David Mura has captured the feeling of the tea ceremony: "The art was not simply the gestures of preparing and sipping the tea, breathing the aroma of the leaves, heavy as incense. After you finish drinking, you take the cup, the saucer, lift each up, examine it in the light. Turn it over, note who made it. Hold it loosely, lightly, sense the texture. Even cleaning up was an art; wiping the tray in six strokes, starting with a half moon; folding the towel as intricately as origami. More precise than a surgeon, nothing left to chance.''[6]

Zen seeks to concentrate the mind through the scrupulous adherence to ceremonial practice and rote learning. It will produce a master player, one who is not distracted by fear of losing or by the chance that his move will reveal something of his soul. As a goal of therapy, expertness, as Zen produces it, appears to be the antithesis of the well-rounded personality.

As well as I can determine, the philosophical origins of well-roundedness are found in the *Meditations* of the Roman emperor Marcus Aurelius (A.D. 121–180). This book shows a man facing death by journeying into the depths of his soul. Thereby, he discovers the relative unimportance of shame culture. Social pretense, relationships with others, your good name, your reputation, your memory will be eradicated by the grim reaper. Thus you should cultivate and purify your soul and rediscover the divinity that lives within you. Cleanse your sins to act in justice.

Marcus Aurelius derived the idea of well-roundedness from Empedocles, whose own relationship with death was sealed when he threw himself into the mouth of a volcano. Remove your self, Aurelius meditated, from past and future, from the opinions of others, to live unaffected by anything that you cannot control. As you ''keep yourself aloof and unspotted from all that destiny can do,'' you live ''in independence, doing what is just, consenting to what befalls, and speaking what is true. . . .'' Having become ''what Empedocles calls a 'totally rounded orb, in its own rotundity joying,' '' you will ''be concerned solely with the life which you are now living, the life of the present moment, then until death comes you will be able to pass the rest of your days in freedom from all anxiety, and in kindliness and good favor with the deity within you.''[7]

From Socrates to Montaigne and beyond, Western philosophy has based its psychology on learning how to face death. This idea suggests that the more you detach yourself from social networks, the less you will be missed. The individual who makes this sacrifice will also be rewarded with something that surpasses social custom . . . that is, love.

"The soul attains her perfectly rounded form," Aurelius wrote, when she is "bathed in a radiance which reveals to her the world and herself in their true colours."[8] Above all, well-roundedness means completeness and perfection, harmonizing all the different parts of one's soul, both the good and the bad.

Well-roundedness means accepting guilt and expiating it to form a more complete personality, one that is less beholden to others. Relieved from obligations to transitory social forms, the soul becomes self-sufficient and self-contained in goodness.

Succeeding in the world on the world's terms does not matter. Being in touch with one's feelings does. One is taught to take responsibility for one's mistakes, not by being ashamed, but by feeling guilt. It does not matter how you look to others; what matters is how you feel about yourself.

Psychotherapies that work uniquely from a shame cultural mode —especially cognitive therapies—do not ordinarily deal with neurosis: they deal with delimited symptoms, like depression and anxiety, or with repairing the problems of a specific relationship. They prescribe exercises that would be useful for anyone with the same problem; they do not often sympathize with the uniquely personal quality of the individual's agony.

To succeed with that approach you need to have a clearly defined problem, and a compliant patient who can follow instructions and suspend disbelief. As with swordsmanship, the patient has to understand the game, know the rules, and accept the value of playing it. Cognitive therapy works by restoring the patient's sense of shame.

Examine a simple case. A patient had been unable to drive a car because he was afraid of hitting a pedestrian. He was cured by being instructed to imagine scenes in which he ran over someone deliberately. As Paul Wachtel summarized the case, reported by B. W. Feather and J. M. Rhoads: "After imagining a number of scenes in which he pictured himself thoroughly enjoying increasingly more ghastly acts of aggression with his car, his anxiety diminished markedly and he was able to begin a graduated set of actual driving tasks that culminated, in two weeks, in his being able to drive anywhere in the city and even across the state."[9]

Here the technique was invented by behavioral therapists; forasmuch it is no less cognitive. It is not based on the typical reward-punishment model, but involves observing oneself from the point of view of others.

When the patient sees himself choosing *deliberately* to perform irresponsible actions, he then can imagine how he would look to others if he did these things of his own volition, and had to be held accountable for them. By learning to measure his own responsibility, he revived his sense of shame.

Previously he had been struggling against uncontrollable impulses to run down pedestrians. His attempts at mastering his impulses, however, represented a constant punishment for having the impulses in the first place. Afraid to drive a car, he might as well have been imprisoned.

Similarly, someone who has the habit of emptying the contents of the refrigerator into his mouth during an eating binge is responding to what feels like an uncontrollable urge. In fact, as long as he defines himself asocially, his appetites will be beyond his control.

To resocialize his appetite he should stand outside himself to imagine what his colleagues would think if they were watching him. Or, he may imagine himself *choosing* to consume greater and greater quantities of food. If he accompanies this with increased participation in social activities, the hold of his compulsion will be lessened. Food consumption is normally regulated by the ritual aspect of eating meals.

Were this man to feel guilt over his binge, he could either purge the contents of his stomach or flagellate his rebellious flesh. Neither will prevent the next binge. Only when his sense of shame overrides the guilt mechanism for dealing with appetite will he find himself on the road to cure.

Many cases are not as clear and focused as these. A neurotic patient, for example, may not trust authority because he was abused by an authority figure in the past. A patient who had been given bad advice by a previous therapist will not give very much credence to the guidance of a current therapist. Some neurotics will make it a point of honor to disobey instructions. Also, the more the surrounding culture is saturated with guilt the less likely that people will find that shame culture techniques can address their problems. It is one thing to be incapable of trusting authority for personal reasons; it is quite another to subscribe to an ideology that declares all authority figures corrupt.

Cognitive therapies assume that psychological problems are bad habits. A phobia represents the habit of thinking that extreme danger lurks . . . in flying on an airplane, in being in a crowd, in seeing a snake, and so on. Habitual thoughts constitute beliefs. They do not represent wishes, as psychoanalytic theory would have it. Cognitive therapists do not argue that the patient fears crowds because he really wants to be molested by a stranger.

Whatever trauma inaugurated the patient's fear of the dark, whatever meanings have been attached to light and dark, the treatment will test his beliefs against reality: Do you have any reason to fear the dark? What could lie in wait in the dark? Has anyone you know ever been attacked in a dark alley? . . . and so on.

Anxiety is taken to be an exaggeration of realistic fears that have not been moderated by the work of adult reason. It is reasonable for a person to pull back from a precipice; it is an exaggeration to avoid all tall buildings because of a fear of falling through a window. Distinct from psychoanalytic approaches, cognitive theory believes in the patient's capacity to think his way out of his problems.

If the patient is largely functional, with only an isolated area of dysfunction, then his established skills in solving some problems can be called upon to solve other problems.

Whereas psychoanalysis began with hysteria, taken to be a disorder of desire, cognitive therapy began with depression, a disorder of identity. If the depressed patient has gotten into the habit of deprecating his efforts and believing himself to be a total failure, cognitive therapy will attack those beliefs by testing them against information the patient provides about his own life. The voice telling him he is worthless is countered by a more credible authority pointing to examples that refute the hypothesis.

Discarding a bad habit, changing a dysfunctional behavior, modifying a long-standing belief, all these can only take place accompanied by embarrassment. No one likes to see himself thinking like a child or holding superstitious beliefs, especially if he has defended those beliefs to other people. Furthermore, no one accepts easily the thought that mindless, meaningless, even unnecessary fears have crippled his efforts over a number of years.

To avoid facing shame it is easier to think that one has good reason to be afraid, only one does not know what it is, that one is correct to believe in one's worthlessness, needing only some sympathy, and that symptoms reveal hidden truths that need to be integrated into one's well-rounded personality.

The great paradox of psychotherapy—namely, that people suffering from mental disorder are not totally enthusiastic about the possibility of cure—does not derive, as Freud believed, from patients' fear of accepting their own depravity, but rather from their unwillingness to admit to the silliness of what they had previously taken to be the most important thing in their lives.

While cognitive therapy may serve as a paradigm, its duration is too short to constitute a true retraining. It does not have the time to guide the patient to establish good habits, to analyze the life situations he finds himself in, and to do the work of reconstituting his history. Eliminating symptoms and moderating emotional pain are only the beginning of the therapeutic process.

The most significant limitation of cognitive therapy is that it does not allow the time for the agonizing work of facing shame. Often it takes considerable time and effort for the patient to face the shame of his past failures and to learn new ways of dealing with present difficulties. And however much the patient learns different modes of cognitive processing, the rest of his entourage, not privy to these activities, will continue to expect him to remain as he was.

The fewer the sessions the more the therapist is dealing with a generic person—a problem without a face. He will usually seek to dispel this notion by taking a history and adding to it the knowledge he gleans by observing the patient's appearance and attuning himself to the more subtle forms of gestural communication.

Of course, the automatic thoughts that produce depression tend to be generic and nonpersonalized: I am a failure, I am worthless, I never get anything right. The cognitive treatment will often conflict with the patient's agenda: to share the pain, to be recognized as a person, to hear remarks that are suited to his and not everyone's problems.

It may appear that the patient is looking to be taken as an individual with a soul. Cognitive therapists are successful when they suspend such demands. Their success is sometimes mitigated for failing to recognize that behind the demand the patient requires that someone give him face.

An inexperienced therapist, of whatever stripe, is least likely to address different patients differently; the experienced therapist, the most. Short-term treatments, whether cognitive, behavioral, or psychopharmacological, rely on the least information about the patient and run the greatest risk of making a mistake for simple lack of information. This rule is basic to human conversation: you must always be more guarded about what you are saying with people you barely know. You would not want to brag about how wonderfully your child is doing if you knew nothing about your interlocutor's child.

Long-term treatments obviously collect mountains of information about the patients involved. When they model themselves on psychoanalysis, they make the mistake of validating this information only to the extent that it reflects on the patient's psyche.

A classically trained Freudian analyst will care about dreams and fantasies, intentions and motivations, and will systematically disregard the patient's real world experiences. Psychoanalysis has never been in the business of giving face.

What the theory dictates and what has happened in the practice of psychoanalysts over the past century have often diverged. Much of value is contained in the collective experience of a century of psychoanalytic psychotherapy, despite the often tortured attempts to theorize it.

The history of psychoanalytic theory constitutes a series of revisions of Freud. These revisions often have taken place in an atmosphere of bitter contention. Conflicts between Freud's defenders and detractors have produced a lively debate about his ideas. In the past I participated in this debate on the side of the defenders . . . mistakenly, as I now recognize.

Freud maintains his influence for having produced a coherent and consistent psychology. The value of the theory must, I now believe, be delimited. Freud produced a psychology, but it is hardly the only psychology. His theories describe accurately the way that someone who has been traumatized attempts unsuccessfully to deal with his torment through the mechanisms of guilt. Freud stands out for providing one of the fullest theories of guilt culture.

But there is more to psychology than guilt, and making guilt the primary motivating factor in psychology leaves too many issues untouched. Primary among them is depression; Freudian theory overemphasizes anxiety at the expense of depression. It exaggerates the importance of desire and ignores problems of Self and identity. It does so because it does not provide an adequate understanding of shame. As Helen Block Lewis was among the first to note in her *Shame and Guilt in Neurosis* psychoanalytic treatments have often fallen short for failing to deal with shame.

A psychoanalytic approach to the driving phobia discussed above would provide a better description of the patient's inner conflict. At the same time, it would therapeutically be less effective. This seeming paradox has bedeviled psychoanalysis throughout its existence.

Psychoanalysis would see the man as torn between his true wish to run down pedestrians and his guilt over this wish. He punishes himself for his wishes by renouncing the advantages that accrue to someone who drives a car.

Labeling the patient's fantasies of killing pedestrians as his true wish, even the truth of his being, defines the psychoanalytic approach. This wish can never be expunged; the best to be hoped for is that the patient accepts the wish as his and finds a way to control it.

To accept the wish as his own the patient will construct a personal emotional history that shows where the wish came from and what it means. Past wishes to hurt or maim; past aggressive actions like cutting up salamanders; past feelings about automobile accidents witnessed or heard about . . . all of these will produce a picture of the patient as latent homicidal maniac. If he is afraid of driving his car, now he will believe that he has good reason. Phobic patients often seek to discover the reason behind the fear, believing erroneously that the truth will set them free.

This history makes the phobia meaningful, but at a high price. Normal life experiences will be expunged from this new history; events where the patient acted courageously and properly will become irrelevant; feelings and fantasies of being a solid citizen will pale in significance next to the picture of the patient as incipient criminal. He has now discovered that he is the pawn of powerful psychic forces that he can only attempt to harness. Strengthening the control mechanism—what Freud called the ego—coupled with expiatory rites—what Freud called accepting castration—is prescribed as the means to overcome the phobia.

However satisfying we find this description—it has more narrative force than the cognitive exercise we saw above—it is less effective therapeutically.

In the cognitive exercise the therapist eliminates the taboo over thinking about running people down with a car. Imagine yourself doing what you fear, he declares. Imagine yourself doing it as the result of a conscious command, not of some powerful unconscious impulse that your conscious mind is struggling against. As you see yourself being commanded to entertain certain homicidal wishes, you will normally ask yourself whether this is really who you are. You will feel shame at responding to the instruction to perform an action that your moral being finds revolting.

Your shame will depend on this: however powerful the imagined voice that is commanding you to commit criminal actions, you always have a choice—to obey or to rebel. And here, driving well is the only face-saving act of rebellion. Were you to renounce your car you would be accepting the tyrant's view of you as being a homicidal maniac.

To reject that view, you will make it a point of honor to reassert yourself by driving your car responsibly, following the rules of the road, respecting other drivers and pedestrians, and so on.

Psychotherapy should provide a moral education in saving face. Call it rebuilding self-respect, gaining an identity, or restoring a sense of self, but it must surpass soul searching and self-castigation.

The patient needs to learn how to do the right thing in the right way at the right time with the right person. No psychotherapist can provide proper guidance under these circumstances unless he knows whom he is dealing with, and what the patient is dealing with, in detail. Negotiating the difficulties of everyday social life is far more complicated than addressing an isolated symptom like a phobia.

Situations do exist where the proper course of action is self-evident and would be the same no matter who the person was—anyone who abuses a public trust must apologize and resign, no matter what the extenuating circumstances.

Such occasions are rare, but certainly not insignificant. Normally, a psychotherapist uses his knowledge of the person and the circumstances he is confronting to offer guidance. He may propose a new analysis of the situation, or even a course of action that the patient had disregarded. The therapist must do this without having the patient feel coerced. He does so by giving the patient face: taking him to be an honorable person seeking to act morally.

The therapist discovers enough information to provide the proper guidance only by asking direct questions. Paradoxically, allowing his patient to say whatever comes to mind in psychoanalytic free association serves to mask vital information. By encouraging dissociated thinking, free association tells the patient that concentration on a specific issue is counterproductive.

Where the cognitive approach to phobia de-emphasizes the cause to concentrate on the solution, psychodynamic therapy attempts to address historical roots without overly concerning itself with whether the problem remains in force. It may assume that an incident of traumatic abuse produced the neurosis, or else that his parents' failure to provide a healthy emotional environment drove the person into illness.

Too often psychodynamic therapy seems like historical research into a forgotten crime. Some therapists believe that they have overcome Freud's belief in the primacy of fantasy over reality, but they have remained firmly entrenched in a guilt cultural mode of operation. Whereas Freud believed that patients should learn to expiate their own sinful impulses, contemporary therapists hold that the crime was real and that cure will involve cleansing the patient's guilt by transferring it to someone else.

The clinical strategy based on remembering the past was invented by Freud, even though he came to believe—wrongly, it now appears—that his patients had exaggerated their claims of having been sexually abused. Before he got to this point, Freud had treated his patients by seeking to induce their recollection of repressed memories of childhood trauma. This approach provided a deeper understanding of the patient's psychology. In many ways it still does.

Take one of Freud's pre-psychoanalytic cases of a phobia, dating to the end of the last century. A patient named Emma[10] was afraid of going into a clothing store alone. She was suffering from a form of agoraphobia.

Through Freud's probing, she first recalled that when she was twelve "she went into a shop and saw the two assistants laughing together." She believed that they were laughing at her clothes. She next recollected a time when she was eight and went into a shop to buy candy. Then "the shopkeeper had grabbed at her genitals through her clothes." Despite this, she had gone back a second time. "She now reproached herself for having gone there the second time, as though she had wanted in that way to provoke the assault."

Was she suffering her phobia because she was ashamed, or because she felt guilty? I speculate that her suffering was caused by her belief that she had wanted to be sexually abused; she blamed herself. Imagine that she felt herself tempted to return, perhaps because she needed new clothes, and interpreted this temptation as meaning that she liked being abused. If the sinful impulse existed within her soul, there would be nothing she could do to prevent its recurrence—except refusing to go out in public. To control the impulse she punished herself by confining herself to her home. She covered her shame by folding it into a mental conflict.

Teaching this woman that she wants to be molested will not cure her of anything. For her to be cured she would have to recognize that her experience of shame was an isolated incident, one she had never wished for, and that she has no impulses that would normally put her in danger.

Even if she did have erotic fantasies containing abuse, this does not mean that she wished for them to take place in reality, even less that they drove her into a shop where the owner would molest her. Knowing that something can occur in reality is quite different from believing that it must.

She experienced shame at being exposed involuntarily to the importunities of a stranger. Whether she wanted it or not, he still knows more of her privacy than she wished. Her shame is this knowledge of having been exposed. Her phobia is an exaggeration of the danger of it happening again, based on her belief that she wished it to happen. What does the molester say to his victim if not: you know you really wanted it. If you tell anyone, you will be confessing your sinful wishes.

Now take this one step further. The normal response to an offensive gesture is anger. To save face the best reaction would have been an immediate exclamation of disapproval—even to the point of slapping the shopkeeper's face. This would have aborted the abuse and publicly shamed the abuser. The patient's failure to react in the right way at the right time signifies—to herself and to her abuser—that she believes she might have provoked the abuse because she might have wanted it.

She may have concluded that she did not wish to accuse the shopkeeper after the fact, because this would only draw attention to her own failure to respond appropriately. Nevertheless, her understanding that she might have reacted differently should arm her for possible future confrontations. The real reason she returned to the shop was to attempt to get it right the second time, not because she liked being abused. Understanding these points would have constituted her moral education in saving face.

Patients who try to forget their sexual traumas have a good reason to do so. Accusing them of obstructing justice is disrespectful of their attempts to deal with their traumas. Long-term psychotherapy affords patients the opportunity to face shame in private with someone who respects them sufficiently not to think less of them for exposing their shame.

In some cases it may be useful for a patient to confront someone who was abusive in the past; affording the abuser an opportunity to apologize and to repair a broken relationship may have psychological value. Only in the most extreme cases should patients be encouraged toward public denunciation, indictment, and prosecution.

Contemporary therapists have opposed this attitude because they feel that childhood sexual abuse is everywhere, and that it must be exposed. Only with the punishment of all those responsible can society be cleansed of this scourge. Among the leaders of this movement is Alice Miller.

Whether her approach was as original as it claimed, it certainly had a profound effect on American society. Whereas Freud's theory had promoted a guilt narrative based on the universality of children's wishes to commit crimes against their parents, the new theorists asserted the universality of parents' impulses to commit crimes against their children.

Alice Miller and friends have taken things well beyond the question of how to treat the individual victim of abuse. Miller has attempted to draw all individuals into a group where their identity is based on their having been victims of abuse. Thereby, she has sought to create a band of innocents within a culture of guilt.

It is as though parents were being put on the couch, found guilty, and coerced into submitting to manifold ways of controlling their impulses to molest children. Through this issue we have seen the dawning of a culture that purveys psychotherapeutic insights into everyone's home by making us all either actual or potential child molesters.

Many proponents of this movement have noticed the importance of the victim's shame. Victims of abuse act like people who have been ostracized by society. They are withdrawn and isolated, feel responsible for what happened to them, fear social contacts, and cannot trust any authority figures. But rather than face and overcome the shame of their situations, they mask it by continuing to act in the role of silent victim, making their suffering a permanent indictment of society.

Therapists have sought to compensate for the silence by

shouting about abuse, seeing it everywhere. To help the person who feels alone with his pain, these therapists have wanted to make the traumatized condition a norm. Instead of dividing the world between those who had healthy experiences of childhood and those who were abused, the new theories divide the world between those who recall their traumas and those who remain blind to the truth. Thus victims can now display with pride the emotional scars they have received at the hands of their parents.

However often they speak about shame, these therapists are selling guilt. Adults are guilty; children are innocent. In place of Freud's mythic crime story we have real crimes being committed within just about all families. If you are not aware of this, you are even more guilty because you are sustaining a conspiracy of silence.

In the eyes of Alice Miller the sexual abuse of children has always been ubiquitous. She describes it as "the situation of the child as it has existed unchanged for millennia, at least in our culture. The link between parents' need for erotic fulfillment and their right to use and punish the child is such an inherent feature of our culture that until recently its legitimacy had been questioned by very few."[11] Several pages later she continues, "The tendency for adults to use their children as best they can to meet all their needs is so widespread and so taken for granted in world history that most people do not refer to this form of sexual abuse as a perversion. . . ."[12]

This movement goes beyond normal psychotherapy because it intends to cure all society. But if child molestation is as pervasive as these people think, then the only solution would be increased policing of the relationship between parent and child. To say that a child ought to respect a parent according to the principles of filial piety would simply open the child to salacious abuse.

Nevertheless, the fact that so many people find Alice Miller and her ilk persuasive suggests that sexual abuse of children has increased in America in recent years. Rather than see it as an occasion to overthrow the authority of parents, we ought to see it as a symptom of the breakdown of parental authority. Authority is always subject to abuse. Nevertheless, encouraging people to denounce their parents and promoting familiarity between parents and their children is likely to increase, not decrease, abuse. At present, child abuse in America is addressed through the mechanisms of guilt culture. And yet, in a courtroom there are two sides to each story: prosecution and defense. Each will have some supporters, no matter the verdict. When community opinion is divided, the effect of stigmatization is diminished. The more often such charges are leveled, the more they are subject to doubt.

The issue debated in courtrooms is one that has bedeviled psychology at least since Freud: How truthful are memories of childhood events? Considering the consequences of a charge of child abuse, should society grant credence to fuzzy memories? And a new issue has come to plague the field of psychology: Does a constellation of behaviors constitute presumptive evidence for the reality of childhood sexual abuse? Has every withdrawn, sullen, antisocial child been the victim of a child molester?

The individual victim, bearing witness in court to a long-forgotten crime, has become the prototype of the psychotherapy patient. Has the practice of psychotherapy, concerned as it now is with recovering such memories and attaching appropriate affect to them, unconsciously taken as its model the kind of coaching an attorney would offer a witness?

In the United States public discussion of these issues has taken the form that we would normally expect from a guilt culture. As Daniel Goleman reported, ''The debate [over the reliability of adult memories of child molestation] has implications beyond the therapy session, as a mounting number of adults who remember sexual abuse in childhood are being urged to sever all ties with their families, and even sue their parents for damages. And now some parents, saying they have been falsely accused, are suing the therapists involved for medical malpractice.''[13]

While most therapists—I would contend that this even applies to most Freudians—accept their patients' stories, it has also been shown experimentally that patients can be induced to believe in the reality of events that did not happen.[14] And recent studies have shown that young children do not always tell the truth when they testify in these cases. Goleman summarized these studies: "Researchers have found new evidence that persistent questioning can lead young children to describe elaborate accounts of events that never occurred, even when at first they denied them."[15]

How pervasive is child abuse in human society? If Alice Miller is right, every family is a small tyranny that needs to be destroyed in order to save the individual members. If Miller is simply the victim of her own hyperbole and if families are not conspiracies to protect sexual predators, then her form of therapy will become the problem. In reinforcing the patient's sense of isolation, it will be leading him to believe in the power of infantile trauma in order to rationalize his withdrawal from society.

Evidently, child abuse really happens; it need not be sexual in content; the father may not be the principal perpetrator. The broad category of abuse is another way of saying that many children are socialized with the values of guilt culture. They know physical punishment as the primary sanction against bad behavior; they live in fear of beatings and harangues. They come to believe that an angry parent can only be reacting to their own bad behavior; they accept their punishment as just deserts. Eventually, they will decide that they can forestall further punishment by purifying their own souls of their tendencies to be bad—or, that they must continue to misbehave in order to justify the treatment they receive.

When a child is abused systematically by his parents, he will come to count that behavior as a way of showing passionate regard. People whose only recognition has consisted in abuse tend to see formal ceremonies as false, empty, and meaningless. Bowing and curtsying do not have the emotional intensity of abusive behavior and therefore seem to have a weaker claim to truth.

Such people gravitate toward those who affirm their truth, whether by offensive words or offensive deeds. Since their self-esteem hinges on receiving some kind of passionate response, they do engage in durable relationships based on abuse. They do not seek to modify behavior because they believe that the fault is within their souls. As they numb themselves to abuse, they believe that they are using the experience to further psychic growth.

Someone who has often been victimized will disregard people who are not abusive, because he has never known, and therefore does not believe, that they exist. Forming a relationship with a kind person can produce an initial feeling of depersonalization. The alternative is a self-imposed isolation, a refusal to interact with others derived from a conviction that the truth will always win out.

Clinically, it is insufficient to focus entirely on recalling past incidences of abuse. Since the patient's ability to choose friends and form relationships has been damaged, he will require guidance from a therapist if he is to build a new life on other terms. When you embark on a journey through uncharted territory, you seek a guide. When your moral compass has been damaged, you may need both correction and a guide. The same pertains to the psychotherapy of traumatic abuse.

Guilt and shame cultures propose alternative therapies. The one teaches the transcendent value of love; the other demonstrates the value of respect. The one inculcates passion, the other group membership. The one wants you to create within your own soul; the other wants you to be a player in the marketplace.

If psychotherapists seek to restore the value of respect for their patients, they must practice it themselves with their patients. Shame culture is based on feelings of pride, not feelings of shame. Only the practice of respect confirms group membership.

Psychotherapy takes place in a private space; its communications are covered by rules of professional secrecy. But is its space sacred or profane? Do the rules of respect operate there, or are they suspended to achieve a release of tension? Clearly, patients are encouraged by therapists to speak their minds and to avoid censoring their thoughts. They are thus permitted to face shame in private instead of in more public places. And they should understand that what is normal in private can be abnormal in public. No one should learn from therapy that he should put his shame on public display. His humility, yes; his shame, no.

Psychotherapy is not an exercise in shamelessness. Insulting behavior ought not to be legal tender, on the part of either participant. A patient has the right to unload his anger on the therapist, but he ought not to be encouraged to do so. If the patient lashes out at his therapist instead of defending himself at work, he should be brought to feel some shame for saying the wrong thing to the wrong person. If the patient has reason to be angry at the therapist, an apology by the therapist may be in order.

A patient may well learn to face shame without revealing all his secrets. Respect for the patient's privacy is a fundamental rule of therapy. Only if the patient is allowed to maintain his dignity as a social being can the therapist expect him to face the shame of an occasional and uncharacteristic failure.

Without information about the reality of the patient's life, no therapist can offer useful guidance. If the therapist does not respect privacy, he will disregard the patient's social existence and only accept admissions of guilt as valid material. When a therapist only cares about the patient's intrapsychic productions, he disrespects the patient's ability to function in the world.

Psychotherapy functions by granting respect to the patient; it will stall if it pretends to offer a space where no rules pertain and anything goes. Rationalizing such a practice on the ground that it frees the patient from repression does no honor to the profession. Its most likely consequences are self-deprecating depression and self-aggrandizing mania.

Psychoanalysts have noted that some patients show substantial improvement after only a very few sessions. Given their bias, they have attributed this ''transference cure'' to the love the patient feels for the analyst. I believe, on the contrary, that someone who thinks that he is unworthy of dignified treatment will gain stability from the fact that a person with authority receives him politely, listens to what he has to say, and enters into a contract with him. The patient will certainly have feelings for such a person: calling this romantic love in all cases is a gross exaggeration.

Other aspects of psychoanalysis have been less salutary. Traditionally, the principal ways therapists have failed to respect their patients derive from Freudian psychoanalysis. Some of its presuppositions need to be examined here. They have extensive influence, and represent a guilt cultural mode of therapy.

The initial benefits of the ceremonial quality of the analytic relationship are often undermined by a practice of disrespect.

How does a practice of disrespect work in psychoanalysis? First, the patient's existence in the outside world and his ability to solve problems in that world are ignored. Therapists thus orient their approach toward the inner workings of the patient's mind or the transference relationship with the therapist. Second, the patient is demeaned when the therapist considers that only romance matters, and that the patient's other involvements and obligations must relate to that. Making transference love the motor of cure suggests that the only real problem is desire. If you know your desire, all will be well. Third, almost nothing that the patient says is taken at face value. Analytic interpretation seeks hidden meanings that invariably concern sexual crimes.

Freud articulated the basis for these practices in his paper "Observations on Transference-Love." Freud wrote, "I have already let it be understood that analytic technique requires of the physician that he should deny to the patient who is craving for love the satisfaction she demands. The treatment must be carried out in abstinence. By this I do not mean physical abstinence alone, nor yet the deprivation of everything that the patient desires, for perhaps no sick person could tolerate this. Instead, I shall state it as a fundamental principle that the patient's need and longing should be allowed to persist in her, in order that they may serve as forces impelling her to do work and make changes, and that we must beware of appeasing those forces by means of surrogates.

And what we could offer would never be anything else than a surrogate, for the patient's condition is such that, until her repressions are removed, she is incapable of getting any real satisfaction."[16]

From the Freudian perspective, sexual energy is the motor that drives the human machine. Blocking its expression produces frustration and thus incentive for treatment. Freud saw sexual desires as the truth of one's being. If he was right, then face is a convenient mask that creates a social group where everyone is denying his sexual deviance.

Freud understood well that neurotics require myths to organize their experiences. And he sought to provide them. From the beginning, he declared that the mythic structure of the Oedipus complex was the meaning of human experience.

The Oedipus myth shows a detective who discovers that he himself is the criminal he is seeking. As ruler of Thebes, Oedipus is instructed to find the murderer of King Laius; only justice will deliver the city from its degeneration. Eventually, Oedipus learns that he himself is the killer; that his wife is his mother, that his children are his half siblings, and so on. In tearing his eyes out and going into exile, he exacts punishment on himself.

Freud proposed his myths—both the social myth of the primal horde and its individualized version in the Oedipus complex—as the basis for human psychology. He held that men compete with each other because they want to possess women. Concerns for prestige dissimulate the real motives. There is nothing dignified about human behavior when this is seen as its truth.

But if the Oedipus myth is saying that younger men are competing with older men for older women, this would be a bizarre and largely inaccurate description of human behavior. Not because it never happens, but because it certainly does not happen all the time; it does not even happen very often.

To propose that younger men desire younger women because older women are taboo adds nothing to our understanding. Sexual attraction does not require this theoretical contortion to be intelligible.

The Freudian interest in narrative leads to the recommendation that a trauma be integrated into a patient's history as a relevant event that sheds meaning on his life. When it replaces the emphasis on trauma with a concern for desire, this approach recommends that a reconstructed primal fantasy be integrated as the formative element in the patient's history. The better to round out his personality.

From the perspective of shame, an incident of traumatic abuse should be segregated from the patient's life history. While the patient may well believe with Freud that, given human nature, such events are inevitable and beyond repair, the therapist ought to think otherwise.

It is more persuasive in a courtroom to present a victim as having been ruined for life, but no one should communicate this to a patient. The therapist must hold that the trauma was not inevitable, that it might not have happened, that it was more an accident than a necessity. This does not mean that he will show no sympathy for the fact that it did happen, but he should not rely overly on the weak curative effect of commiseration.

If we are thinking of a simple mugging, it is relatively easy for the victim to think that he might not have been in a particular place at a particular time. With child abuse it is more difficult for the victim to think that he might have had different parents, belonged to a different community or to a different species. It is also difficult for us to imagine a child possessing the social skills required to offer a face-saving response.

The most difficult kind of shame a victim will have to deal with concerns having acquiesced to abuse. In terms of shame, forced consent still counts as having made a decision to consent. The trauma does not, as Freud may suggest, derive from the victim's having wished the abuse, but from his having performed an action that compromises his moral integrity. And this failure is known to someone else.

Legally a victim who consents under threat of violence is innocent, and no molester can use such consent as a defense. From the perspective of shame the consent represents a decision even if it was only the better of two unacceptable options.

Some people would use the idea of forced consent to abrogate decision making in favor of becoming a pure victim. Shame does not know such distinctions. Nor does it care for claims that would explain away the decision because we know the motivation. Even with the best motivation—self-preservation—the victim of abuse will still experience shame . . . for having chosen to accept it.

The most powerful means of degrading people, of causing them to lose face, is to make them consent to the act whereby they are humiliated, to force them to choose it. In the Chinese underworld the worst disgrace is to force someone to eat his excrement. Beyond reversing the natural order, the worst part is that the victim colludes in his own shaming.

A rape victim is forced to betray herself, to consent to her own degradation in order, at times, to save her life. If she comes forward she will be revealing her own decision, and she must take some responsibility for that decision. The inculpation of the rapist will not in itself serve to erase her shame.

Consider her as faced with something like Sophie's choice. In William Styron's novel of that name, a mother is forced by a Nazi doctor at Auschwitz to choose which of her two children will die; if she does not choose one, both will be murdered. Faced with this "choice," Sophie chose one. No reproach is imaginable, no guilt conceivable; nevertheless she is haunted by the shame of having selected her child for execution.

With shame, the pain is mental; the process of decision making has been subjugated to the will of a despot. And yet the victim still feels responsible.

If the victim thinks of himself as powerless, then he will feel powerless to discard the aftereffects of the trauma. If things could not have been otherwise, then he will conclude that things can never be otherwise. Knowing his innocence will not mitigate his feeling of having participated in his own degradation.

Facing shame here means what it always means: accepting temporary ostracism so that the sincerity of one's apology will lead to reintegration. And it also means that the individual who admits to a fault will make every effort to avoid any actions or inactions that would cause members of the group to recall his shame.

And let us be very clear about what it does not mean. It does not imply that showing off one's wounds makes one more lovable to others. People who love you for your suffering are happy to see it continue. In place of the dire task of seeking to be readmitted into a group, you form love relationships based on sympathy.

Some forms of psychotherapy too easily allow the patient to mask shame by exploiting the therapist's sympathy or by accepting that true love will solve all problems. Love's blindness does not prevent others from seeing you; it allows you to pretend that you do not see them seeing you.

With the most extreme experiences of shame, like that of Sophie, love will never be enough. The love of a good man will not restore her self-respect, any more than good sex will. Only the feeling of belonging to a group would provide the support required to allow her to face her shame.

The same applies to people who have almost definitively ruined their lives through the abuse of alcohol, drugs, gambling, or other addictions. An alcoholic must face the shame of his behavior. Such afflictions are treated most effectively through the artificial groups clustered under the banner of the recovery movement.

When alcoholics manage to make themselves into social pariahs, it becomes difficult to reintegrate them into the groups that used to form their lives. To respond to this problem, some therapies have offered people membership in artificial groups like Alcoholics Anonymous. It is too easy to mock such groups. They have maintained an excellent treatment record and deserve to be studied respectfully.

To face his shame the alcoholic stands up at a meeting and declares himself to be an alcoholic. He is not seeking sympathy and will not receive any. His membership in the group requires that he continually make the effort to overcome his alcoholism and to avoid behaviors that are associated with it. He is accepted as an honorable member of the community—his behavior is not policed. His sobriety is based not only on his ability to feel shame for having been an alcoholic but also on his capacity to reconstruct his life in the world.

The groups provide an immediate sense of belonging. Membership is granted without question, and attendance at meetings is voluntary. The regularity of the meetings organizes the lives of many members. New members are granted sponsors—more experienced members they can call in times of trouble. The group tells them that they are no longer alone, that other people will always be there for them, that they belong to something.

AA or Al-Anon meetings should lead the individual to function effectively in other groups. If the movement becomes a cult that seeks to sever all other attachments, it becomes a problem. No one should be convinced that he will always be unworthy of membership in any of the groups that constitute society.

Different addictions have very different effects on social functioning. Someone who has been an alcoholic or a compulsive gambler and who has destroyed his career and his marriage, who has mistreated his friends and colleagues, might do well to remember that the way others interact with him will most often bear some trace of his previous behavior. But someone whose addiction to food takes place in private and has done no real harm to anyone but himself does not need to overcome such strong expectations in others.

Many people get queasy over the God-talk that inhabits twelve-step programs. Even the nonsectarian references to divinity make movement participants sound at times like converts. The movement is not a religion; it does not minister to anyone's soul. It concerns behavior, not belief; ceremony, not dogma. References to God provide the sense of there being at least one trustworthy leader in a social hierarchy.

For people whose traumas have made it difficult to have confidence in any leadership, this can represent an important achievement. The addict's ability to allow himself to be led, to follow rules, to participate in social rituals under someone's authority, is critical to the therapeutic process.

Invoking a notoriously infallible leader like God comports risks. It may, however, be better to incur this risk than to leave the patient to deal with his problems alone in defiance of all authority.

The process of AA meetings appears to be confessional. I prefer to see it as ceremonial. As the person stands and says, "My name is Jack and I am an alcoholic," thereby following the prescribed form of self-presentation, he is greeted by a chorus of people saying, "Hi, Jack." He does not confess guilt; he offers a formal public apology. The encouragement of others represents the possibility of reintegration, so crucial to shame cultures. It is artifice, not reality, but it shows that shame does not mean being banished forever.

Meetings also respect ceremony by always being organized around an initial concept and ending with the recitation of the same nonsectarian prayer.

Here many alcoholics face their problem for the first time. They accept the validity of the way others see them. This is the first step toward being held accountable for one's actions and toward asserting that those actions are not a reflection of one's true character—even if all members of one's entourage take one to be an alcoholic.

The recovery movement weans the addict from his reliance on the paradigms of guilt culture by offering him those of shame culture. The closer he is to his group the more he will have the sense of wanting to stay "dry" because he feels that others are with him. If he slips and falls off the wagon, the group will not criticize or blame him; he will be left with his own shame. The sense that a slip can be taken as an accidental event, not the inevitable result of a character flaw, removes the typical recourse to the mechanisms of guilt culture.

Twelve-step programs have recognized the importance of repairing relationships in steps 8 and 9. Step 8 reads, "We made a list of all the persons we had harmed, and became willing to make amends to them." Step 9 says, "We made direct amends to such people wherever possible except when to do so would injure them or others."

Making amends involves facing shame by facing the person one has harmed. This requires apology followed by changed behavior to demonstrate sincerity. One cannot just say, "I'm sorry," and then go on as though nothing has happened.

Recovery groups provide us a better model than therapies that are supposed to promote regression in the service of historical research. They do not emphasize reliving the past, but recovering shame in the present so that the past can be reevaluated. This relearning will shed a radically different light on one's history and will require learning new ways to engage in social relations.

While shame may make you feel that nothing can be done, in fact, it is directing you to do something. You may apologize, you may hide your face, you may resign your office; also, you must resolve to act differently in the future and keep scrupulously to this resolve. These are actions that overcome shame.

They do not diminish the immediate pain; in fact, coping with shame in this way assumes that the person has fully experienced the emotion. If you feel guilt, you will assert that whatever you did represented your true unconscious intentions, and that you are ready to submit to reasonable punishment.

Once you have admitted that you intended to harm, have accepted hostile impulses as a fundamental part of your personality, and, in addition, have submitted to punishment, what would stop you from repeating your hurtful action? Fear of punishment becomes less of a deterrent once you have successfully undergone it.

The distinction is germane to the conduct of therapy. Shame will see the mistake as aberrant; guilt will see it as indicative. Shame will require the individual to restore his reputation by engaging in a consistent pattern of proper behavior; guilt will require him to accept his "medicine" and then be more vigilant over his words, thoughts, and deeds.

Shame will tell him what he should be doing; guilt will tell him what he should not be doing. Shame will tell him that he might have done otherwise; guilt will show him why he could not have done otherwise. Shame will provide an education in social skills; guilt will offer a list of limits to be or not to be transgressed.

A therapeutic process based on shaming will assume that the patient acts badly because he has never been taught to act well. With guilt, the process takes the patient to have been physically, sexually, or emotionally abused, and will say that, given his background, it was inevitable that he turned out the way he did.

Psychotherapy ought to be an apprenticeship in shame. What makes the neurotic neurotic is his masking shame with a guilt narrative; therapists ought to be leading their patients out of guilt and innocence into self-respect.

Maturation consists in this: a child is shamed out of his childishness. Behaviors that are inappropriate to his level of socialization are made to appear to be ridiculous, thus something to discard. Simultaneously, he is taught proper behaviors and welcomed back into the group when he shows that he practices them.

As a model of psychotherapeutic change, one that uses shaming techniques with great skill—sometimes excessively—I propose that we examine, in rough outline, military boot camp.

Boot camp transforms boys into men; it produces the transition between adolescence and adulthood. It has always been more effective than the self-involved adolescent identity crisis, itself an individualized attempt to accomplish the same thing.

Erving Goffman defined the transition affected by boot camp. He stated that "the raw recruit . . . initially follows army etiquette in order to avoid physical punishment," but "eventually comes to follow the rules so that his organization will not be shamed and his officers and fellow soldiers will respect him."[17] Thus he moves from guilt culture to shame culture.

At the beginning of basic training a recruit is treated as nearly subhuman. Whether he is actively hazed or just talked down to by everyone around him, he quickly learns that his own value is close to nil. Having no "face" within the organization, he is motivated by fear of punishment.

The recruit is shamed into removing the arrogant pretense of his adolescent behavior. He may have been the toughest guy on the block, he may have been a star halfback, but none of this counts now. He is now an adult, and as an adult, he has not accomplished much of anything. He must prove himself worthy of the honor about to be entrusted in him.

Shame is not used here to exclude someone from a group— that would involve placing a stigma—instead it becomes part of a process of inclusion. To work effectively it must be of relatively short duration; too much shaming will demoralize the recruit and provoke a need to retaliate. Finally, it must be completed by reintegration rituals. Once a man earns his stripes, his achievements must be acknowledged openly in a public ceremony.

When recruits have earned their way into the group, they are treated with the respect appropriate to their rank. Effectively, the ritual humiliation imposed on a recruit represents a zero degree of respect: the amount appropriate to someone who does not have a rank.

Having conquered personal fear, having learned the group's values, having participated in its ceremonies and rituals, having overcome the narcissism of youth, the individual gains an adult identity.

Earning his stripes has given him psychological capital that is recognized in the marketplace and can be invested or spent in the various activities that constitute everyday life.

To understand more fully the difference between therapeutic strategies dictated by shame and guilt, let us examine some clinical situations as they might be presented to a therapist. We will limit ourselves to specific problems, not to an entire case, in order to highlight the different ways of approaching clinical issues.

A man presents himself for treatment with the following complaint: during the course of his everyday activities he has been insulted, offended, even abused. A subordinate spoke down to him—perhaps simply by calling him by an overly familiar form of address—and made him look foolish in front of his colleagues. He did not know how to respond, and so did nothing.

He tells his therapist that he does not know what he did to deserve this treatment, but that he needs to find out. He assumes that his failure to respond shows him to be harboring repressed guilt feelings, which require psychological exploration. If he gets in touch with these feelings no one will ever mistreat him again.

If the therapist is functioning according to guilt culture he will agree that the man cannot respond because he feels an unconscious sense of guilt. The therapist will then seek to discover the cause for that sense of guilt, assuming that once the man knows why he feels guilty, he will submit to proper punishment and no longer feel bad about what happened.

Strictly speaking, such a therapist will not engage himself directly with the practical situation; he will not mention that it is still not too late to respond or that the failure to respond immediately might be justified while the failure to respond in time would be a mistake. He may even see the wish to retaliate as an admission of guilt through denial.

The patient will have learned a specific lesson. First, that his malaise about accepting an insult reflects unresolved guilt; second, that any wish to reassert his own standing is wrong. He may even learn that his competitive drive is a symptom of a deeper conflict requiring therapeutic correction.

If the therapy seeks to restore the man's face it will be conducted differently. The rules of shame culture oblige this man to respond to the offense in order to maintain his position and status. Anyone who allows himself to be treated disrespectfully with impunity will see his authority diminished.

If the patient gains insight but does not behave differently in the outside world, he has simply engaged in an elaborate and costly means of masking his shame.

Where necessary, the therapist should explain this aspect of social gamesmanship and say that the only way for him to overcome his pain is to engage, even belatedly, in an action that will restore his authority.

If the exchange occurred in public, a public repudiation of the subordinate's arrogance would be called for. If the offense was sufficiently serious, he may be obliged to demote or fire the subordinate. The particularities of each set of circumstances will determine what action will be face-saving and what will make him look like a fool.

The patient's guilt feelings—his sense that he deserves the calumny he has been receiving—may well reflect the way he has, as a child, been taught to respond to criticism from his parents or teachers. It may, for him, have become a way of life.

On the other hand, he may have failed to respond to an insult because his mind was elsewhere. His inaction need not reflect anything about his upbringing, but he may well seek to make it a part of a larger pattern.

The longer the patient delays, the more his failure will become significant. He may lose a promotion, see his credibility erode, or have his subordinates become unruly and inefficient. He will not gain comfort for knowing that executive ineptitude is his destiny.

Look at another clinical example. A man presents himself for therapy because he is overwhelmed by resentment over his neighbor's recent promotion. He cannot tolerate the fact that his neighbor's advancement has far outstripped his own meager accomplishments. While the reason may simply be that his neighbor works harder than he does, he still feels demeaned.

He dreams of revenge, and never misses an opportunity to make a disparaging remark about his neighbor. It does not help that his spouse and children are deeply impressed by the neighbor and always take note of the signs of his success.

Here again one may use either of two different therapeutic strategies. Using the paradigm of guilt culture the therapist may declare that these feelings of resentment are irrational and inappropriate to the situation, and that their roots must be sought elsewhere.

Through this intervention the patient stands condemned. Now he will scour his psyche to discover the roots of his resentment —perhaps in his childhood jealousy of his siblings—and to perform some kind of psychic penance to atone for his sins.

The activity of treatment will in the main be taking place within his mind, so he need not apologize to anyone for his previous behavior. Future behavior will demonstrate that he no longer engages in expressions of resentment. Knowing that these feelings are signs of disease, he will do better at policing them.

The crux of the issue will lie in whether the therapist believes that the patient ought to improve his professional standing. From a guilt culture perspective the resentment would be interpreted as coveting his neighbor's possessions.

If therapy is conducted through the principles of shame culture, the response is quite different. The patient should understand his resentment as a call to action; it means that he ought to work harder to advance his own career. Of course, if he feels no resentment of his neighbor's success, he may simply be content with his own position, assuming that it is worthy of respect.

In the case at hand, his neighbor's success has shamed him; it has shown him to be less than he imagines himself to be. Not only has his own pretension been deflated, but the loss of face has also affected his family. This is hardly his neighbor's fault;

nor is it the fault of anyone in his past whose success showed him a truer picture of his accomplishments than he was willing to admit.

Rather than rail about his neighbor's success, he should develop a strategy to gain the recognition due him. He may even model it on what his neighbor has done. If the neighbor has done better because he works twice as hard, the patient should take that as a lesson.

Guiding a patient to a more constructive approach to problems only represents the beginning of a therapeutic process. Ordinarily, the patient has a personal stake in his habitual behaviors, and is unlikely to suffer change gladly.

If this man has been peppering dinner table conversation with deprecating remarks about his workaholic neighbor, any modification of his own work habits may easily be thrown in his face. His own words will now come back to haunt him; also, if his wife, for example, had been advising this change, he will risk making it appear that he is following her orders.

Inevitably, a man who has always behaved one way and now learns another will engage in a serious revision of his past history. Often people persist in making the same mistake in order to mask shame. Once a man has demonstrated that the mistake was unnecessary, he will recognize his past failures as such and experience shame for them.

One consequence of changing a typical mode of action is a profound sense of shame for not having done it before. Someone who has always chosen confrontation over compromise will have an initial rush of pride when he learns to negotiate a dispute. This will soon be followed by a wave of shame for the occasions in the past in which he could have done the same. With the sense of new success comes that of wasted opportunity.

This shame is the most difficult emotion a therapist has to deal with. Certainly, he does not encourage it: shame is something that the individual has to recognize himself. The patient will experience it in his own way at his own time when he is ready to do so. One does not want to encourage the patient to avoid the emotion, but one does not want to force it on him either.

Also, someone may come to the conclusion that he has made a mistake when he has not. A man may decide that his marriage has been a mistake. He has discovered that he should have married Betty instead of Sue. Should he feel shame for his marriage?

Since this decision has produced many consequences, breaking it is not a simple matter. The fact that he really loves Sue will not count for very much next to the amount of damage he is about to cause. As long as his marriage is not a battlefield, where everyday explosions have damaged all members of his family, his sense of shame about whom he should have loved sounds like so much egoism. Shame exists only when one has failed a social obligation; no one has a social obligation to marry his true love.

It is one thing to discard one's habit of compulsive gambling, quite another to jettison a wife and children. Therapists ought to limit the label of addictive behavior to antisocial activities.

In shame culture the prototypical therapeutic act is an apology. If you inadvertently hurt someone's feelings, you offer an immediate apology to signify that you accept responsibility for the gesture but that it does not represent your feelings for that person. If you fail to apologize, the gesture becomes an expression of hostile intent.

A second important therapeutic act is to take a mistake as inadvertent and laugh it off through the use of self-deprecating humor.[18] Throughout her book *Shame and Guilt in Neurosis*, Helen Block Lewis emphasized the therapeutic effectiveness of laughter. Used as a sign of humility, it often serves elegantly as a way to take back what was said.

In shame culture, mistakes, offenses, and even some forms of abuse can be retracted because they are not taken as a meaningful representation of the person's true intentions. The real person is the one who apologizes, not the one who slips up. Mistakes are not integrated, but discarded.

As represented by psychoanalysis, guilt culture assumes that when you inadvertently hurt someone's feelings your action represents an unacknowledged intention. You ought then to accept the hostility as your own, suffer your punishment, and guard against acting it out again.

One of the hallmarks of psychoanalytic treatment is the analyst's refusal to allow the patient to apologize. Slips of the tongue and forgotten appointments are taken as signposts leading to the patient's unconscious intentions. They are supposed to represent what the patient would be saying if he were not constrained by the repressive rules of social interaction.

If the patient is late to an appointment, the analyst will take it to be an expression of hostility toward the analyst. He might interpret it: you made me wait because you want to get back at your father for making you wait until you were eighteen before getting a driving license. Not only is the patient not allowed to apologize for a fault that may have been caused by a breakdown on the subway, but he is being treated as a petulant and vindictive adolescent.

These concepts led Freud to articulate a rule that obliged the patient to say whatever came to mind without censorship. The fundamental rule of psychoanalysis induces the patient to practice what is called free association, a disconnected speech where no importance is placed on logical connection or coherence. It is rationalized as a means by which the patient will recall infantile traumas by using language in an infantile way. The search for psychoanalytic truth can proceed only when the rules of social propriety are suspended.

Children often seem to be saying whatever comes to mind, without censorship and without regard for the feelings of others. Since the calculus of shame only applies to them partially, their non sequiturs and general failure to engage in conversation count as charming. Such uses of language promote laughter rather than hurt feelings.

The therapeutic usefulness of "free association" is subject to question. More problematical is the application of this same principle to conversation outside therapeutic settings. Speaking what comes to mind and unburdening oneself no matter what the consequences are consistent with guilt culture and function in some circles as an accepted rule of social conduct. Evidently, this encourages people to act as if they had no shame.

When an adult must choose between constraints on free expression and offending his neighbor, he ought always to prefer the constraints. The former will produce a semblance of harmony, the latter a permanent drama.

Saying whatever comes to mind without regard for the consequences works perfectly for children and also for those whose words have no social importance. If no one is listening or if no one cares what you say, then you can use language to ventilate whatever you please. Why should this be an ideal condition?

Using language more poetically and speaking more freely might be justified on the grounds that it promotes intimacy and romance. Poetry, after all, is the language of love. Its seductive powers, however, function best in private spaces, and will ultimately yield to the social obligations inherent in any relationship. You cannot justify words that publicly humiliate your lover on the grounds that you were just speaking what came to mind.

Speaking openly and freely in public denotes someone whose words do not count for much because he occupies a lowly place on the social hierarchy.

Problems arise when therapists propose that modes of communication proper to the boudoir and the nursery should be the paradigms from which all others derive. They are laboring under the false assumption that someone who can speak freely, who is in touch with his feelings, who does not censor his communications, will naturally find happiness in love, friendships, and work.

Ultimately, this is not what psychotherapy ought to be about. By encouraging patients to withdraw from the world to get in touch with their infantile feelings, it does them a disservice. Shame culture is based on the marketplace, not the nursery. Each person seeks to increase his prestige, thus to have more influence on the formulation of policy; prestige means having a greater say in the way the group acts.

The higher one is in a hierarchy, the more careful one has to be about what one says. In order to maintain credibility, a leader must exercise considerable caution before saying anything. When a leader speaks, he engages the group's prestige, sets policy, and gives the group's word. An American president's musings on tax policy may cause corporate officers all over the country to readjust their business plans or even modify investment and hiring plans.

What you can and cannot say in public depends on your place in a hierarchy, your level of authority, your proximity to policy-making decisions and implementation. It depends on how much and what kind of face you have relative to your interlocutor.

As your authority increases, the stakes involved in your decisions also increase, and more people and things are affected. Any individual who attains an august position recognizes quickly that his statements are no longer self-expressions but count as policy indications guiding future behavior. Those who hear them are obliged to take them as such and to situate themselves accordingly.

Also, if a negotiation is taking place, it is better to avoid being straightforward and taking a strong position. If you know that you will eventually have to compromise your position, you should not put forth words that you are going to have to eat.

Policy is not poetry; it must be precise, to the point, relevant, and intelligible. Otherwise no one would be able to implement it. There is no place for ambiguity in the secretary of state's instructions to his diplomats.

Assertions about the fundamentally creative nature of language are academically compelling but would make it impossible to have a policy or be responsible for its consequences. An individual or government that does not have a policy to deal with one or another person, place, or thing will be put on the defensive and will be reacting to policy initiatives from others. At the limit, you will become a character in someone else's drama.

A policy is a principle defining how a government or an individual will deal with a particular problem or situation. It cannot be invented of whole cloth; it is usually inherited from one's predecessors, and retained or modified depending on how effective it proves to be.

A government will have policies that define its dealings with foreign governments: policies may promote or avoid trade and cultural exchanges, they may seek to contain an aggressive adversary or to attack it. A government will have a policy for directing the nation's economic affairs; it may wish to promote free enterprise, business formation, and capital expansion. Or, it may decide to slow down rampant development in the interest of preserving environmental sanctuaries.

But individuals also have policies to deal with situations where they act in the world. Parents, for example, have many policies for bringing up their children. In our culture they will have policies concerning allowances, homework, bedtime, play dates, after-school activities, and so on.

In addition, parents will also set policies that their children will adopt in the conduct of their own lives. The parents' beliefs and values, the importance granted to education versus athletics, the proper behavior regarding friendship and dating, the way one conducts oneself in the world as a representative of the family— these are policies that a child inherits from his parents.

Many people who consult psychotherapists are suffering from an excess of individuality. They feel isolated and disconnected, they lack a clear sense of belonging to social groups, and they are missing the sense of purpose a group would give. Often they attempt to compensate by developing their individuality to absurd degrees: rejecting the goals, standards, and policies of society. Unfortunately, too many psychologists encourage them in this direction by idealizing a self-sufficient, self-contained, autonomous, independent personhood.

One implication of this litany of self-containment is that the individual should never count on other people, but must learn to function on his own. Must he also become someone others cannot count on?

I believe there is a quantity of sadness behind the mask of the well-rounded personality. Based on a vision of human loneliness, it says that it is best not to concentrate on one or two areas of expertise because you will not be able to rely on others to fulfill other social functions. A woman must have a career because there is every chance that her husband will not be able or will not want to support her or her children. A man must learn all aspects of child care because he cannot count on his wife to be there to do it.

To concentrate all one's efforts on making oneself into a grand creation—whether through therapy or not—points the individual away from the world into himself. His self may then open itself to him in splendor, but that vision will eventually reveal itself to be a mirage blinding him to the approaching abyss.

The risk with a well-rounded personality is that it prematurely becomes an angel. Instead let us understand that relations between people in society are best undertaken when individuals adhere to principles of ethical behavior, when they take care not to hurt the feelings of others, when they respect their own and their friends' privacy, when they understand that self-exposure and shamelessness are the enemies of good personal relations.

In today's America, national unity is so distant a memory that many believe it never existed. The national purpose is tattered because we have abandoned the practice of respect. We scoff at ceremony, trample on rituals, disregard courtesy, and repugn propriety.

Beseiged by the forces of disorder we expend energy keeping danger at bay. Seeing omens of destruction everywhere we grasp at solutions offered by guilt culture: more police, more courts, more prisons, more litigation, more regulation, more lawyers. And we do it all in the name of the individual.

Are we peering into the abyss that constitutes the truth of human nature? Freud thought so. People want nothing other than "to satisfy their aggressiveness on [their neighbor], to use him sexually without his consent, to seize his possessions, to humiliate him, to cause him pain, to torture and to kill him.''[19]

If this is our truth, then draconian punishment inflicted by a pitiless conscience is our best recourse. Such pessimism breeds despair; paralyzed by terror people seek only to ensure individual survival. Cut off from their social moorings they fall into depression.

The same Freud provided an apt description of the depressed individual: "Feelings of shame in front of other people . . . are lacking in the melancholic, or at least they are not prominent in him. One might emphasize the presence in him of an almost opposite trait of insistent communicativeness which finds satisfaction in self-exposure.''[20]

How many psychotherapists take these traits to be hallmarks of cure?

Of course, we do not want anyone to sneak around avoiding others because he always feels ashamed. We want him to recall his own dignity, to restore his pride, to regain his reputation.

We want the depressed individual to save face; and he cannot do it if he is isolated from the groups that sustain his identity. We want him to build his reputation, to avoid confrontation, to fulfill his duties, to honor his commitments, to be good to his word, and to participate fully in the ceremonies and rituals that constitute the social order.

Personal dignity may assert itself in opposition to a decadent leadership, but it can only do so in the name of an honorable tradition. Making utopia the standard will permit limitless criticism of social reality, but yearning after unattainable goals has always paved the way for despotism.

Saving face means acting as a responsible member of a functioning group and gaining identity from its successes. Good character involves many traits: from good manners to proper attire, from consideration for others to loyalty to the nation.

But we know that people have committed abominations, as they would have it, to save face.

Human beings have built concentration camps, killed their spouses, maimed and mutilated their enemies, because a failure to do so would have counted as a dishonor. But let us not forget that those who defeated despotism also had a sense of honor, one that prevailed for not having to assert itself at someone's expense.

Physical punishment and ignorant superstition characterize guilt, not shame cultures. And yet, once these become common practice, they are perpetuated as social obligations providing group membership, status, and prestige. If everyone wears a mask then each will be identified in public according to that mask; eventually people may even forget that there is a face behind the mask.

Do we need a set of God-given moral laws to separate those groups worthy of emulation from those that require opprobrium? Do we need more religious belief and more ideological conformity?

The problem is not that we have the wrong values but that our public conduct belies our protestations of virtue. Would we not be better off requiring more civilized behavior from our citizens, more dignity from our leaders, more loyalty from our coworkers, more respect from our children, and more courtesy from our mates? No matter what they believe, where they worship, or for whom they vote.

The principles that allow groups to function are simple: an organized group will be more successful than a collection of individuals seeking self-actualization; a group whose rewards are distributed fairly will be more stable than one where gross disparities of wealth exist; a group in which most members are accorded respect and in which happiness consists in cooperative engagement in a common enterprise will excel over one that promotes the good of the individual over the good of the group.

A group that indulges in conflict will leave its neighbors no other way to save face than fighting back. Being involved in permanent conflict wastes both human and material resources and produces economic calamity. Avoiding conflict at all costs is servile.

In the not too distant past we turned a blind eye to the monsters in our midst. We lived as though our government were run by decent public servants and as though our families provided respite from the travails of the marketplace. Doubtless, we erred.

Now, however, we see nothing but monsters. We impugn the motives of all government officials and believe that a good family is one whose horrors have not yet been revealed. This too is an error, in many ways greater than the one it sought to correct.

A good family can reject any member who corrupts its reputation. If there are no good families or good governments then we will need to welcome monsters into our communities, offer them compassion, and pray that their next victim will be someone else.

Saving face in the midst of such calamity will require that we reconcile ourselves to our institutions, not because we do not know where they failed us but because we can see, beyond their failures, what they have provided us. Belaboring failure produces more of the same. It is easier to turn a small success into a larger one than to draw success from the habits of failure.

In place of our monomaniacal emphasis on Self, we should refocus on the larger group by taking special pains in choosing our leaders. In a democratic society our leaders should show the best of our character to ourselves and to the world.

We should end our romance with telegenic candidates who lack the qualifications for office. We should seek leaders of unimpeachable character who command respect, not quasi-celebrities who lack a sense of shame. We should reject crusading ideologues who divide the nation and choose leaders whose primary interest is the national interest. We should ask how much prestige a leader brings to office, not how much prestige he will take from it.

Identifying the qualities we seek in those who would guide us places us in a far better position to know which qualities we should use to guide ourselves.

Acknowledgments

It may be true that "words cannot express . . ." but under the circumstances they will have to do.

It takes a lot of work to turn a tree into a book. I could not have done it alone. Among those who have graciously offered me their advice, counsel, and friendship, I want to thank especially:

David Levine for first suggesting that I write this book and for sharing his wisdom through countless conversations about its different topics.

My brother David for offering the benefit of his knowledge about politics and foreign policy and simply for always being there.

Sherry Turkle for reading the inelegant early drafts and offering advice that proved a consistently valuable guide throughout.

Ronald Ostrow for helping me to connect my flights of fancy to the real world of business and commerce, and inviting me to present some of my ideas to the managers of his company, Lea-Ronal, Inc.

Stanley Cohen for his unexampled generosity of spirit, incomparable wit, and willingness to share his expertise about law, business, and Asian culture.

Abraham David Christian for sharing his deep knowledge of human relationships and his irrepressible irreverence.

M Mark for being M Mark.

The largest share of my gratitude belongs to my editor, Victoria Wilson. Vicky guided the project from the first rough outlines to the final words, from the largest issues of organizational structure to the smallest ones of word choice. She did so with tact and brilliance. Her rigorous professional attitude and willingness to stick with a project that had its problems in transit merit my most sincere thanks.

Tom Dyja assisted me on the most difficult aspects of the project; without him this book would not exist. Tom often knew what I wanted to say before I did; he offered expert guidance and mature judgment. I am most appreciative of his unflinching honesty.

My agent, Charlotte Sheedy, knew what to do with my initial proposal and knew what I needed when I needed it. She placed the book where I wanted it placed; I am very grateful.

To Neeti Madan of the Sheedy Agency and to Lee Buttala of Knopf my thanks for being friendly and encouraging voices on the phone and for handling the production process with good cheer and great competence.

All faults, flaws, errors, and mistakes—of omission and commission—are entirely my responsibility.

Notes

Introduction

1. In terms of economic games, this point is made by Thurow in *Head to Head*.
2. See Kotkin's *Tribes*, chap. 5.
3. For a full analysis see "A Billion Consumers," in *The Economist*, October 30, 1993.
4. Louis Kraar's "Asia 2000," in *Fortune*, October 5, 1992, 113.
5. In his book *Aidos*, Cairns provides an extensive analysis of the literature on shame and guilt cultures, most especially in relation to classical Greek cultures.
6. Shain's *The Myth of American Individualism*, 3, 66, 98, 112, 268.
7. Wood's *The Radicalism of the American Revolution*, 19–20.
8. Ibid., 351, 355, 356.
9. Ibid., 8.
10. Shain's *The Myth of American Individualism*, 195.
11. Elkins and McKitrick's *The Age of Federalism*, 264.
12. Peyrefitte's *The Immobile Empire* recounts the attempt by the British king to share the discoveries of scientific and technological revolutions with the Chinese emperor. The emperor's lack of interest had devastating consequences for the Chinese people.
13. Schlesinger's *The Disuniting of America*, 28.
14. See Kotkin's *Tribes*, 46.
15. Pogrebin has remarked on the importance of keeping secrets in traditional Jewish families: "I see too that the main stimulus for stockpiling secrets

in my family was the fear of shame." In *Deborah, Golda, and Me,* 13–14.

16. Fisher and Ury's *Getting to Yes,* 28–29.
17. Montesquieu's *De l'Esprit des Lois,* bk. VIII, chap. 21, no. 3.
18. See Austin, ed. *Japan: The Paradox of Progress,* 245 and passim.
19. A full account of the conflict between Hamilton and Jefferson can be found in Elkins and McKitrick's *The Age of Federalism.* Also, Beer argues the connection between Hamiltonian Federalism and Abraham Lincoln in *To Make a Nation,* 162.
20. Quoted in Elkins and McKitrick's *The Age of Federalism,* 269.
21. Elkins and McKitrick's *The Age of Federalism,* 19.
22. McDonald's *Alexander Hamilton,* 121.
23. Elkins and McKitrick's *The Age of Federalism,* 282.
24. Tocqueville's *Democracy in America,* vol. 2, 235.
25. Ibid., 236.
26. Huntington's *American Politics,* 4.
27. "Address at Sanitary Fair, Baltimore, Maryland," April 18, 1864, in Lincoln's *Selected Speeches and Writings,* 422.
28. Key has argued in *Public Opinion and American Democracy,* chapter 2, that Americans do not agree on an ideology. See also Robert McCloskey's "The American Ideology," in Kammen, ed., *The Contrapuntal Civilization.*
29. See Elkins and McKitrick's *The Age of Federalism,* 497, 516. For example, "So the first President of the United States could be very testy about his honor and reputation. . . . His every care must be to preserve the safety of the country and the government over which he had been summoned to preside, and this required at the very least, the country's presenting a united face to an outside world only too happy to divide it."
30. Wood's *The Radicalism of the American Revolution,* 196.
31. Ibid., 205–6.
32. Ibid., 209.

I   *A Conflict of Cultures?*

1. Shrivastava's *Bhopal,* 100.
2. Ibid., 101.
3. Clyde Haberman, "Jetliner Crashes with 524 Aboard in Central Japan," *The New York Times,* August 13, 1985, A1 & A6.
4. Ibid.
5. See Clark's *The Japanese Company,* 125–26.
6. de Bary's *The Trouble with Confucianism,* 12.
7. Erikson's *Childhood and Society,* 253.
8. Point made by Democritus and Plato. See Cairns's *Aidos,* 364, 388.
9. See Cairns's *Aidos,* 364, 388.
10. Benedict's *The Chrysanthemum and the Sword,* 222.

11. Ibid., 223.
12. Ibid., 219.
13. Ibid., 220.
14. Dore's *Taking Japan Seriously*, vii.
15. Ibid., vii–viii.
16. The point is presented at length by Braithwaite in *Crime, Shame, and Reintegration*.
17. Chu's *The Asian Mind Game*, 115.
18. Emerson's "Self-Reliance," in *Essays: First and Second Series*, 31.
19. Benedict's *Patterns of Culture*, 2.
20. Benedict's *The Chrysanthemum and the Sword*, 112.
21. Vogel's *Japan as Number One*, 146–48.
22. Lasch's "For Shame," 32.
23. Eberhard's *Guilt and Sin in Traditional China*, 3.
24. Ibid., 3.
25. Fischer's *Albion's Seed*, 84.
26. Ibid., 85.
27. Ibid., 86.
28. Freud's *Standard Edition*, vol. xv, 145.
29. Ibid., 147.
30. Schama's *Citizens*, 858 (see also 643).

2   Facing Trauma: America in Vietnam

1. For a full study of this process, see Billings-Yun's *Decision Against War*.
2. Ibid., 106.
3. Ibid., 151.
4. Charlton and Moncrieff's *Many Reasons Why*, 77.
5. Ball's "JFK's Big Moment," in *The New York Review of Books*, Feb. 13, 1992.
6. Ibid.
7. Theodore Draper, "McNamara's Peace," in *The New York Review of Books*, May 11, 1995, 8.
8. Kissinger's *White House Years*, 296.
9. Quoted in Karnow's *Vietnam: A History*, 24.
10. Charlton and Moncrieff's *Many Reasons Why*, 124.
11. Johnson's, *The Vantage Point*, 68.
12. Ibid., 274.
13. In Karnow's *Vietnam: A History*, 25.
14. Clark Clifford maintained consistency in his view of the responsibility of executive leadership. When his First American Bankshares was revealed to be a front for the rogue Bank of Credit & Commerce International, Mr. Clifford and his associate Robert Altman vigorously maintained their innocence, which a court affirmed in the case of Mr. Altman. Neither of

them took any real responsibility for their roles as American frontmen for B.C.C.I.

15. Kissinger's *White House Years*, 292.
16. Ibid., 295.
17. Mickey Kaus, "Who's Sorry Now," in *The New Republic*, May 1, 1995, 6.
18. Kissinger's, *White House Years*, 228.

3 The Great American Cultural Revolution

1. This concept was proposed by Wurmser in his book *The Mask of Shame*.
2. Lance Morrow's "The Temping of America," in *Time*, March 29, 1993, 41.
3. Huntington's *American Politics*, 134, 141, and passim.
4. Ibid., 141.
5. Ibid., 175 (see also 178, 188, 191).
6. Ibid., 11.
7. Ibid., 15.
8. Among the many works on the Great American Cultural Revolution, see Magnet's *The Dream and the Nightmare*.
9. See Lifton's *Thought Reform and the Psychology of Totalism*.
10. Halberstam's *The Reckoning*, 54.
11. Ibid., 497.
12. Ibid., 51.
13. Morrow's "The Temping of America," 40.
14. Thurow's *Head to Head*, 137.
15. "The Death of Corporate Loyalty," in *The Economist*, April 3, 1993, 63–64.
16. Chu's *The Asian Mind Game*, 130–31.
17. See Magnet's *The Dream and the Nightmare* on these points.
18. On this topic see Howard's *The Death of Common Sense*.
19. Olson's *The Litigation Explosion*, 2.
20. Ibid., 31.
21. Vogel's *The Four Little Dragons*, 235.
22. Jencks's *Rethinking Social Policy*, 53–54.
23. Roszak's "Green Guilt and Ecological Overload," in *The New York Times*, June 9, 1992, A27.
24. Mary Beth Regan's "An Embarrassment of Clean Air," in *Business Week*, May 31, 1993, 34.
25. Ibid., 34.
26. Hacker's *Two Nations*, 63.
27. Ibid., 64.
28. Ibid., 19.
29. Ibid., 50 ff.

30. See Jencks's *Rethinking Social Policy*, 68–69.
31. See, among many statements to this effect, the remarks of Andrew Billingsley of Howard University, quoted in Lemann's *The Promised Land*, 177.
32. Schlesinger's *The Disuniting of America*, 90 and passim.
33. Jencks's *Rethinking Social Policy*, 63.
34. Schlesinger's *The Disuniting of America*, 130.
35. Jencks's *Rethinking Social Policy*, 141.
36. Ibid., 63.
37. Joe Klein's "Principle or Politics?" in *Newsweek*, June 14, 1993, 29.
38. Ellis Cose's "Rage of the Privileged Class," in *Newsweek*, November 15, 1993, 63.

4 Family Secrets

1. For a concise summary see Kennedy's *Preparing for the Twenty-First Century*, 305–8. For a more comprehensive study see "Coming Top: A Survey of Education," in *The Economist*, November 21, 1992.
2. Kennedy's *Preparing for the Twenty-First Century*, 197 (see also 308).
3. On the importance of family among the Puritan settlers in New England, see Fischer's *Albion's Seed*, 69 ff.
4. On these points, see Kotkin's *Tribes*.
5. Iwao's *The Japanese Woman*, 81–82.
6. See Fox-Genovese's *Within the Plantation Household*, 61.
7. Iwao's *The Japanese Woman*, 81.
8. See Posner's *Sex and Reason*, 91.
9. Ibid., 90.
10. Iwao's *The Japanese Woman*, 80.
11. Epstein's *Children of the Holocaust*, 19.
12. Quoted in Epstein's *Children of the Holocaust*, 215.
13. Quoted in Epstein's *Children of the Holocaust*, 124.
14. Quoted in Epstein's *Children of the Holocaust*, 116–7.
15. Recounted in Segev's *The Seventh Million*, 6–10.
16. Quoted in Epstein's *Children of the Holocaust*, 29.
17. Epstein's *Children of the Holocaust*, 35.
18. Cash's *The Mind of the South*, 99.
19. Wallerstein's "Children After Divorce: Wounds that Don't Heal," in *The New York Times Magazine*, January 23, 1989, 42. See also Wallerstein's larger study, *Second Chances: Men, Women and Children a Decade After Divorce*.
20. See A. Cherlin et al., "Longitudinal Studies of the Effects of Divorce on Children in Great Britain and the United States," in *Science*, June 7, 1991, 1,386–9.

21. Wallerstein's "Children After Divorce," 43. See also Etzioni's *The Spirit of Community*, 73–77.
22. "The Bargain Breaks," in *The Economist*, December 26, 1992–January 8, 1993, 37–40.
23. Ibid.
24. Quoted in "The Bargain Breaks" in *The Economist*, December 26, 1992–January 8, 1993. See also Cherlin's *Marriage, Divorce, Remarriage:* Revised and Enlarged Edition, Cambridge, Mass., 1992.
25. Schwartz's *The World of Thought in Ancient China*, 101.
26. Ibid., 70.
27. Lifton's *Thought Reform and the Psychology of Totalism*, 361. Lifton is quoting a traditional book that provided moral education to Chinese children, *Twenty-Four Examples of Filial Piety.*
28. Quoted in Lifton's *Thought Reform and the Psychology of Totalism*, 361.
29. Freud's *Standard Edition*, vol. xv, 189.
30. Schwartz's *The World of Thought in Ancient China*, 23.
31. Ibid., 24.
32. Ibid., 23.
33. Spence's *The Search for Modern China*, 125.
34. Fischer's *Albion's Seed*, 74–75.
35. Tocqueville's *Democracy in America*, vol. 2, 47.
36. Peyrefitte's *The Immobile Empire*, 363.
37. For a full study of this, see Levy's *Chinese Footbinding.*
38. Chang's *Wild Swans*, 24.
39. Max Weber's, "The Religions of Asia," in *Selections*, 200.
40. MacGowan's *Sidelights on Chinese Life*, 34.
41. A movie like *Farewell, My Concubine*, which takes place in post-imperial China, shows graphically how important beatings were to the training of opera singers. The first Ming emperor, Hongwu, held almost daily public canings in the courtyard of the Imperial Palace. In a guilt culture, sanctions associated with physical pain are pervasive.
42. Most particularly by Wyatt-Brown in, among other works, *Honor and Violence in the Old South.*
43. Ibid., 60–61.
44. Cash's *The Mind of the South*, 69.
45. See Paula Giddings's "The Last Taboo," in Toni Morrison, ed., *Race-ing Justice, En-Gendering Power.*
46. Nell Irvin Painter's "Hill, Thomas, and the Use of Sexual Stereotype," in Toni Morrison, ed., *op. cit.*, 212.
47. Cash's *The Mind of the South*, 85.
48. Quoted in Fischer's *Albion's Seed*, 304.
49. Ibid., 86.
50. Ibid., 73.

51. Wyatt-Brown's *Honor and Violence in the Old South*, 126–7. See also Fox-Genovese's *Within the Plantation Household*, 115 ff.

52. See Wyatt-Brown's *Honor and Violence in the Old South*, 92.

53. Ibid., 71.

54. Fox-Genovese's *Within the Plantation Household*, 63.

55. Lifton's *Thought Reform and the Psychology of Totalism*, 383.

56. In his essay "In Opposition to Liberalism," quoted in Lifton's *Thought Reform and the Psychology of Totalism*, 383.

57. Chang's *Wild Swans*, 290.

58. Ibid., 270–71.

59. Anna Quindlen's "Threshold of Pain," in *The New York Times*, March 3, 1993, A25.

60. Stacey and Shupe's *The Family Secret*, 1–2.

61. Quoted in *The New York Times*, April 1, 1993, A1.

62. A good collection of essays on this topic is Martin Duberman, Vicinus, and Chauncey's *Hidden from History*. See also Sedgwick's *The Epistemology of the Closet*.

63. David Halperin's "Sex Before Sexuality: Pederasty, Politics, and Power in Classical Athens," in Duberman, Vicinus, and Chauncey's *Hidden from History*, 50.

64. Tocqueville's *Democracy in America*, vol. 2, 205–6.

65. Fischer's *Albion's Seed*, 79.

66. See Posner's *Sex and Reason*, 45, 47, 51 and passim.

5 Love and Marriage

1. See Daniel Goleman's "Pain of Unrequited Love Afflicts the Rejecter, Too," in *The New York Times*, February 9, 1993, C1 and C9.

2. Tannen's *You Just Don't Understand*, 42–47.

3. Posner's *The Feminine Mistake*, 113.

4. Ibid., 121.

5. Beck's *Love Is Never Enough*, 80.

6. See Posner's *The Feminine Mistake*, 86–91.

7. Anne Tsui, Terri Egan, Charles O'Reilly III's "Being Different: Relational Demography and Organizational Attachment" (unpublished paper), provided by Tsui, Graduate School of Management, University of California, Irvine.

8. Sowell's *Race and Culture*, 85.

9. Pharr's *Losing Face*, 30–31.

10. See also Posner's *Sex and Reason*, 318.

6 The New Face of Psychotherapy

1. Durkheim's *Suicide*, 334.
2. Suzuki's *Zen and Japanese Culture*, 62.
3. Ibid., 70.
4. Benedict's *The Chrysanthemum and the Sword*, 235–36.
5. Suzuki's *Zen and Japanese Culture*, 206.
6. Mura's *Turning Japanese*, 90–91.
7. Aurelius's *Meditations*, bk. 12, sect. 3.
8. Ibid., bk. 11, sect. 12.
9. Wachtel's *Psychoanalysis and Behavior Therapy*, 119.
10. In Freud's "Project for a Scientific Psychology," *Standard Edition*, vol. 1, 353–56.
11. Alice Miller, *Thou Shalt Not Be Aware*, 109.
12. Ibid., 114.
13. Daniel Goleman, "Childhood Trauma: Memory or Invention," in *The New York Times*, July 21, 1992, C1 and C5. See also "Memories Lost and Found," in *U.S. News and World Report*, November 29, 1993, 52–63.
14. Ibid.
15. Daniel Goleman, "Studies Reveal Suggestibility of Very Young as Witnesses," in *The New York Times*, June 11, 1993, A1.
16. In Freud's *Standard Edition*, vol. XII, 165.
17. Erving Goffman's *The Presentation of Self in Everyday Life*, 20.
18. See also Ibid., 53n.
19. Freud's *Standard Edition*, vol. XXI, 111.
20. Freud, ibid., vol. XIV, 247.

References

Anderson, Mary. *Hidden Power: The Palace Eunuchs of Imperial China.* Buffalo, N.Y.: Prometheus Books, 1990.

Archibald, Katherine. *Wartime Shipyard.* Berkeley, Calif.: University of California Press, 1947.

Aristotle. *The Complete Works,* vol. II. Ed. Jonathan Barnes. Princeton: Princeton University Press, 1984.

Aurelius, Marcus. *Meditations.* Trans. Maxwell Staniforth. Baltimore, Md.: Penguin, 1964.

Austin, Lewis, ed. *Japan: The Paradox of Progress.* New Haven, Conn.: Yale University Press, 1976.

Baldwin, James. *Nobody Knows My Name: More Notes of a Native Son.* New York: Dial Press, 1961.

Ball, George. "JFK's Big Moment." *The New York Review of Books,* February 13, 1992.

Bayley, David. *Forces of Order: Police Behavior in Japan and the United States.* Berkeley: University of California Press, 1976.

Beck, Aaron. *Love Is Never Enough.* New York: HarperCollins, 1989.

Beer, Samuel. *To Make a Nation: The Rediscovery of American Federalism.* Cambridge, Mass.: Harvard University Press, 1993.

Benedict, Ruth. *The Chrysanthemum and the Sword.* Boston: Houghton Mifflin, 1946.

———. *Patterns of Culture.* Boston: Houghton Mifflin, 1934.

Billings-Yun, Melanie. *Decision Against War: Eisenhower and Dien Bien Phu, 1954.* New York: Columbia University Press, 1988.

Bly, Robert. *Iron John: A Book About Men.* New York: Vintage, 1992.

Bond, Michael Harris, ed. *The Psychology of the Chinese People.* New York: Oxford University Press, 1986.

Bornoff, Nicholas. *Pink Samurai: Love, Marriage and Sex in Contemporary Japan.* New York: Pocket Books, 1991.

Braithwaite, John. *Crime, Shame, and Reintegration.* Cambridge: Cambridge University Press, 1989.

Brown, Bert. "The Effects of the Need to Maintain Face in Interpersonal Bargaining." *Journal of Experimental Social Psychology* 4 (1968): 107–22.

Buruma, Ian. *The Wages of Guilt.* New York: Farrar, Straus, Giroux, 1994.

Cairns, Douglas. *Aidos: The Psychology and Ethics of Honour and Shame in Ancient Greek Literature.* New York: Oxford University Press, 1993.

Carroll, John. *Guilt: The Grey Eminence Behind Character, History, and Culture.* London: Routledge & Kegan Paul, 1985.

Carroll, Michael. *The Cult of the Virgin Mary.* Princeton: Princeton University Press, 1986.

Cash, W. J. *The Mind of the South.* New York: Vintage, 1991.

Chang, Jung. *Wild Swans: Three Daughters of China.* New York: Simon & Schuster, 1991.

Chao, Paul. *Chinese Kinship.* Boston, Mass: Routledge & Kegan Paul, 1983.

Charlton, Michael, and Anthony Moncrieff. *Many Reasons Why: The American Involvement in Vietnam.* London: Scolar Press, 1978.

Cherlin, Andrew. *Marriage, Divorce, Remarriage.* Revised and enlarged edition. Cambridge, Mass.: Harvard University Press, 1992.

Christopher, Robert. *The Japanese Mind.* New York: Fawcett Columbine, 1984.

Chu, Chin-ning. *The Asian Mind Game: Unlocking the Hidden Agenda of the Asian Business Culture.* New York: Rawson Assoc., 1991.

Clark, Rodney. *The Japanese Company.* New Haven, Conn.: Yale University Press, 1979.

Deal, Terrence, and Allen Kennedy. *Corporate Cultures: The Rites and Rituals of Corporate Life.* Reading, Mass.: Addison Wesley, 1982.

de Bary, W. T. *The Trouble with Confucianism.* Cambridge, Mass.: Harvard University Press, 1991.

———. "Chinese Despotism and the Confucian Ideal: A Seventeenth Century View." In Fairbank, John K., ed. *Chinese Thought and Institutions.* Chicago: University of Chicago Press (1957): 163–233.

Dent, David. "The New Black Suburbs." *The New York Times Magazine,* June 14, 1992.

Dionne, E. J., Jr. *Why Americans Hate Politics.* New York: Simon & Schuster, 1991.

Dore, Ronald. *Taking Japan Seriously: A Confucian Perspective on Leading Economic Issues.* London: Athlone Press, 1987.

Draper, Theodore. "Who Killed Communism?" *The New York Review of Books,* June 11, 1992.

Duberman, Martin, Martha Vicinus, and George Chauncey, Jr., eds. *Hidden from History: Reclaiming the Gay and Lesbian Past*. New York: Meridian/ Penguin, 1990.

Durkheim, Emile. *Suicide: A Study in Sociology*. New York: Free Press, 1951.

Eberhard, Wolfram. *Guilt and Sin in Traditional China*. Berkeley: University of California Press, 1967.

Elkins, Stanley and Eric McKitrick. *The Age of Federalism*. New York: Oxford University Press, 1993.

Elshtain, Jean Bethke. *Public Man; Private Woman: Women in Social and Political Thought*. Princeton: Princeton University Press, 1981.

Emerson, Ralph Waldo. *Essays: First and Second Series*. New York: Vintage, 1990.

Epstein, Helen. *Children of the Holocaust: Conversations with Sons and Daughters of Survivors*. New York: Penguin, 1988.

Erikson, Erik. *Childhood and Society*, 2nd ed. New York: Norton, 1963.

Erikson, Kai T. *Wayward Puritans: A Study in the Sociology of Deviance*. New York: Wiley, 1966.

Etzioni, Amitai. *The Spirit of Community: Rights, Responsibilities, and the Communitarian Agenda*. New York: Crown, 1993.

Fairbank, John K. *China: A New History*. Cambridge, Mass.: Harvard University Press, 1992.

Fairbank, John K., ed. *Chinese Thought and Institutions*. Chicago: University of Chicago Press, 1957.

Fallows, James. *Looking at the Sun*. New York: Pantheon, 1994.

Fingleton, Eamonn. *Blindside: Why Japan Is Still on Track to Overtake the U.S. by the Year 2000*. Boston: Houghton Mifflin, 1995.

Fischer, David Hackett. *Albion's Seed: Four British Folkways in America*. New York: Oxford University Press, 1989.

Fisher, Roger, and William Ury. *Getting to Yes: Negotiating Agreement Without Giving In*, 2nd ed. New York: Penguin, 1991.

Flexner, James Thomas. *Washington: The Indispensable Man*. Boston: Little, Brown, 1974.

Fossum, Merle, and Marilyn Mason. *Facing Shame: Families in Recovery*. New York: Norton, 1986.

Fox-Genovese, Elizabeth. *Within the Plantation Household: Black and White Women of the Old South*. Chapel Hill, N.C.: University of North Carolina Press, 1988.

Freud, Sigmund. *The Standard Edition of the Complete Psychological Works*. London: Hogarth Press, 1971.

Fukuyama, Francis. *The End of History and the Last Man*. New York: Free Press, 1992.

Genovese, Eugene. *The Slaveholder's Dilemma: Freedom and Progress in Southern Conservative Thought, 1820–60*. Columbia, S.C.: University of South Carolina Press, 1992.

Glazer, Nathan. *Affirmative Discrimination: Ethnic Inequality and Public Policy*. New York: Basic Books, 1975.

Glendon, Mary Ann. *Rights Talk: The Impoverishment of Political Discourse*. New York: Free Press, 1991.

Goffman, Erving. *Interaction Rituals: Essays on Face-to-Face Behavior*. New York: Pantheon, 1982.

———. *The Presentation of Self in Everyday Life*. New York: Doubleday, 1959.

Goldman, Marshall. *What Went Wrong with Perestroika*. New York: Norton, 1991.

Goleman, Daniel. "The Self: From Tokyo to Topeka, It Changes." *The New York Times*, March 7, 1989.

Hacker, Andrew. *Two Nations: Black, White, Separate, Hostile, Unequal*. New York: Scribner's, 1992.

Halberstam, David. *The Reckoning*. New York: Pocket Books, 1987.

———. *The Best and the Brightest*. New York: Random House, 1972.

Haley, John. "Sheathing the Sword of Justice in Japan: An Essay on Law without Sanctions." *The Journal of Japan Studies* 8, no. 2 (summer 1982).

Hamilton, Alexander, James Madison, and John Jay. *The Federalist*. Jacob Cooke, ed. Middletown, Conn.: Wesleyan University Press, 1961.

Harre, Rom, ed. *The Social Construction of Emotions*. Oxford: Basil Blackwell, 1986.

Hendry, Joy. *Becoming Japanese: The World of the Preschool Child*. Manchester: Manchester University Press, 1986.

Herring, George. *America's Longest War: The United States and Vietnam, 1950–1975*. Philadelphia: Temple University Press, 1986.

Hill, Thomas. *Autonomy and Self-Respect*. New York: Cambridge University Press, 1991.

Himmelfarb, Gertrude. *The De-Moralization of Society: From Victorian Virtues to Modern Values*. New York: Knopf, 1995.

Hollander, Paul. *Anti-Americanism*. New York: Oxford University Press, 1992.

Howard, Philip. *The Death of Common Sense: How Law Is Suffocating America*. New York: Random House, 1994.

Hsu, Francis L. K. *Under the Ancestor's Shadow*. Stanford: Stanford University Press, 1971.

Hu, Hsien Chin. "The Chinese Concepts of 'Face.' " *American Anthropologist* 46 (January–March 1944): 45–64.

Hughes, Robert. *Culture of Complaint: The Fraying of America*. New York: Oxford University Press, 1993.

Huntington, Samuel. "The Clash of Civilizations." *Foreign Affairs* 72, no. 3 (summer 1993): 22–49.

———. *American Politics: The Promise of Disharmony*. Cambridge, Mass.: Harvard University Press, 1981.

Iwao, Sumiko. *The Japanese Woman: Traditional Image and Changing Reality.* New York: Free Press, 1993.

James, William. *The Principles of Psychology.* Cambridge, Mass.: Harvard University Press, 1981.

Jencks, Christopher. *Rethinking Social Policy: Race, Poverty, and the Underclass.* Cambridge, Mass.: Harvard University Press, 1992.

Johnson, Lyndon. *The Vantage Point: Perspectives of the Presidency, 1963–69.* New York: Holt, Rinehart, Winston, 1971.

Kammen, Michael. *People of Paradox: An Inquiry Concerning the Origins of American Civilization.* New York: Knopf, 1972.

Kammen, Michael, ed. *The Contrapuntal Civilization: Essays Toward a New Understanding of American Experience.* New York: Knopf, 1971.

Karen, Robert. "Shame." *The Atlantic* 269, no. 2 (February 1992).

Karnow, Stanley. *Vietnam: A History.* New York: Viking, 1991.

Kaufman, Gershen. *The Psychology of Shame.* New York: Springer, 1989.

Kaus, Mickey, "Who's Sorry Now," in *The New Republic,* May 1, 1995, 6.

Kennedy, Paul. *Preparing for the Twenty-First Century.* New York: Random House, 1993.

———. *The Rise and Fall of the Great Powers.* New York: Knopf, 1989.

Key, V. O. *Public Opinion and American Democracy.* New York: Knopf, 1961.

Kissinger, Henry. *White House Years.* Boston: Little, Brown, 1979.

Kitihara, Michio. *Children of the Sun: The Japanese and the Outside World.* New York: St. Martin's Press, 1989.

Klein, Michael, ed. *The Vietnam Era: Media and Popular Culture in the U.S. and Vietnam.* London: Pluto Press, 1990.

Kondo, Dorinne. *Crafting Selves: Power, Gender, and Discourses of Identity in a Japanese Workplace.* Chicago: University of Chicago Press, 1990.

Kotkin, Joel. *Tribes: How Race, Religion and Identity Determine Success in the New Global Economy.* New York: Random House, 1992.

Kraar, Louis, "Asia 2000," in *Fortune,* October 5, 1992, 111–13.

Kristof, Nicholas. "China Update: How the Hardliners Won." *The New York Times Magazine,* November 12, 1989.

Landry, Bart. *The New Black Middle Class.* Berkeley, Calif.: University of California Press, 1987.

Lasch, Christopher. "For Shame." *The New Republic,* August 10, 1992.

Lehman, David. *Signs of the Times: Deconstruction and the Fall of Paul de Man.* New York: Simon & Schuster, 1991.

Lemann, Nicholas. *The Promised Land: The Great Black Migration and How It Changed America.* New York: Knopf, 1991.

Levenson, Joseph. *Confucian China and Its Modern Fate: A Trilogy.* Berkeley, Calif.: University of California Press, 1958.

Levy, Howard S. *Chinese Footbinding: The History of a Curious Erotic Custom.* London: Spearman, 1966.

Lewis, Helen Block, ed. *The Role of Shame in Symptom Formation.* Hillsdale, N.J.: Erlbaum Assoc., 1987.

Lewis, Helen Block. *Shame and Guilt in Neurosis.* New York: International Universities Press, 1971.

Lewis, Michael. *Shame: The Exposed Self.* New York: Free Press, 1991.

Lifton, Robert Jay. *Thought Reform and the Psychology of Totalism: A Study of "Brainwashing" in China.* New York: Norton, 1963.

Lincoln, Abraham. *Selected Speeches and Writings.* New York: Vintage, 1992.

Livingston, Jon, et al., eds. *Postwar Japan: 1945 to the Present.* New York: Pantheon, 1973.

Lynd, Helen Merrell. *On Shame and the Search for Identity.* New York: Harcourt Brace, 1958.

MacDonald, Heather. "The 'Diversity' Industry." *The New Republic*, July 5, 1993, 22–25.

MacGowan, John. *Sidelights on Chinese Life.* Philadelphia, Pa.: Lippincott, 1907.

Magnet, Myron. *The Dream and the Nightmare: The Sixties' Legacy to the Underclass.* New York: Morrow, 1993.

March, Robert. *The Japanese Negotiator: Subtlety and Strategy Beyond Western Logic.* Tokyo and New York: Kodansha, 1988.

Marsella, Anthony, George DeVos, and Francis L. K. Hsu. *Culture and Self: Asian and Western Perspectives.* New York: Tavistock, 1985.

McDonald, Forrest. *Alexander Hamilton: A Biography.* New York: Norton, 1979.

McNamara, Robert. *In Retrospect: The Tragedy and Lessons of Vietnam.* New York: Times Books, 1995.

Metzger, Thomas. *Escape from Predicament: Neo-Confucianism and China's Evolving Political Culture.* New York: Columbia University Press, 1977.

Mill, John Stuart. *On Liberty and Other Writings.* Ed. Stefan Collini. Cambridge, England: Cambridge University Press, 1989.

Miller, Alice. *Thou Shalt Not Be Aware.* New York: Farrar, Straus, Giroux, 1984.

———. *The Drama of the Gifted Child.* New York: Basic Books, 1981.

Minami, Hiroshi. *Psychology of the Japanese People.* Tokyo: University of Tokyo Press, 1971.

Modigliani, Andre. "Embarrassment, Face-work, and Eye Contact." *Journal of Personality and Social Psychology* 17 (1971): 15–24.

Montesquieu, Charles. *De l'Esprit des Lois.* Paris: Editions Garnier frères, 1969.

Morris, Ivan. *The Nobility of Failure: Tragic Heroes in the History of Japan.* New York: Holt, Rinehart, Winston, 1975.

Morrison, Toni, ed. *Race-ing Justice, En-gendering Power: Essays on Anita Hill, Clarence Thomas, and the Construction of Social Reality.* New York: Pantheon, 1992.

Morrow, Lance, "The Temping of America," in *Time*, March 29, 1993, 40–41.

Mosher, Steven. *China Misperceived: American Illusions and Chinese Reality.* New York: Basic Books, 1990.

Mouer, Ross, and Yoshio Sugimoto. *Images of Japanese Society: A Study in the Social Construction of Reality.* New York: Routledge & Kegan Paul, 1990.

Mura, David. *Turning Japanese: Memoirs of a Sansei.* New York: Doubleday, 1992.

Nakane, Chie. *Japanese Society.* Berkeley, Calif.: University of California Press, 1972.

Nathanson, Donald. *Shame and Pride: Affect, Sex, and the Birth of the Self.* New York: Norton, 1992.

Nichols, Michael. *No Place to Hide.* New York: Simon & Schuster, 1991.

Olson, Walter. *The Litigation Explosion: What Happened When America Unleashed the Lawsuit.* New York: Dutton, 1991.

Peters, Tom. *Liberation Management.* New York: Knopf, 1992.

Peyrefitte, Alain. *The Immobile Empire.* New York: Knopf, 1992.

Pharr, Susan. *Losing Face: Status Politics in Japan.* Berkeley, Calif.: University of California Press, 1990.

Phelps, Timothy, and Helen Winternitz. *Capital Games.* New York: Hyperion, 1992.

Pogrebin, Letty Cottin. *Deborah, Golda, and Me: Being Female and Jewish in America.* New York: Doubleday, 1992.

Posner, Judith. *The Feminine Mistake: Women, Work, and Identity.* New York: Warner Books, 1992.

Posner, Richard. *Sex and Reason.* Cambridge, Mass.: Harvard University Press, 1992.

Pye, Lucian. *The Spirit of Chinese Politics.* Cambridge: Harvard University Press, 1992.

Rawls, John. *A Theory of Justice.* Oxford: Oxford University Press, 1973.

Reich, Robert. *The Work of Nations.* New York: Knopf, 1991.

Reischauer, Edwin O. *The Japanese Today: Change and Continuity.* Cambridge, Mass.: Harvard University Press, 1988.

Richie, Donald, and Kenkichi Ito. *The Erotic Gods: Phallicism in Japan.* Tokyo: Zufushinsha, 1967.

Roszak, Theodore. "Green Guilt and Ecological Overload." *The New York Times*, June 9, 1992, A27.

Rowland, Diana. *Japanese Business Etiquette.* New York: Warner Books, 1985.

Sabini, J., and M. Silver. "Envy." In Harre, Rom, ed. *The Social Construction of Emotions.* Oxford: Oxford University Press (1986): 167–83.

Salisbury, Harrison. *The New Emperors: China in the Era of Mao and Deng.* Boston: Little, Brown, 1992.

———. *A Time of Change.* New York: Harper & Row, 1988.

Schama, Simon. *Citizens: A Chronicle of the French Revolution.* New York: Knopf, 1989.

Schlesinger, Arthur M., Jr. *The Disuniting of America: Reflections on a Multicultural Society.* New York: Norton, 1992.

Schneider, Carl. *Shame, Exposure, and Privacy.* Boston: Beacon Press, 1977.

Schwartz, Benjamin. *The World of Thought in Ancient China.* Cambridge, Mass.: Harvard University Press, 1985.

Sedgwick, Eve Kosofsky. *Epistemology of the Closet.* Berkeley, Calif.: University of California Press, 1990.

Segev, Tom. *The Seventh Million: The Israelis and the Holocaust.* New York: Hill & Wang, 1993.

Shain, Barry Alan. *The Myth of American Individualism: The Protestant Origins of American Political Thought.* Princeton: Princeton University Press, 1994.

Shapiro, David. *Psychotherapy of Neurotic Character.* New York: Basic Books, 1989.

Shotter, John. *Social Accountability and Selfhood.* Oxford: Oxford University Press, 1984.

Shrivastava, Paul. *Bhopal: Anatomy of a Crisis.* Cambridge, Mass.: Ballinger, 1987.

Singer, Kurt. *Mirror, Sword, and Jewel: A Study of Japanese Characteristics.* New York: Braziller, 1973.

Smith, Arthur. *Chinese Characteristics.* New York: F. H. Revell, 1894.

Smith, Robert John. *Japanese Society: Tradition, Self, and the Social Order.* New York: Cambridge University Press, 1983.

Solomon, Richard. *Mao's Revolution and the Chinese Political Culture.* Berkeley, Calif.: University of California Press, 1971.

Sowell, Thomas. *Race and Culture: A World View.* New York: Basic Books, 1994.

Spence, Jonathan. *In Search of Modern China.* New York: Norton, 1990.

Stacey, Judith. *Patriarchy and Socialist Revolution in China.* Berkeley, Calif.: University of California Press, 1993.

Stacey, William A., and Anson Shupe. *The Family Secret: Domestic Violence in America.* Boston: Beacon Press, 1983.

Stover, Leon. *China: An Anthropological Perspective.* Pacific Palisades, Calif.: Goodyear, 1976.

Suleiman, Susan Rubin. *The Female Body in Western Culture: Contemporary Perspectives.* Cambridge, Mass.: Harvard University Press, 1986.

Suzuki, D. T. *Zen and Japanese Culture.* New York: Pantheon, 1959.

Tannen, Deborah. *You Just Don't Understand: Women and Men in Conversation.* New York: Morrow, 1991.

Taylor, Gabriele. *Pride, Shame, and Guilt: Emotions of Self-Assessment.* Oxford: Oxford University Press, 1985.

Thomas, Gordon. *Chaos Under Heaven: The Shocking Story of China's Search for Democracy.* Secaucus, N.J.: Carol Publishing Group, 1991.

Thurow, Lester. *Head to Head: The Coming Economic Battle Among Japan, Europe, and America.* New York: Morrow, 1992.

Tocqueville, Alexis de. *Democracy in America,* vols. 1 and 2. New York: Vintage, 1990.

Turkle, Sherry. "Revolutions in Mind: Computers are Changing the Way We Think." *The Journal of Computing and Society* 1 (1990): 83–106.

Turkle, Sherry, and Seymour Papert. "Epistemological Pluralism: Styles and Voices within the Computer Culture." *Signs* 16, no. 1 (autumn 1990).

Turner, John. *Social Influence.* Bristol, Pa.: Open Press, 1991.

Vogel, Ezra. *The Four Little Dragons: The Spread of Industrialization in East Asia.* Cambridge, Mass.: Harvard University Press, 1991.

———. *Japan as Number One: Lessons for America.* Cambridge, Mass.: Harvard University Press, 1979.

Wachtel, Paul. *Psychoanalysis and Behavior Therapy.* New York: Basic Books, 1989.

Wallerstein, Judith. *Second Chances: Men, Women, and Children a Decade After Divorce.* New York: Ticknor & Fields, 1989.

Wasserstrom, Jeffrey, and Elizabeth Perry. *Popular Protest and Political Culture in Modern China: Learning from 1989.* Boulder, Colo.: Westview Press, 1992.

Weber, Max. *Selections in Translation.* Ed. W. G. Runciman. Cambridge: Cambridge University Press, 1978.

Whitehead, Barbara Dafoe. "Dan Quayle Was Right." *The Atlantic Monthly,* April, 1993.

Williams, Bernard. *Shame and Necessity.* Berkeley: University of California Press, 1993.

Wilkins, Lee. *Shared Vulnerability: The Media and American Perceptions of the Bhopal Disaster.* New York: Greenwood Press, 1987.

Williams, Lena. "Dos and Don'ts of Office Etiquette: Has Rudeness Gotten Out of Hand?" *The New York Times,* May 29, 1991.

Wilson, James Q. *The Moral Sense.* New York: Free Press, 1993.

Wilson, Richard W. *The Moral State.* London: Collier Macmillan, 1974.

———. *Learning to Be Chinese.* Cambridge, Mass.: MIT Press, 1972.

Wolferen, Karel, van. *The Enigma of Japanese Power.* New York: Knopf, 1990.

Wood, Gordon. *The Radicalism of the American Revolution.* New York: Knopf, 1991.

Wurmser, Leon. *The Mask of Shame.* Baltimore: Johns Hopkins University Press, 1981.

Wyatt-Brown, Bertram. *Honor and Violence in the Old South.* New York: Oxford University Press, 1986.

Yang, C. K. "The Functional Relationship Between Confucian Thought and

Chinese Religion.'' In Fairbank, John K., ed. *Chinese Thought and Institutions.* Chicago: University of Chicago Press (1957): 291–309.

Yang, Lien-Sheng. ''The Concept of *Pao* as a Basis for Social Relations in China.'' In Fairbank, John K. ed. *Chinese Thought and Institutions.* Chicago: University of Chicago Press (1957): 269–90.

Index

abortion, 190
absolute standards of morality, 28
addiction, treatment for, 273–6, 283
advertising, 237
affirmative action, 121, 133–5
Against Our Will (Brownmiller), 226
agoraphobia, 261–2
AIDS, 191
Alcoholics Anonymous, 273–6
alienation of the sexes, 205–6
Altman, Robert, 297*n*14
America, *see* United States
American Bar Association, 118
American Revolution, 6–7, 157
ancestor worship, 38, 162
Anderson, Warren, 19
Anglo-American tribe, 8–9
Antigone (Sophocles), 77
Apocalypse Now (film), 84–6, 90
apology
    psychoanalysis and, 284
    in shame cultures, 283
    Vietnam War and, 72, 77
appearance, 10

aristocracy, 156–7
Aristotle, 45
arts and entertainment industry, 110
Ashby, Hal, 86
Asian Mind Game, The (Chu), 115
automobile industry, 107–8

baby boomers, 4–5
Baldwin, James, 124–5
Ball, George, 65, 66, 67
Bank of Credit and Commerce International, 297*n*14
Barr, Callie, 177
beatings, 171, 300*n*41
Beck, Aaron, 213
"Being Different: Relational Demography and Organizational Attachment" (Tsui, Egan, and O'Reilly), 216–17
Belli, Melvin, 19
Benedict, Ruth, 5, 28, 29, 37, 41, 249
Bhopal poison gas incident, 19–20

A NOTE ON THE TYPE

*The text of this book was set in a typeface called Times
New Roman, designed by Stanley Morison for* The Times
(London), and introduced by that newspaper in 1932.

*Among typographers and designers of the twentieth century, Stanley
Morison was a strong forming influence, as typographical adviser to the
Monotype Corporation of London, as a director of two distinguished
English publishing houses, and as a writer of sensibility,
erudition, and keen practical sense.*

Composed by PennSet, Inc., Bloomsburg, Pennsylvania

*Printed and bound by The Haddon Craftsmen, a division of R. R. Donnelley
& Sons, Scranton, Pennsylvania*

Designed by Iris Weinstein